FEET
and
TOES

ON A PATH THAT PLEASES GOD

Jack Sorg

ISBN 978-1-63961-869-9 (paperback)
ISBN 978-1-63961-870-5 (digital)

Christian Faith Publishing
832 Park Avenue
Meadville, PA 16335
www.christianfaithpublishing.com

Printed in the United States of America

Contents

Preface 5
The Path 7

Understanding the Path

What Are We Talking About? 11
Where Are We Going? 20
Where Do We Find the Way We Should Walk? 27
How Do We Recognize the Wrong Path and Stay on the Right? ...35
How Much Holy Conduct Is Holy Enough? 47
What Is a Wrong Path of Holiness? 53
What Is the Key to True Holiness? 66
Who Did It Best? 77

Walking the Path

How? *Faith*: The Foundation
    Virtue: Walking Worthy by Putting Off and Putting On 89
How? *Knowledge*: Growing in Understanding 112
How? *Self-Control*: Self-Discipline and Assessing Instead
    of Condemning Others 119
How? *Patient Endurance*: Accepting Where God Puts Us
    and What He Allows in Our Lives 132

How? *Godliness*: Following God's Example of Response to
Listeners and Nonlisteners..144

How? *Brotherly Kindness*: Understanding Our Freedom in
Christ and Its Limits under the Law of Liberty.................177

How? The Law of *Love*: Serving God and Others with
Sacrificial Love 202

Can We Say It More Simply?...225

Preface

Bob glanced quickly at his watch. He and Jill had been in the store only twenty minutes, but they needed to leave immediately to be on time for their dinner engagement. He walked past the ends of the drugstore display rows and finally found his wife reading a novel near the bookrack.

"So buy it, and let's go," he urged.

She did not respond, and he knew she was deep into the story.

When he repeated his request a little louder, she calmly looked up, smiled, put the book back in the rack, and sweetly said, "I don't need to buy it. I've already read it."

"You couldn't have! We've only been here twenty minutes!"

Crisply walking toward the front door, she emphasized, "I read the first chapter and the last. That's all you need to read in a novel like that."

This book on the Christian walk is no simple novel from which a couple of chapters can give the sense of the whole. Each chapter gives a clearer grasp of the previous while leading to the next. To better understand a walk that pleases God, *take this book as a whole.*

My intended readers are fellow born-again believers in the Lord Jesus, who wish to grow in grace, knowledge of Christ, unity, and fruitfulness but who struggle in their Christian growth. You may be confused about how holiness and love should come together in our life. You may not understand the contrast of personal virtue and self-righteousness. Perhaps, you were handed a list of rules, then heard about Christian liberty and are left wondering where the truth lies. You may not be sure if you can ever please God. This book brings together scripture that clarifies these issues and others of our life path.

The book is a fast read for the parts that are familiar and easily understood. But when you find a part that is confusing, or questionable, or troubling, or convicting, please pause to look up the scripture in the endnotes for that section. Aside from my stories, I have documented almost every sentence with scripture and have noted those verses in the endnotes. The Word of God is what the Spirit of God uses to teach us and to bring us into a right path for our life.

Many thousands of books have been written about Bible truth. For certain, this book does not cover everything. However, it does cover some of the key issues of a path that pleases God.

The Path

The path, I must find it,
    While wandering as a child in this wilderness world.
Trees grew to mark the way,
    To shade it and make the path easier.
Some lost their leaves,
    Covering the way, obscuring it.
The call comes again to follow
    God's path of holiness and love.
The path, the path, I can find it,
    While wandering as a child in this wilderness world.

Understanding the Path

What Are We Talking About?

One June day, my son, Matthew, looked at a sign that read, "The path to the mountaintop starts here." Near a suspension bridge, the path began its crawl up Grandfather Mountain in Western North Carolina. Behind him lay the parking lot and scores of tourists buying souvenirs of the mountain but not attempting to climb it. Matthew decided to scale it. Stepping onto the trail with some friends, he had no idea what lay ahead.

For short distances the hiking was an easy stroll. However, most of the trail crept uphill; over rocks; through wooded ravines; across small open meadows and around muddy patches, constantly turning and twisting. Signs warned the travelers to stay on the path for their own safety. When the way was not obvious, blue paint on the stones or trees showed the correct route.

Several parts of the path made use of sturdy ladders to climb otherwise impossible rock cliffs. Across slanted smooth stone faces, a steel cable provided a handhold for the hikers to pull themselves along. The rugged trail made my son sweaty and dirty. His shoes became caked with mud. At times, he doubted if he could go on, but his friends encouraged and helped him.

Arriving on the summit of the mountain, Matthew was rewarded with a sense of accomplishment and a wonderful view of the whole region.

The Start of Our Path That Pleases God

Everyone treads a path through this life. When we become Christians, we start on a new path of separation from the world unto God. This *beginning* of being *set apart unto God*, also called *initial sanctification*, occurs the day that we repent of our sin, ask His forgiveness, and trust in Christ for eternal.[1] This salvation beginning is by the spiritual "work" of believing.[2] We start by grace through faith, without any physical works, because Christ paid the whole price of redemption with His own blood.[3]

On that eventful day, we spiritually die to the world and are born into the family of God.[4] As newborn babes, we start the path of new life in Christ.[5]

The Finish of Our Earthly Path

Just as Matthew could see the mountain peak on and off, yet several times misjudged the distance yet to go, none of us know the day that we will leave this world behind and reach the end of our journey. However, our physical separation from this earth by death or rapture will bring us into God's very presence in heaven.[6] On that glorious day, we will gain a new immortal body, stand before Him, and enjoy His presence forever.[7] That *final separation from* the world and the flesh, *unto* God, brings the believer into complete and *final sanctification* (what some call *glorification*).

The Path between the Start and Finish

A tortuous path wound *from* Matthew's first step *to* his last on the mountaintop. For most of the way he struggled. Only a few patches of wide level ground permitted easy walking. Often, he crawled along narrow passages, across rock faces, up ladders, and around the mud. A few times he paused to rest and search for the right marker, staying out of areas indicated by chains and warning signs.

The life path we now tread between our initial and final sanctification is called *progressive sanctification*. This trail is not an easy stroll across the field of life. God's Word describes the path with words like *avoiding, fleeing, watching, laboring, being vigilant, denying ourselves,* and *serving.*[8] Through this new life, we progressively move *from* the world *to* God, growing in Christlike conduct.[9] We are servants of God, following His will, striving to please Him.[10]

When speaking just about sanctification, we most often mean the time of *progressive sanctification.* This is where the soles of our feet tread the ground of this life, our daily steps toward eternity.

Different Paths with the Same Two Questions

Each person's life path before God is different because we are born into diverse cultures and belief systems.[11] Moreover, we are dissimilar in our physical, emotional, mental abilities;[12] our life circumstances;[13] and God's calling.[14] But regardless of the differences, we all face the same two questions:

1. *Where are our feet now?* Where are we spiritually on our life's path? Are we walking a path that is pleasing to God?[15]
2. *Which way are our toes pointing?* Are they in the right direction on the path or another direction? Are we looking to God and His Word,[16] or are we seeking the ways of the world and the flesh?[17] When our toes are in the wrong direction, we will be off the path shortly.[18]

In the path of this life what is our goal?
Matthew's goal was a small patch of ground on
the top of a mountain. Is our goal a place?
Where are we going?

Notes

¹ For there is not a just man upon earth, that doeth good, and sinneth not. (Eccles. 7:20)

I tell you, Nay: but, except ye repent, ye shall all likewise perish. (Luke 13:3)

For the wages of sin is death; but the gift of God is eternal life through Jesus Christ our Lord. (Rom. 6:23)

Through this man [Christ] is preached unto you the forgiveness of sins. (Acts 13:38b)

Testifying...repentance toward God, and faith toward our Lord Jesus Christ. (Acts 20:21)

In whom we have redemption through his blood, the forgiveness of sins, according to the riches of his grace. (Eph. 1:7)

Look upon mine affliction and my pain; and forgive all my sins. (Ps. 25:18)

For thou, Lord, art good, and ready to forgive; and plenteous in mercy unto all them that call upon thee. (Ps. 86:5)

That if thou shalt confess with thy mouth the Lord Jesus, and shalt believe in thine heart that God hath raised him from the dead, thou shalt be saved. For with the heart man believeth unto righteousness; and with the mouth confession is made unto salvation. For the scripture saith, Whosoever believeth on him shall not be ashamed. For there is no difference between the Jew and the Greek: for the same Lord over all is rich unto all that call upon him. For whosoever shall call upon the name of the Lord shall be saved. (Rom. 10:9–13)

² This is the work of God, that ye believe on him whom he hath sent. (John 6:29b)

The just shall live by faith. (Rom. 1:17b)

³ For by grace are ye saved through faith; and that not of yourselves: it is the gift of God: Not of works, lest any man should boast. (Eph. 2:8–9)

Not by works of righteousness which we have done, but according to his mercy he saved us. (Titus 3:5a)

Forasmuch as ye know that ye were not redeemed with corruptible things, as silver and gold, from your vain conversation received by tradition from your fathers; But with the precious blood of Christ, as of a lamb without blemish and without spot. (1 Pet. 1:18–19)

In whom we have redemption through his blood, the forgiveness of sins, according to the riches of his grace. (Eph. 1:7)

⁴ Know ye not, that so many of us as were baptized into Jesus Christ were baptized into his death? Therefore we are buried with him by baptism into death: that like as Christ was raised up from the dead by the glory of the Father, even so we also should walk in newness of life. For if we have been planted together

in the likeness of his death, we shall be also in the likeness of his resurrection: Knowing this, that our old man is crucified with him, that the body of sin might be destroyed, that henceforth we should not serve sin. For he that is dead is freed from sin. Now if we be dead with Christ, we believe that we shall also live with him: Knowing that Christ being raised from the dead dieth no more; death hath no more dominion over him. For in that he died, he died unto sin once: but in that he liveth, he liveth unto God. Likewise reckon ye also yourselves to be dead indeed unto sin, but alive unto God through Jesus Christ our Lord. (Rom. 6:3–11)

In whom also ye are circumcised with the circumcision made without hands, in putting off the body of the sins of the flesh by the circumcision of Christ: Buried with him in baptism, wherein also ye are risen with him through the faith of the operation of God, who hath raised him from the dead. And you, being dead in your sins and the uncircumcision of your flesh, hath he quickened together with him, having forgiven you all trespasses; Blotting out the handwriting of ordinances that was against us, which was contrary to us, and took it out of the way, nailing it to his cross. (Col. 2:11–14)

Jesus answered and said unto him, Verily, verily, I say unto thee, Except a man be born again, he cannot see the kingdom of God... Marvel not that I said unto thee, Ye must be born again. (John 3:3, 7)

But as many as received him, to them gave he power to become the sons of God, even to them that believe on his name. (John 1:12)

5 Therefore if any man be in Christ, he is a new creature: old things are passed away; behold, all things are become new. (2 Cor. 5:17)

As ye have therefore received Christ Jesus the Lord, so walk ye in him. (Col. 2:6)

6 For we know that if our earthly house of this tabernacle were dissolved, we have a building of God, an house not made with hands, eternal in the heavens. (2 Cor. 5:1)

Therefore we are always confident, knowing that, whilst we are at home in the body, we are absent from the Lord: (For we walk by faith, not by sight:) We are confident, I say, and willing rather to be absent from the body, and to be present with the Lord. (2 Cor. 5:6–8)

7 Beloved, now are we the sons of God, and it doth not yet appear what we shall be: but we know that, when he shall appear, we shall be like him; for we shall see him as he is. (1 John 3:2)

So shall we ever be with the Lord. (1 Thess. 4:17b)

After this I beheld, and, lo, a great multitude, which no man could number, of all nations, and kindreds, and people, and tongues, stood before the throne, and before the Lamb, clothed with white robes, and palms in their hands; And cried with a loud voice, saying, Salvation to our God which sitteth upon the throne, and unto the Lamb. (Rev. 7:9–10)

In thy presence is fulness of joy; at thy right hand there are pleasures for evermore. (Ps. 16:11b)

8 Timothy, keep that which is committed to thy trust, avoiding profane and vain babblings, and oppositions of science [or "knowledge"] falsely so called. (1 Tim. 6:20)

Flee also youthful lusts: but follow righteousness, faith, charity, peace, with them that call on the Lord out of a pure heart. (2 Tim. 2:22)

Praying always with all prayer and supplication in the Spirit, and watching thereunto with all perseverance and supplication for all saints. (Eph. 6:18)

Be sober, be vigilant; because your adversary the devil, as a roaring lion, walketh about, seeking whom he may devour. (1 Pet. 5:8)

Whereunto I also labour, striving according to his working, which worketh in me mightily. (Col. 1:29)

With good will doing service, as to the Lord, and not to men. (Eph. 6:7)

Then said Jesus unto his disciples, if any man will come after me, let him deny himself, and take up his cross, and follow me. (Matt. 16:24)

9 Forgetting those things which are behind, and reaching forth unto those things which are before, I press toward the mark for the prize of the high calling of God in Christ Jesus. (Phil. 3:13b–14)

For we are his workmanship, created in Christ Jesus unto good works, which God hath before ordained that we should walk in them. (Eph. 2:10)

But grow in grace, and in the knowledge of our Lord and Saviour Jesus Christ. (2 Pet. 3:18a)

10 Neither yield ye your members as instruments of unrighteousness unto sin: but yield yourselves unto God, as those that are alive from the dead, and your members as instruments of righteousness unto God... But now being made free from sin [initial sanctification], and become servants to God, ye have your fruit unto holiness [progressive sanctification], and the end everlasting life [final sanctification]. (Rom. 6:13, 22)

I beseech you therefore, brethren, by the mercies of God, that ye present your bodies a living sacrifice, holy, acceptable unto God, which is your reasonable service. And be not conformed to this world: but be ye transformed by the renewing of your mind, that ye may prove what is that good, and acceptable, and perfect, will of God. (Rom. 12:1–2)

Not with eyeservice, as men pleasers; but as the servants of Christ, doing the will of God from the heart. (Eph. 6:6)

That ye might walk worthy of the Lord unto all pleasing, being fruitful in every good work, and increasing in the knowledge of God. (Col. 1:10)

Furthermore then we beseech you, brethren, and exhort you by the Lord Jesus, that as ye have received of us how ye ought to walk and to please God, so ye would abound more and more... For this is the will of God, even your sanctification. (1 Thess. 4:1, 3a)

That he no longer should live the rest of his time in the flesh to the lusts of men, but to the will of God. (1 Pet. 4:2)

11 And how hear we every man in our own tongue, wherein we were born? Parthians, and Medes, and Elamites, and the dwellers in Mesopotamia, and in Judaea, and Cappadocia, in Pontus, and Asia, Phrygia, and Pamphylia, in Egypt, and in the parts of Libya about Cyrene, and strangers of Rome, Jews and proselytes, Cretes and Arabians, we do hear them speak in our tongues the wonderful works of God. (Acts 2:8–11)

For though I be free from all men, yet have I made myself servant unto all, that I might gain the more. And unto the Jews I became as a Jew, that I might gain the Jews; to them that are under the law, as under the law, that I might gain them that are under the law; To them that are without law, as without law, (being not without law to God, but under the law to Christ,) that I might gain them that are without law. To the weak became I as weak, that I might gain the weak: I am made all things to all men, that I might by all means save some. (1 Cor. 9:19–22)

12 For ye see your calling, brethren, how that not many wise men after the flesh, not many mighty, not many noble, are called: But God hath chosen the foolish things of the world to confound the wise; and God hath chosen the weak things of the world to confound the things which are mighty; And base things of the world, and things which are despised, hath God chosen, yea, and things which are not, to bring to nought things that are: That no flesh should glory in his presence. (1 Cor. 1:26–29)

For the body is not one member, but many. If the foot shall say, Because I am not the hand, I am not of the body; is it therefore not of the body? And if the ear shall say, Because I am not the eye, I am not of the body; is it therefore not of the body? If the whole body were an eye, where were the hearing? If the whole were hearing, where were the smelling? But now hath God set the members every one of them in the body, as it hath pleased him. And if they were all one member, where were the body? But now are they many members, yet but one body. (1 Cor. 12:14–19)

13 But I would ye should understand, brethren, that the things which happened unto me have fallen out rather unto the furtherance of the gospel; So that my bonds in Christ are manifest in all the palace, and in all other places. (Phil. 1:12–13)

Are they ministers of Christ? (I speak as a fool) I am more; in labours more abundant, in stripes above measure, in prisons more frequent, in deaths oft. Of the Jews five times received I forty stripes save one. (2 Cor. 11:23–24)

14 Now there are diversities of gifts, but the same Spirit. And there are differences of administrations, but the same Lord. And there are diversities of operations, but it is the same God which worketh all in all. But the manifestation of the Spirit is given to every man to profit withal. For to one is given by the Spirit the word of wisdom; to another the word of knowledge by the same Spirit; To another faith

by the same Spirit; to another the gifts of healing by the same Spirit; To another the working of miracles; to another prophecy; to another discerning of spirits; to another divers kinds of tongues; to another the interpretation of tongues: But all these worketh that one and the selfsame Spirit, dividing to every man severally as he will. (1 Cor. 12:4–11)

¹⁵ Blessed are they that keep his testimonies. (Ps. 119:2a)

O lord, thou hast searched me, and known me. Thou knowest my downsitting and mine uprising, thou understandest my thought afar off. Thou compassest my path and my lying down, and art acquainted with all my ways. For there is not a word in my tongue, but, lo, O LORD, thou knowest it altogether... Search me, O God, and know my heart: try me, and know my thoughts. (Ps. 139:1–4, 23)

For the ways of man are before the eyes of the LORD, and he pondereth all his goings. (Prov. 5:21)

I the LORD search the heart, I try the reins, even to give every man according to his ways, and according to the fruit of his doings. (Jer.17:10)

Great in counsel, and mighty in work: for thine eyes are open upon all the ways of the sons of men: to give every one according to his ways, and according to the fruit of his doings. (Jer. 32:19)

Who is wise, and he shall understand these things? prudent, and he shall know them? for the ways of the LORD are right, and the just shall walk in them: but the transgressors shall fall therein. (Hos. 14:9)

Now therefore thus saith the LORD of hosts; Consider your ways... Thus saith the LORD of hosts; Consider your ways. (Hag. 1:5, 7)

Be ye therefore followers of God, as dear children... For ye were sometimes darkness, but now are ye light in the Lord: walk as children of light... See then that ye walk circumspectly, not as fools, but as wise... Wherefore be ye not unwise, but understanding what the will of the Lord is. (Eph. 5:1, 8, 15, 17)

That ye would walk worthy of God, who hath called you unto his kingdom and glory. (1 Thess. 2:12)

I therefore, the prisoner of the Lord, beseech you that ye walk worthy of the vocation wherewith ye are called...that ye henceforth walk not as other Gentiles walk, in the vanity of their mind, Having the understanding darkened, being alienated from the life of God through the ignorance that is in them, because of the blindness of their heart: Who being past feeling have given themselves over unto lasciviousness, to work all uncleanness with greediness. But ye have not so learned Christ. (Eph. 4:1, 17b–20)

For we are his workmanship, created in Christ Jesus unto good works, which God hath before ordained that we should walk in them. (Eph. 2:10)

¹⁶ And that seek him with the whole heart. (Ps. 119:2b)

And now, Israel, what doth the LORD thy God require of thee, but to fear the LORD thy God, to walk in all his ways, and to love him, and to serve the LORD thy God with all thy heart and with all thy soul, To keep the commandments of the LORD, and his statutes, which I command thee this day for thy good? (Deut. 10:12–13)

And keep the charge of the LORD thy God, to walk in his ways, to keep his statutes, and his commandments, and his judgments, and his testimonies, as it is written in the law of Moses, that thou mayest prosper in all that thou doest, and whithersoever thou turnest thyself. (1 Kings 2:3)

When thou saidst, Seek ye my face; my heart said unto thee, Thy face, LORD, will I seek. (Ps. 27:8)

He that hath my commandments, and keepeth them, he it is that loveth me: and he that loveth me shall be loved of my Father, and I will love him, and will manifest myself to him. Judas saith unto him, not Iscariot, Lord, how is it that thou wilt manifest thyself unto us, and not unto the world? Jesus answered and said unto him, If a man love me, he will keep my words: and my Father will love him, and we will come unto him, and make our abode with him. He that loveth me not keepeth not my sayings: and the word which ye hear is not mine, but the Father's which sent me. (John 14:21–24)

[17] Blessed are they that keep his testimonies, and that seek him with the whole heart... I thought on my ways, and turned my feet unto thy testimonies. I made haste, and delayed not to keep thy commandments... I will keep thy precepts with my whole heart. (Ps. 119:2, 59–60, 69b)

But seek ye first the kingdom of God, and his righteousness; and all these things shall be added unto you. (Matt. 6:33)

I beseech you therefore, brethren, by the mercies of God, that ye present your bodies a living sacrifice, holy, acceptable unto God, which is your reasonable service. And be not conformed to this world: but be ye transformed by the renewing of your mind, that ye may prove what is that good, and acceptable, and perfect, will of God. (Rom. 12:1–2)

[18] Hold up my goings in thy paths, that my footsteps slip not. (Ps. 17:5)

I thought on my ways, and turned my feet unto thy testimonies... I have refrained my feet from every evil way, that I might keep thy word. (Ps. 119:59, 101)

Ponder the path of thy feet, and let all thy ways be established. (Prov. 4:26)

Therefore we ought to give the more earnest heed to the things which we have heard, lest at any time we should let them slip. (Heb. 2:1)

Where Are We Going?

While preparing to travel to West Africa for the first time, I was asked by some, "Where are you going?" The sense of their question was about a location, so I answered accordingly, "To Liberia." However, our goal was not just a location but a person, Pastor James. He was going to help us explore opportunities for our mission work in that country. Our objective was more than a place; it was an individual who would be overseeing our days and opening doors of ministry in Liberia.

To a Person

In our daily walk through this life, our focus must be a Person, the Lord.[1] Getting closer to Him, becoming more like Him in our own heart and life separates us from the world and the old fleshly ways.[2] So also, the eternal goal of our journey is not just a heavenly place but God Himself, especially in the person of Jesus Christ.[3] The end of our path shines with the glory of God in Christ.[4] The Lord promises that He will never abandon us,[5] and we will be with Him forever.[6]

Our Glorious God

What makes God eligible to be the whole goal of our life? How does He qualify for that position? What puts Him above all? God created and owns this whole universe, right down to the ground upon which we stand.[7] He created us and gave us life.[8]

We occupy one small place in this world for a very short time.[9] By contrast, God is everywhere present[10] and is eternal.[11] This magnificent creation displays His glorious wisdom and power.[12] Moreover, He holds all power in heaven and earth.[13] This power makes Him the sovereign ruler and judge of all creation and the affairs of men.[14] What He plans and decrees will be accomplished.[15]

God already knows all things; He is omniscient.[16] He knows the end from the beginning.[17] He knows us completely: our actions, words, motives, even our thoughts before we think or say them![18] God does not need to be taught the truth or guided to the truth before He works. He is Truth and works all things according to the counsel of His own will.[19] Such wisdom is beyond our comprehension.[20]

While He does not need our help, He has left us commands to follow[21] and does seek to work through us (our prayers, words, actions)[22] so that He may bless us.[23] Our wisest choice is to look to Him for our life path.[24]

God is *the* eternal Sovereign.[25] He is *the* Authority of our life and *the* Goal of our life, especially in the Person of Christ.[26]

But how do we know the path for our feet?
Has God provided enough light about Himself and His way?

Notes

[1] And thou shalt love the Lord thy God with all thy heart, and with all thy soul, and with all thy mind, and with all thy strength: this is the first commandment. (Mark 12:30)

[2] Brethren, I count not myself to have apprehended: but this one thing I do, forgetting those things which are behind, and reaching forth unto those things which are before, I press toward the mark for the prize of the high calling of God in Christ Jesus. (Phil. 3:13–14)

Wherefore seeing we also are compassed about with so great a cloud of witnesses, let us lay aside every weight, and the sin which doth so easily beset us, and let us run with patience the race that is set before us, Looking unto Jesus the author and finisher of our faith. (Heb. 12:1–2a)

[3] And he is the head of the body, the church: who is the beginning, the firstborn from the dead; that in all things he might have the preeminence. For it pleased the Father that in him should all fulness dwell. (Col. 1:18–19)

Wherefore God also hath highly exalted him, and given him a name which is above every name: That at the name of Jesus every knee should bow, of things in heaven, and things in earth, and things under the earth; And that every tongue should confess that Jesus Christ is Lord, to the glory of God the Father. (Phil. 2:9–11)

[4] And now, O Father, glorify thou me with thine own self with the glory which I had with thee before the world was. (John 17:5)

But speaking the truth in love, may grow up into him in all things, which is the head, even Christ. (Eph. 4:15)

But we are bound to give thanks always to God for you, brethren beloved of the Lord, because God hath from the beginning chosen you to salvation through sanctification of the Spirit and belief of the truth: Whereunto he called you by our gospel, to the obtaining of the glory of our Lord Jesus Christ. (2 Thess. 2:13–14)

Who [God's Son] being the brightness of his [God's] glory, and the express image of his person, and upholding all things by the word of his power, when he had by himself purged our sins, sat down on the right hand of the Majesty on high. (Heb. 1:3)

[5] And he said, My presence shall go with thee, and I will give thee rest. (Exod. 33:14)

Be strong and of a good courage, fear not, nor be afraid of them: for the LORD thy God, he it is that doth go with thee; he will not fail thee, nor forsake thee... And the LORD, he it is that doth go before thee; he will be with thee, he will not fail thee, neither forsake thee: fear not, neither be dismayed. (Deut. 31:6, 8)

Have not I commanded thee? Be strong and of a good courage; be not afraid, neither be thou dismayed: for the LORD thy God is with thee whithersoever thou goest. (Josh. 1:9)

6 For God so loved the world, that he gave his only begotten Son, that whosoever believeth in him should not perish, but have everlasting life... He that believeth on the Son hath everlasting life: and he that believeth not the Son shall not see life; but the wrath of God abideth on him. (John 3:16, 36)

Let not your heart be troubled: ye believe in God, believe also in me. In my Father's house are many mansions: if it were not so, I would have told you. I go to prepare a place for you. And if I go and prepare a place for you, I will come again, and receive you unto myself; that where I am, there ye may be also. (John 14:1–3)

Therefore we are always confident, knowing that, whilst we are at home in the body, we are absent from the Lord:... We are confident, I say, and willing rather to be absent from the body, and to be present with the Lord. (2 Cor. 5:6, 8)

7 In the beginning God created the heaven and the earth. (Gen. 1:1)

These are the generations of the heavens and of the earth when they were created, in the day that the LORD God made the earth and the heavens. (Gen. 2:4)

Who hath prevented me, that I should repay him? whatsoever is under the whole heaven is mine. (Job 41:11)

The heavens are thine, the earth also is thine: as for the world and the fulness thereof, thou hast founded them. (Ps. 89:11)

Hast thou not known? hast thou not heard, that the everlasting God, the LORD, the Creator of the ends of the earth, fainteth not, neither is weary? There is no searching of his understanding. (Isa. 40:28)

Thou art worthy, O Lord, to receive glory and honour and power: for thou hast created all things, and for thy pleasure they are and were created. (Rev. 4:11)

8 And the LORD God formed man of the dust of the ground, and breathed into his nostrils the breath of life; and man became a living soul. (Gen. 2:7)

Thus saith God the LORD, he that created the heavens, and stretched them out; he that spread forth the earth, and that which cometh out of it; he that giveth breath unto the people upon it, and spirit to them that walk therein. (Isa. 42:5)

I have made the earth, and created man upon it: I, even my hands, have stretched out the heavens. (Isa. 45:12a)

9 Whereas ye know not what shall be on the morrow. For what is your life? It is even a vapour, that appeareth for a little time, and then vanisheth away. (James 4:14)

10 Whither shall I go from thy spirit? or whither shall I flee from thy presence? If I ascend up into heaven, thou art there: if I make my bed in hell, behold, thou art there. If I take the wings of the morning, and dwell in the uttermost parts of the sea; Even there shall thy hand lead me, and thy right hand shall hold me. (Ps. 139:7–10)

11 Thy throne is established of old: thou art from everlasting. (Ps. 93:2)

Even from everlasting to everlasting, thou art God. (Ps. 90:2b)

12 LORD, how manifold are thy works! in wisdom hast thou made them all. (Ps. 104:24a)

The LORD by wisdom hath founded the earth; by understanding hath he established the heavens. (Prov. 3:19)

He hath made the earth by his power, he hath established the world by his wisdom, and hath stretched out the heavens by his discretion. (Jer. 10:12)

13 God hath spoken once; twice have I heard this; that power belongeth unto God. (Ps. 62:11)

Ah Lord GOD! behold, thou hast made the heaven and the earth by thy great power and stretched out arm, and there is nothing too hard for thee. (Jer. 32:17)

14 And he shall judge the world in righteousness, he shall minister judgment to the people in uprightness. (Ps. 9:8)

The mighty God, even the LORD, hath spoken, and called the earth from the rising of the sun unto the going down thereof… He shall call to the heavens from above, and to the earth, that he may judge his people… And the heavens shall declare his righteousness: for God is judge himself. (Ps. 50:1, 4, 6)

Say among the heathen that the LORD reigneth: the world also shall be established that it shall not be moved: he shall judge the people righteously… Before the LORD: for he cometh, for he cometh to judge the earth: he shall judge the world with righteousness, and the people with his truth. (Ps. 96:10, 13)

And I saw a great white throne, and him that sat on it, from whose face the earth and the heaven fled away; and there was found no place for them. And I saw the dead, small and great, stand before God; and the books were opened: and another book was opened, which is the book of life: and the dead were judged out of those things which were written in the books, according to their works. And the sea gave up the dead which were in it; and death and hell delivered up the dead which were in them: and they were judged every man according to their works. (Rev. 20:11–13)

15 And said, O LORD God of our fathers, art not thou God in heaven? and rulest not thou over all the kingdoms of the heathen? and in thine hand is there not power and might, so that none is able to withstand thee? (2 Chron. 20:6)

The counsel of the LORD standeth for ever, the thoughts of his heart to all generations. (Ps. 33:11)

Say unto God, How terrible art thou in thy works! through the greatness of thy power shall thine enemies submit themselves unto thee... He ruleth by his power for ever. (Ps. 66:3, 7a)

16 Great is our Lord, and of great power: his understanding is infinite. (Ps. 147:5)

In whom are hid all the treasures of wisdom and knowledge. (Col. 2:3)

17 Remember the former things of old: for I am God, and there is none else; I am God, and there is none like me, 10 Declaring the end from the beginning, and from ancient times the things that are not yet done. (Isa. 46:9–10a)

18 For thou, even thou only, knowest the hearts of all the children of men. (1 Kings 8:39b)

For the ways of man are before the eyes of the Lord, and he pondereth all his goings. (Prov. 5:21)

Thou knowest my downsitting and mine uprising, thou understandest my thought afar off. Thou compassest my path and my lying down, and art acquainted with all my ways. For there is not a word in my tongue, but, lo, O LORD, thou knowest it altogether. (Ps. 139:2–4)

19 Shall any teach God knowledge? seeing he judgeth those that are high. (Job 21:22)

Who hath directed the Spirit of the Lord, or being his counsellor hath taught him? With whom took he counsel, and who instructed him, and taught him in the path of judgment, and taught him knowledge, and shewed to him the way of understanding? (Isa. 40:13–14)

My counsel shall stand, and I will do all my pleasure. (Isa. 46:10b)

In whom also we have obtained an inheritance, being predestinated according to the purpose of him who worketh all things after the counsel of his own will. (Eph. 1:11)

20 the depth of the riches both of the wisdom and knowledge of God! How unsearchable are his judgments, and his ways past finding out! (Rom. 11:33)

For my thoughts are not your thoughts, neither are your ways my ways, saith the LORD. For as the heavens are higher than the earth, so are my ways higher than your ways, and my thoughts than your thoughts. (Isa. 55:8–9)

21 And he said to them all, If any man will come after me, let him deny himself, and take up his cross daily, and follow me. (Luke 9:23)

If any man serve me, let him follow me; and where I am, there shall also my servant be: if any man serve me, him will my Father honour. (John 12:26)

For even hereunto were ye called: because Christ also suffered for us, leaving us an example, that ye should follow his steps. (1 Pet. 2:21)

22 am the true vine, and my Father is the husbandman... Abide in me, and I in you. As the branch cannot bear fruit of itself, except it abide in the vine; no more can ye, except ye abide in me. I am the vine, ye are the branches: He that abideth in me, and I in him, the same bringeth forth much fruit: for without me ye can do nothing... Herein is my Father glorified, that ye bear much fruit; so shall ye be my disciples. (John 15:1, 4–5, 8)

23 Blessed is the man that walketh not in the counsel of the ungodly, nor standeth in the way of sinners, nor sitteth in the seat of the scornful. But his delight is in the law of the Lord; and in his law doth he meditate day and night. And he shall be like a tree planted by the rivers of water, that bringeth forth his fruit in his season; his leaf also shall not wither; and whatsoever he doeth shall prosper. (Ps. 1:1–3)

Praise ye the Lord. Blessed is the man that feareth the Lord, that delighteth greatly in his commandments. (Ps. 112:1)

24 Shew me thy ways, O LORD; teach me thy paths. 5 Lead me in thy truth, and teach me: for thou art the God of my salvation; on thee do I wait all the day. (Ps. 25:4–5)

Blessed art thou, O LORD: teach me thy statutes... Teach me, O LORD, the way of thy statutes; and I shall keep it unto the end. (Ps. 119:12, 33)

The fear of the LORD is the beginning of wisdom: and the knowledge of the holy is understanding. (Prov. 9:10)

25 Thine, O Lord, is the greatness, and the power, and the glory, and the victory, and the majesty: for all that is in the heaven and in the earth is thine; thine is the kingdom, O Lord, and thou art exalted as head above all. Both riches and honour come of thee, and thou reignest over all; and in thine hand is power and might; and in thine hand it is to make great, and to give strength unto all. (1 Chron. 29:11–12)

The Lord is King for ever and ever. (Ps. 10:16a)

And I heard as it were the voice of a great multitude, and as the voice of many waters, and as the voice of mighty thunderings, saying, Alleluia: for the Lord God omnipotent reigneth. (Rev. 19:6)

26 If ye then be risen with Christ, seek those things which are above, where Christ sitteth on the right hand of God... And whatsoever ye do in word or deed, do all in the name of the Lord Jesus, giving thanks to God and the Father by him... And whatsoever ye do, do it heartily, as to the Lord, and not unto men; Knowing that of the Lord ye shall receive the reward of the inheritance: for ye serve the Lord Christ. (Col. 3:1, 17, 23–24)

Where Do We Find the Way
We Should Walk?

Stepping away from Raimundinha's bed, I wanted to be wrong about the diagnosis. Our Amazon jungle hospital had few laboratory tests and almost none of the medicines needed to care for her. Searching in the back of a consultation room where we kept our medical reference books, I found one of the largest. Paging past the list of contributing experts, I searched the table of contents and found the article I needed to read.

My suspicions were confirmed that this twelve-year-old girl had all the possible signs and symptoms of a deadly illness. Her parents did not have the money to transport her hundreds of miles to the big city for specialist care. So we gave her the only the medicine we had. She improved generally but very little in her kidney function.

During this time, my daughter, Elizabeth, began to read to her and to share the Gospel. One evening Raimundinha prayed and received the Lord as her Savior. She avidly read God's Word and other Christian literature. As she grew spiritually, her body weakened. Repeatedly, she asked to go to church so she could fellowship and worship with other believers. However, each time she became well enough to leave the hospital, her non-Christian parents would whisk her off to their home thirty miles downriver.

In the coming months, her kidney function worsened, and we admitted her again to the hospital. Her parents finally granted permission for us to carry her (literally) to church. She rejoiced in the only service she ever attended as if it were her birthday party. That afternoon she went to her home and a few weeks later died.

The Need

The medical text I read had over three hundred authors who had done original research and intelligently brought it together. They wrote from the background of tremendous reading, study, and experience to help others in time of need. The book told me the truth about Raimundinha's illness and what things could be done for her. Knowing *our* needs, would the eternal, omniscient, loving God do less?[8]

We need wise answers, especially to the fundamental questions of life. What is life about? Why am I here? Where am I going? What should I be doing? Can I find peace in my life situation? Can I find forgiveness and healing for my heart and soul? What are the right answers? Where is the best and ultimate source for that information?

The Answer

God spoke.[1]

God's Word, the Bible, is not just another book, or even another inspirational book. The Bible is from our Creator Who loves us so much that He sent His only Son to die for us.[2] It tells us how to live this life and how to prepare for the next through the Lord Jesus Christ.[3] Unlike any writings from human minds, Scripture has inspiration, authority, unity, and sufficiency on the fundamental issues of life.

The word *"inspiration"*[4] is used in only one verse in the Bible.[5] However, the truth is emphasized repeatedly throughout the Bible that the Scripture comes from God,[6] is eternal,[7] and is true.[8]

God's Word is *God's Word* on the subject of life.[9] His Word is our light for the right path.[10] There is no higher authority and no better place to learn of our proper walk and relationship to Him.[11]

The medical textbook writers' backgrounds, writings, labor, and esteem from colleagues gave their words authority. Since *The*

Sovereign God gave the Scriptures, it is *The Authority* and light on how we should follow Christ and live pleasing to the Lord.[12]

In my medical book, a small group of editors labored to tie together the articles of many authors. One article mentions a disease complication, even as another enlarges on that complication, and another explains connections to further illnesses. While over forty men wrote the Bible, it has just *one Author* and should be understood as a *unified* book. Because it comes from one Perfect Author, the Bible comments on itself—that is, we can compare scriptures from one part of the Old or New Testament to those of another for more complete understanding on a subject.[13]

The basic medical assumptions and concepts of modern health care are constantly changing. However, the *sufficiency* of Scripture means that in all cultures it is always the final authority for learning how to live pleasing to God.[14] It transcends generations and cultures.[15] The principles are there on how to act in all situations. By the Scriptures and God's grace, we can live our lives on a path acceptable to God.[16]

The Bible is *inspired*, "God breathed," and given to us by our Creator. Since the Author is God, Scripture has the *authority* to teach us. Because it has one Author, it has the *unity* of a single book. Able to make us complete (or "perfect"), it is the *sufficient* basis for our Christian walk and the standard for our faith.

The Caution

Because the Bible is inspired, Christian writers of any age must be careful in interpreting scripture, that they are not changing the meaning of the text. The Scriptures themselves must not be altered to conform to our own ideas. Adding the tradition or precepts of men amounts to extrabiblical revelation and is condemned.[17] Such opinions violate each standard set by the Word of God: *His* inspiration, *His* authority, *His* unity, and *His* sufficiency. And basing Christian conduct on man's opinion can lead us away from scriptural principles.[18]

If "one jot or one tittle" is so firmly established,[19] then "chapter and verse" should certainly be our standard of doctrine and practice. Men's opinions can be considered if based on scripture; but scriptural concepts, "chapter and verse," can be trusted.[20]

How do we find a God-pleasing path of life?
By studying His Word.[21]

And on such a path,
what does His Word tell us to avoid?

Notes

1   will instruct thee and teach thee in the way which thou shalt go. (Ps. 32:8a)

    And Jesus answered him, saying, It is written, That man shall not live by bread alone, but by every word of God. (Luke 4:4)

2   For God so loved the world, that he gave his only begotten Son, that whosoever believeth in him should not perish, but have everlasting life. (John 3:16)

3   Now to him that is of power to stablish you according to my gospel, and the preaching of Jesus Christ, according to the revelation of the mystery, which was kept secret since the world began, But now is made manifest, and by the scriptures of the prophets, according to the commandment of the everlasting God, made known to all nations for the obedience of faith. (Rom. 16:25–26)

4   "Inspiration" in the Greek is *theopneustos*: *Theos*, "God"; *pneoto*, "breathe." So *inspiration* means "God breathed" or "divinely breathed." (Robert Young, *Young's Analytical Concordance to the Bible* [Grand Rapids: Eerdmans Publishing Co., 1984], 517).

5   All scripture is given by inspiration of God, and is profitable for doctrine, for reproof, for correction, for instruction in righteousness. (2 Tim. 3:16)

6   I know, O LORD, that thy judgments are right, and that thou in faithfulness hast afflicted me... For ever, O LORD, thy word is settled in heaven... The entrance of thy words giveth light; it giveth understanding unto the simple... Righteous art thou, O LORD, and upright are thy judgments... Thy righteousness is an everlasting righteousness, and thy law is the truth... The righteousness of thy testimonies is everlasting: give me understanding, and I shall live... Thou art near, O LORD; and all thy commandments are truth. Concerning thy testimonies, I have known of old that thou hast founded them for ever... Thou art near, O LORD; and all thy commandments are truth. (Ps. 119:75, 89, 130, 137, 142, 144, 151–152, 160)

    And Micaiah said, As the Lord liveth, what the Lord saith unto me, that will I speak. (1 Kings 22:14)

7   The grass withereth, the flower fadeth: but the word of our God shall stand for ever. (Isa. 40:8)

    Heaven and earth shall pass away, but my words shall not pass away. (Matt. 24:35; Luke 21:33)

    But the word of the Lord endureth forever. And this is the word which by the gospel is preached unto you. (1 Pet. 1:25)

8   He is the Rock, his work is perfect: for all his ways are judgment: a God of truth and without iniquity, just and right is he. (Deut. 32:4)

    Thy word is true from the beginning: and every one of thy righteous judgments endureth forever. (Ps. 119:160)

9   The law of the Lord is perfect, converting the soul: the testimony of the Lord is sure, making wise the simple. The statutes of the Lord are right, rejoicing the heart: the commandment of the Lord is pure, enlightening the eyes. The fear of the Lord is clean, enduring forever: the judgments of the Lord are true and righteous altogether... Moreover by them is thy servant warned: and in keeping of them there is great reward. (Ps. 19:7–9, 11)

Thy testimonies also are my delight and my counsellors... I have chosen the way of truth: thy judgments have I laid before me. (Ps.119:24, 30)

For the commandment is a lamp; and the law is light; and reproofs of instruction are the way of life. (Prov. 6:23)

And now, brethren, I commend you to God, and to the word of his grace, which is able to build you up, and to give you an inheritance among all them which are sanctified. (Acts 20:32)

10   .Thy word is a lamp unto my feet, and a light unto my path... The entrance of thy words giveth light; it giveth understanding unto the simple. (Ps. 119:105, 130)

For the commandment is a lamp; and the law is light; and reproofs of instruction are the way of life. (Prov. 6:23)

11   Shew me thy ways, O Lord; teach me thy paths. Lead me in thy truth, and teach me: for thou art the God of my salvation; on thee do I wait all the day. (Ps. 25:4–5)

Order my steps in thy word: and let not any iniquity have dominion over me... The righteousness of thy testimonies is everlasting: give me understanding, and I shall live. (Ps. 119:133, 144)

12   All scripture is given by inspiration of God... That the man of God may be perfect, throughly furnished unto all good works. (2 Tim. 3:16a, 17)

For this cause also thank we God without ceasing, because, when ye received the word of God which ye heard of us, ye received it not as the word of men, but as it is in truth, the word of God, which effectually worketh also in you that believe. (1 Thess. 2:13)

Then Simon Peter answered him, Lord, to whom shall we go? thou hast the words of eternal life. (John 6:68)

13   Knowing this first, that no prophecy of the scripture is of any private interpretation. For the prophecy came not in old time by the will of man: but holy men of God spake as they were moved by the Holy Ghost. (2 Pet. 1:20–21)

14   All scripture is given by inspiration of God, and is profitable for doctrine, for reproof, for correction, for instruction in righteousness: That the man of God may be perfect, throughly furnished unto all good works. (2 Tim. 3:16–17)

Now we have received, not the spirit of the world, but the spirit which is of God; that we might know the things that are freely given to us of God. Which things also we speak, not in the words which man's wisdom teacheth, but which the Holy Ghost teacheth; comparing spiritual things with spiritual. (1 Cor. 2:12–13)

According as his divine power hath given unto us all things that pertain unto life and godliness, through the knowledge of him that hath called us to glory and virtue... We have also a more sure word of prophecy; whereunto ye do well that ye take heed, as unto a light that shineth in a dark place. (2 Pet. 1:3, 19a)

To the law and to the testimony: if they speak not according to this word, it is because there is no light in them. (Isa. 8:20)

15 The counsel of the Lord standeth forever, the thoughts of his heart to all generations. (Ps. 33:11)

16 Concerning the works of men, by the word of thy lips I have kept me from the paths of the destroyer. Hold up my goings in thy paths, that my footsteps slip not. (Ps. 17:4–5)

The law of the LORD is perfect, converting the soul: the testimony of the LORD is sure, making wise the simple. (Ps. 19:7)

Wherewithal shall a young man cleanse his way? by taking heed thereto according to thy word. With my whole heart have I sought thee: O let me not wander from thy commandments. Thy word have I hid in mine heart, that I might not sin against thee. (Ps. 119:9–11)

And God is able to make all grace abound toward you; that ye, always having all sufficiency in all things, may abound to every good work. (2 Cor. 9:8)

17 What thing so ever I command you, observe to do it: thou shalt not add thereto, nor diminish from it. (Deut. 12:32)

Add thou not unto his words, lest he reprove thee, and thou be found a liar. (Prov. 30:6)

Howbeit in vain do they worship me, teaching for doctrines the commandments of men. (Mark 7:7)

For I testify unto every man that heareth the words of the prophecy of this book, If any man shall add unto these things, God shall add unto him the plagues that are written in this book. (Rev. 22:18)

18 But he answered and said unto them, Why do ye also transgress the commandment of God by your tradition?... But in vain they do worship me, teaching for doctrines the commandments of men. (Matt. 15:3, 9)

To the law and to the testimony: if they speak not according to this word, it is because there is no light in them. (Isa. 8:20)

But though we, or an angel from heaven, preach any other gospel unto you than that which we have preached unto you, let him be accursed. (Gal. 1:8)

Beware lest any man spoil you through philosophy and vain deceit, after the tradition of men, after the rudiments of the world, and not after Christ. (Col. 2:8)

19 For verily I say unto you, Till heaven and earth pass, one jot or one tittle shall in no wise pass from the law, till all be fulfilled. (Matt. 5:18)

20 Hear counsel, and receive instruction, that thou mayest be wise in thy latter end. There are many devices in a man's heart; nevertheless the counsel of the Lord, that shall stand. (Prov. 19:20–21)

[21] This book of the law shall not depart out of thy mouth; but thou shalt meditate therein day and night, that thou mayest observe to do according to all that is written therein: for then thou shalt make thy way prosperous, and then thou shalt have good success. (Josh. 1:8)

Study to shew thyself approved unto God, a workman that needeth not to be ashamed, rightly dividing the word of truth. (2 Tim. 2:15)

How Do We Recognize the Wrong Path and Stay on the Right?

I n September 2005, Hurricane Katrina charged across the Louisiana coast. Besides pouring tons of rain upon the coastal residents, the hurricane pushed the Gulf waters in front of it, causing the dikes around New Orleans to fail. The corrosive seawater carried in thick sediment that covered large parts of the city. Moreover, dangerous chemicals and waste from gas stations, cars, factories, and septic tanks contaminated the murky liquid.

Thousands of residents were caught in the harmful water. TV pictures showed some residents strolling through the flood, apparently without concern. Those who understood the danger got out of the water as fast as they could.

Amazingly, few were harmed by the toxic waters left in Katrina's wake. By contrast, sin is always toxic and deadly.[1] Sin is breaking the Lord's law, going against the righteous God.[2] Many define behavior by dos and don'ts. But sin is greater than any list of don'ts. If we know what is good and do not do it, that is sin.[3] Whatsoever is not done by faith is sin.[4] Finally, Christ put the ultimate indictment against us. He said that if our attitude or thoughts are wrong, we have sinned before God.[5]

Surrounded by Wrong Paths

When we were first saved (initial sanctification), we were radically parted from this sinful world. We became identified completely with Christ in His death on the cross,[6] separated spiritually from the world through the finality of death.[7] This spiritual passage resulted in our being born into life in the family of God.[8] We became a new creation on the inside.[9]

As God's children, are we totally free from sin? No, because we still have our sin-cursed human bodies that the Bible calls the old man[10] and the flesh.[11] In our progressive walk through this world in these bodies, we encounter old and new temptations. Believers are constantly enticed to go back into sin.[12] In very personal terms, Paul described the battle with sin that we all face.[13]

To illustrate our problem, let us consider a man who raced down the road in his car to arrive on time at a meeting. In his haste, he made a wrong turn. Then he ran into a detour. In that part of town, the streets were a confusion of twists and turns. So, in less than a mile, he was no longer sure what direction he was heading. On top of that, vandals had turned around some of the street signs. Within minutes, he was completely lost. His wrong turn came under the influence of a detour, twisting streets, and wrong signs.

We must carefully watch the trail that our feet tread, as a turn into sin quickly leaves us on a confused path. Three influences urge us to point our toes the wrong direction and draw us away from the right way. They are the *flesh*, the *world*, and the *devil*.

The Flesh

Our own fleshly lusts are the primary drive for us to do wrong.[14] We are urged to avoid and not obey those desires.[15] And Scripture lays bare the motives of lust:[16]

- The lust of the flesh: sensual sins to satisfy us physically, from immorality to drunkenness.
- The lust of the eyes: materialism and the desire to meet all our wants.
- The pride of life: selfishness, a thirst for power, and judgment of others. Such pride and lack of submission to God is one of our chief offenses.[17]

We need to consider our weaknesses and pray about them.[18] With the help of the Holy Spirit,[19] we are commanded to actively turn away from those sins, even flee them, and then stay away from them.[20] Such lusts work against the Word of God bearing fruit in our lives.[21]

We must purpose in our hearts to make our bodies servants of righteousness instead of sin.[22] We must *put off* the sin and *put on* right conduct.[23] In another place, this is called *putting on Christ*.[24] Every step of obedience and trust is an act of faith toward Christ.[25] And such acts of faith in not feeding our desires can be painful to our old flesh. Scripture graphically compares it to crucifying the flesh.[26]

The World

This sinful world shows us a disobedient lifestyle and encourages unholy living. In the past, we freely walked in the world's sins.[27] While the examples of these sins have always abounded around us, the pressure is increasing on Christians today due to television, magazines, movies, and the Internet. Many Christians liberally expose themselves to these influences and, in their lives, reap the consequences of shame, loss, and defeat.[28]

My parents and I camped one summer in Yellowstone National Park. On a moonless night, I was crossing the campground with an old flashlight that was low on battery power. In the weak light, I could barely see the trail and tree roots. Pausing to catch my bearings in the starlight, I was stunned to see right in front of me a bear sitting quietly, munching a morsel from a garbage can. In two more paces, I would have walked up his back! I quickly sought a different way back to our tent, because continuing that wrong path would have had disastrous consequences.

The psalmist David contrasts the believer who lives by the light of God's word[29] with those walking the downward path into worldliness. That downward path starts with listening to the world, then walking in their ways, and lastly scorning the good.[30] We are ordered to flee, separate, and stay away from the worldly influences over which we do have control.[31] We should let the sowing in our Christian lives be godly attitudes and conduct and not worldliness.[32]

The Devil

Both the flesh and world are encouraged by the devil.[33] As the "father" of wrongdoing, Satan is the detour expert.[34] He seduced Adam and Eve into disobeying God in the Garden of Eden.[35] Through this first couple, sin passed to all humans, so no one is without sin. We have not only inherited the sin nature in our bodies from Adam, but also everyone has committed sin themselves.[36]

Satan works on the weaknesses and sins of humans,[37] seeking to destroy us.[38] He will be punished for his evil labor, and his followers also will be condemned.[39] As believers, how do we thwart the work of the devil? We have both the command to resist him and the power to do it through the blood of Christ.[40]

The Effect of Sin

We have seen cars crushed by a collision with a drunk driver. That driver drank the alcohol for his own pleasure. But his behavior brought destruction to himself and others. Likewise, sin has the same sweeping impact on us and others. It wounds our mind and body through pornography, sexual impurity, alcohol abuse, and illicit drugs. It harms others through gossip, anger, stealing, or injury. It sets up an idol in the place of God.[41] It causes division among brothers and sisters in the church through bitterness and bad mouthing.[42]

Continue or Repent

For each step into sin, we face a decision of either repenting or continuing on. If we repent, our Father will forgive,[43] but He may still allow us to suffer some of the consequences.[44] We must not be fooled into thinking we can escape punishment for continuing in sin. If we persistently indulge our desires, God, in judgment, may let us have our desires and all the consequences of those sins.[45] He must deal with sin because He cannot deny Himself.[46]

God disciplines His people.[47] He disciplines because He knows that such wrong behavior destroys both us and those around us.[48] In this walk, we must follow the example of our Lord Jesus Christ. God works to totally conform us to the image of His wonderful Son.[49] As everything good begins in God, everything good is brought together in Christ.[50]

In denying fleshly desires, refusing worldly pressures, and fleeing the devil's influence, we are keeping our feet on a right path that is pleasing to God. It is a holy life.

But how much of this should we do? How far should we go? How much holy conduct is enough?

Notes

1   For the wages of sin is death. (Rom. 6:23a)

2   Whosoever committeth sin transgresseth also the law: for sin is the transgression of the law. (1 John 3:4)

    All unrighteousness is sin. (1 John 5:17a)

    For I acknowledge my transgressions: and my sin is ever before me. Against thee, thee only, have I sinned, and done this evil in thy sight. (Ps. 51:3–4a)

3   Therefore to him that knoweth to do good, and doeth it not, to him it is sin. (James 4:17)

4   For whatsoever is not of faith is sin. (Rom. 14:23b)

5   Ye have heard that it was said by them of old time, Thou shalt not kill; and whosoever shall kill shall be in danger of the judgment: But I say unto you, That whosoever is angry with his brother without a cause shall be in danger of the judgment: and whosoever shall say to his brother, Raca, shall be in danger of the council: but whosoever shall say, Thou fool, shall be in danger of hell fire... Ye have heard that it was said by them of old time, Thou shalt not commit adultery: But I say unto you, That whosoever looketh on a woman to lust after her hath committed adultery with her already in his heart. (Matt. 5:21–22, 27–28)

6   Know ye not, that so many of us as were baptized into Jesus Christ were baptized into his death? Therefore we are buried with him by baptism into death... Knowing this, that our old man is crucified with him, that the body of sin might be destroyed, that henceforth we should not serve sin. For he that is dead is freed from sin. (Rom. 6:3–4a, 6–7)

7   But God forbid that I should glory, save in the cross of our Lord Jesus Christ, by whom the world is crucified unto me, and I unto the world. (Gal. 6:14)

8   For ye are all the children of God by faith in Christ Jesus. (Gal. 3:26)

    Behold, what manner of love the Father hath bestowed upon us, that we should be called the sons of God. (1 John 3:1a)

9   Therefore if any man be in Christ, he is a new creature: old things are passed away; behold, all things are become new. (2 Cor. 5:17)

10 Knowing this, that our old man is crucified with him, that the body of sin might be destroyed, that henceforth we should not serve sin. (Rom. 6:6)

    That ye put off concerning the former conversation the old man, which is corrupt according to the deceitful lusts. (Eph. 4:22)

    Lie not one to another, seeing that ye have put off the old man with his deeds. (Col. 3:9)

11 I speak after the manner of men because of the infirmity of your flesh: for as ye have yielded your members servants to uncleanness and to iniquity unto

iniquity; even so now yield your members servants to righteousness unto holiness. (Rom. 6:19)

For I know that in me (that is, in my flesh,) dwelleth no good thing: for to will is present with me; but how to perform that which is good I find not... I thank God through Jesus Christ our Lord. So then with the mind I myself serve the law of God; but with the flesh the law of sin. (Rom. 7:18, 25)

I am crucified with Christ: nevertheless I live; yet not I, but Christ liveth in me: and the life which I now live in the flesh I live by the faith of the Son of God, who loved me, and gave himself for me. (Gal. 2:20)

12 But now, after that ye have known God, or rather are known of God, how turn ye again to the weak and beggarly elements, whereunto ye desire again to be in bondage? (Gal. 4:9)

Set your affection on things above, not on things on the earth... Mortify therefore your members which are upon the earth; fornication, uncleanness, inordinate affection, evil concupiscence, and covetousness, which is idolatry... But now ye also put off all these; anger, wrath, malice, blasphemy, filthy communication out of your mouth. Lie not one to another, seeing that ye have put off the old man with his deeds. (Col. 3:2, 5, 8–9)

For if after they have escaped the pollutions of the world through the knowledge of the Lord and Saviour Jesus Christ, they are again entangled therein, and overcome, the latter end is worse with them than the beginning... But it is happened unto them according to the true proverb, The dog is turned to his own vomit again; and the sow that was washed to her wallowing in the mire. (2 Pet. 2:20, 22)

13 For I know that in me (that is, in my flesh,) dwelleth no good thing: for to will is present with me; but how to perform that which is good I find not. For the good that I would I do not: but the evil which I would not, that I do. Now if I do that I would not, it is no more I that do it, but sin that dwelleth in me. I find then a law, that, when I would do good, evil is present with me. For I delight in the law of God after the inward man: But I see another law in my members, warring against the law of my mind, and bringing me into captivity to the law of sin which is in my members. (Rom. 7:18–23)

14 Keep thy heart with all diligence; for out of it are the issues of life. (Prov. 4:23)

And he said, That which cometh out of the man, that defileth the man. For from within, out of the heart of men, proceed evil thoughts, adulteries, fornications, murders, thefts, covetousness, wickedness, deceit, lasciviousness, an evil eye, blasphemy, pride, foolishness: All these evil things come from within, and defile the man. (Mark 7:20–23)

But every man is tempted, when he is drawn away of his own lust, and enticed. Then when lust hath conceived, it bringeth forth sin: and sin, when it is finished, bringeth forth death. (James 1:14–15)

15 That ye put off concerning the former conversation the old man, which is corrupt according to the deceitful lusts. (Eph. 4:22)

Teaching us that, denying ungodliness and worldly lusts, we should live soberly, righteously, and godly, in this present world. (Titus 2:12)

Let not sin therefore reign in your mortal body, that ye should obey it in the lusts thereof. (Rom. 6:12)

16 Love not the world, neither the things that are in the world. If any man love the world, the love of the Father is not in him. For all that is in the world, the lust of the flesh, and the lust of the eyes, and the pride of life, is not of the Father, but is of the world. (1 John 2:15–16)

17 The wicked, through the pride of his countenance, will not seek after God: God is not in all his thoughts. (Ps. 10:4)

Every one that is proud in heart is an abomination to the Lord. (Prov. 16:5a)

For the day of the Lord of hosts shall be upon every one that is proud and lofty, and upon every one that is lifted up; and he shall be brought low. (Isa. 2:12)

18 Watch and pray, that ye enter not into temptation: the spirit indeed is willing, but the flesh is weak. (Matt. 26:41)

19 Therefore, brethren, we are debtors, not to the flesh, to live after the flesh. For if ye live after the flesh, ye shall die: but if ye through the Spirit do mortify the deeds of the body, ye shall live. (Rom. 8:12–13)

This I say then, Walk in the Spirit, and ye shall not fulfil the lust of the flesh. For the flesh lusteth against the Spirit, and the Spirit against the flesh: and these are contrary the one to the other: so that ye cannot do the things that ye would. (Gal. 5:16–17)

20 Flee also youthful lusts: but follow righteousness, faith, charity, peace, with them that call on the Lord out of a pure heart. (2 Tim. 2:22)

Dearly beloved, I beseech you as strangers and pilgrims, abstain from fleshly lusts, which war against the soul. (1 Pet. 2:11)

As obedient children, not fashioning yourselves according to the former lusts in your ignorance. (1 Pet. 1:14)

21 And the cares of this world, and the deceitfulness of riches, and the lusts of other things entering in, choke the word, and it becometh unfruitful. (Mark 4:19)

22 I speak after the manner of men because of the infirmity of your flesh: for as ye have yielded your members servants to uncleanness and to iniquity unto iniquity; even so now yield your members servants to righteousness unto holiness. (Rom. 6:19)

23 But now ye also put off all these; anger, wrath, malice, blasphemy, filthy communication out of your mouth. Lie not one to another, seeing that ye have put off the old man with his deeds; And have put on the new man, which is renewed in knowledge after the image of him that created him: Where there is neither Greek nor Jew, circumcision nor uncircumcision, Barbarian, Scythian, bond nor free: but Christ is all, and in all. Put on therefore, as the elect of God, holy and beloved, bowels of mercies, kindness, humbleness of mind, meekness,

longsuffering; Forbearing one another, and forgiving one another, if any man have a quarrel against any: even as Christ forgave you, so also do ye. And above all these things put on charity [love], which is the bond of perfectness. (Col. 3:8–14)

24 But put ye on the Lord Jesus Christ, and make not provision for the flesh, to fulfil the lusts thereof. (Rom. 13:14)

25 I am crucified with Christ: nevertheless I live; yet not I, but Christ liveth in me: and the life which I now live in the flesh I live by the faith of the Son of God, who loved me, and gave himself for me. (Gal. 2:20)

26 And he said to them all, If any man will come after me, let him deny himself, and take up his cross daily, and follow me. (Luke 9:23)

And whosoever doth not bear his cross, and come after me, cannot be my disciple. (Luke 14:27)

And they that are Christ's have crucified the flesh with the affections and lusts. (Gal. 5:24)

27 Among whom also we all had our conversation in times past in the lusts of our flesh, fulfilling the desires of the flesh and of the mind; and were by nature the children of wrath, even as others. (Eph. 2:3)

For we ourselves also were sometimes foolish, disobedient, deceived, serving divers lusts and pleasures, living in malice and envy, hateful, and hating one another. (Titus 3:3)

28 What fruit had ye then in those things whereof ye are now ashamed? for the end of those things is death. (Rom. 6:21)

29 But his delight is in the law of the LORD; and in his law doth he meditate day and night. And he shall be like a tree planted by the rivers of water, that bringeth forth his fruit in his season; his leaf also shall not wither; and whatsoever he doeth shall prosper. (Ps. 1:2–3)

Concerning the works of men, by the word of thy lips I have kept me from the paths of the destroyer. (Ps. 17:4)

O send out thy light and thy truth: let them lead me; let them bring me unto thy holy hill, and to thy tabernacles. (Ps. 43:3)

Thy word is a lamp unto my feet, and a light unto my path... The entrance of thy words giveth light; it giveth understanding unto the simple. (Ps. 119:105, 130)

30 Blessed is the man that walketh not in the counsel of the ungodly, nor standeth in the way of sinners, nor sitteth in the seat of the scornful. (Ps.1:1)

31 Enter not into the path of the wicked, and go not in the way of evil men. Avoid it, pass not by it, turn from it, and pass away... The way of the wicked is as darkness: they know not at what they stumble. (Prov. 4:14–15, 19)

Flee fornication. Every sin that a man doeth is without the body; but he that committeth fornication sinneth against his own body. (1 Cor. 6:18)

Wherefore, my dearly beloved, flee from idolatry. (1 Cor. 10:14)

But thou, O man of God, flee these things; and follow after righteousness, godliness, faith, love, patience, meekness. (1 Tim. 6:11)

Flee also youthful lusts: but follow righteousness, faith, charity, peace, with them that call on the Lord out of a pure heart. (2 Tim. 2:22)

32 Be not deceived; God is not mocked: for whatsoever a man soweth, that shall he also reap. For he that soweth to his flesh shall of the flesh reap corruption; but he that soweth to the Spirit shall of the Spirit reap life everlasting. And let us not be weary in well doing: for in due season we shall reap, if we faint not. (Gal. 6:7–9)

33 And you hath he quickened, who were dead in trespasses and sins; Wherein in time past ye walked according to the course of this world, according to the prince of the power of the air [the devil], the spirit that now worketh in the children of disobedience: Among whom also we all had our conversation in times past in the lusts of our flesh, fulfilling the desires of the flesh and of the mind; and were by nature the children of wrath, even as others. (Eph. 2:1–3)

34 Ye are of your father the devil, and the lusts of your father ye will do. He was a murderer from the beginning, and abode not in the truth, because there is no truth in him. When he speaketh a lie, he speaketh of his own: for he is a liar, and the father of it. (John 8:44)

35 And the Lord God said unto the woman, What is this that thou hast done? And the woman said, The serpent beguiled me, and I did eat. (Gen. 3:13)

36 Wherefore, as by one man sin entered into the world, and death by sin; and so death passed upon all men, for that all have sinned (Rom. 5:12)

37 Wherein in time past ye walked according to the course of this world, according to the prince of the power of the air, the spirit that now worketh in the children of disobedience. (Eph. 2:2)

38 Be sober, be vigilant; because your adversary the devil, as a roaring lion, walketh about, seeking whom he may devour. (1 Pet. 5:8)

39 He that committeth sin is of the devil; for the devil sinneth from the beginning. For this purpose the Son of God was manifested, that he might destroy the works of the devil. (1 John 3:8)

Let no man deceive you with vain words: for because of these things cometh the wrath of God upon the children of disobedience. (Eph. 5:6)

And I saw the dead, small and great, stand before God; and the books were opened: and another book was opened, which is the book of life: and the dead were judged out of those things which were written in the books, according to their works… And whosoever was not found written in the book of life was cast into the lake of fire. (Rev. 20:12, 15)

Then shall he say also unto them on the left hand, Depart from me, ye cursed, into everlasting fire, prepared for the devil and his angels. (Matt. 25:41)

40 Submit yourselves therefore to God. Resist the devil, and he will flee from you. (James 4:7)

Ye are of God, little children, and have overcome them: because greater is he that is in you, than he that is in the world. (1 John 4:4)

And they overcame him by the blood of the Lamb, and by the word of their testimony; and they loved not their lives unto the death. (Rev. 12:11)

41 Wherefore, my dearly beloved, flee from idolatry. (1 Cor. 10:14)

Mortify therefore your members which are upon the earth; fornication, uncleanness, inordinate affection, evil concupiscence, and covetousness, which is idolatry. (Col. 3:5)

Wherefore laying aside all malice, and all guile, and hypocrisies, and envies, and all evil speakings. (1 Pet. 2:1)

For rebellion is as the sin of witchcraft, and stubbornness is as iniquity and idolatry. (1 Sam. 15:23a)

42 But if ye bite and devour one another, take heed that ye be not consumed one of another. (Gal. 5:15)

Let all bitterness, and wrath, and anger, and clamour, and evil speaking, be put away from you, with all malice: And be ye kind one to another, tenderhearted, forgiving one another, even as God for Christ's sake hath forgiven you. (Eph. 4:31–32)

Looking diligently lest any man fail of the grace of God; lest any root of bitterness springing up trouble you, and thereby many be defiled. (Heb. 12:15)

43 Wherefore doth a living man complain, a man for the punishment of his sins? Let us search and try our ways, and turn again to the LORD. Let us lift up our heart with our hands unto God in the heavens. (Lam. 3:39–41)

Having therefore these promises, dearly beloved, let us cleanse ourselves from all filthiness of the flesh and spirit, perfecting holiness in the fear of God. (2 Cor. 7:1)

If we confess our sins, he is faithful and just to forgive us our sins, and to cleanse us from all unrighteousness. (1 John 1:9)

44 Thou answeredst them, O LORD our God: thou wast a God that forgavest them, though thou tookest vengeance of their inventions. (Ps. 99:8)

For he that soweth to his flesh shall of the flesh reap corruption; but he that soweth to the Spirit shall of the Spirit reap life everlasting. (Gal. 6:8)

45 They soon forgat his works; they waited not for his counsel: But lusted exceedingly in the wilderness, and tempted God in the desert. And he gave them their request; but sent leanness into their soul. (Ps. 106:13–15)

Wherefore God also gave them up to uncleanness through the lusts of their own hearts, to dishonour their own bodies between themselves:... For this cause God gave them up unto vile affections...and receiving in themselves that recompence of their error which was meet. (Rom. 1:24, 26a, 27b)

46 If we believe not, yet he abideth faithful: he cannot deny himself. (2 Tim. 2:13)

47 Thou shalt also consider in thine heart, that, as a man chasteneth his son, so the Lord thy God chasteneth thee. (Deut. 8:5)

If his children forsake my law, and walk not in my judgments; If they break my statutes, and keep not my commandments; Then will I visit their transgression with the rod, and their iniquity with stripes. (Ps. 89:30–32)

And ye have forgotten the exhortation which speaketh unto you as unto children, My son, despise not thou the chastening of the Lord, nor faint when thou art rebuked of him: 6 For whom the Lord loveth he chasteneth, and scourgeth every son whom he receiveth. (Heb. 12:5–6)

48 From whence come wars and fightings among you? come they not hence, even of your lusts that war in your members? Ye lust, and have not: ye kill, and desire to have, and cannot obtain: ye fight and war, yet ye have not, because ye ask not. Ye ask, and receive not, because ye ask amiss, that ye may consume it upon your lusts. (James 4:1–3)

49 For we are his workmanship, created in Christ Jesus unto good works, which God hath before ordained that we should walk in them. (Eph. 2:10)

And we know that all things work together for good to them that love God, to them who are the called according to his purpose. For whom he did foreknow, he also did predestinate to be conformed to the image of his Son, that he might be the firstborn among many brethren. (Rom. 8:28–29)

As ye have therefore received Christ Jesus the Lord, so walk ye in him. (Col. 2:6)

He that saith he abideth in him ought himself also so to walk, even as he walked. (1 John 2:6)

50 That in the dispensation of the fulness of times he might gather together in one all things in Christ, both which are in heaven, and which are on earth; even in him. (Eph. 1:10)

How Much Holy Conduct
Is Holy Enough?

O ur jungle hospital in Brazil kept a very clean operating room. But every few months a tiny insect wandered in past three sets of closed doors. One day a black dot flew past my eyes, made a couple of tight turns, and landed in the middle of my operating field. My patient's open wound was clean except for the insect. If we simply hid the problem by closing the wound, infection would develop. Instead, we killed the insect, cut out the area its tiny feet touched, and separated those instruments and that piece of flesh from the field.

All of us have experienced multiple spots of sin landing in our lives.[1] With showy good works we may try to hide what lies beneath. Or perhaps we have been completely covered by sin, like festering sores obvious to all.[2] By contrast, God does not have even one tiny speck of evil or secret error to hide from us.[3]

God's Holiness

The Lord is completely pure, righteous, and holy in *all* that He says and does[4] and in *every part* of His eternal and infinite being.[5] Holiness is absolute moral, sinless perfection, and God Himself defines it.[6] What is holy is of the Lord.[7]

How holy is holy enough? He calls us to *His* holiness. This call is not an option for believers but is *His* standard and command[8] and *not our* ideas of "good behavior."[9]

Our Pursuit of His Holiness

A person who pursues holiness is seeking to walk separate from the world[10] and be pleasing to God.[11] The Lord wants us to leave the deeds of the flesh and walk in His paths, led by His Spirit.[12]

While living in our old bodies, we have not yet attained His holiness.[13] If we say we have attained sinless perfection, we deceive ourselves.[14] We must continually be on guard about our attitude, actions, and speech.[15] Through this life, He is constantly working in us to conform us to the image of His Son.[16]

The Fruit of Holiness

Some state that a strong stand on holiness kills the Christian spirit of love, forgiveness, and kindness. However, following God's righteous path does not deaden the Christian life but makes us flourishing and fruitful.[17] The fruit of His Spirit's presence includes love, long-suffering, gentleness, and goodness toward others.[18]

Learning and following His righteousness opens the door to a productive Christian walk,[19] bringing blessing, peace, and joy.[20]

The Lord is preparing us for that day when we shall see Him. We shall stand before His throne filled with His righteousness, joy, and godly pleasure forever.[21]

God has called us to *His* holiness.

**But why are some Christians so turned off
when others talk of holy living and righteous behavior?
One reason is the damaging impact of a wrong path to holiness
that looks right to some.**

Notes

[1] Who can say, I have made my heart clean, I am pure from my sin? (Prov. 20:9)

For there is not a just man upon earth, that doeth good, and sinneth not. (Eccles. 7:20)

For all have sinned, and come short of the glory of God. (Rom. 3:23)

[2] For mine iniquities are gone over mine head: as an heavy burden they are too heavy for me. My wounds stink and are corrupt because of my foolishness. (Ps. 38:4–5)

The whole head is sick, and the whole heart faint. From the sole of the foot even unto the head there is no soundness in it; but wounds, and bruises, and putrifying sores: they have not been closed, neither bound up, neither mollified with ointment. (Isa. 1:5b–6)

[3] Thou art of purer eyes than to behold evil, and canst not look on iniquity. (Hab. 1:13)

For thou art not a God that hath pleasure in wickedness: neither shall evil dwell with thee. (Ps. 5:4)

There is no unrighteousness in him. (Ps. 92:15b)

[4] Every word of God is pure. (Prov. 30:5a)

The Lord is righteous in all his ways, and holy in all his works. (Ps. 145:17)

[5] O Lord God of Israel, thou art righteous. (Ezra 9:15)

Thus saith the high and lofty One that inhabiteth eternity, whose name is Holy; I dwell in the high and holy place. (Isa. 57:15a)

Thy testimonies are very sure: holiness becometh thine house, O LORD, forever. (Ps. 93:5)

[6] Holy (Hebrew, *qodesh*) means "set apart"; most common of several words for "holy" in the Old Testament, being used in 385 verses; usually translated "holy," "most holy," "holiness" (example: Leviticus 22:32, "Neither shall ye profane my holy name; but I will be hallowed among the children of Israel: I am the Lord which hallow you."). In the New Testament: Holy (Greek, *hagios*) means "separate," "set apart," "holy"; used in 218 verses and usually translated as the adjective "holy" (example: 1 Peter 1:15–16, "But as he which hath called you is holy, so be ye holy in all manner of conversation; Because it is written, Be ye holy; for I am holy.") (Young, 487–8).

[7] Give unto the LORD the glory due unto his name; worship the LORD in the beauty of holiness. (Ps. 29:2)

Exalt the Lord our God, and worship at his holy hill: for the Lord our God is holy. (Ps. 99:9)

And one cried unto another, and said, Holy, holy, holy, is the LORD of hosts. (Isa. 6:3a)

8   That ye would walk worthy of God, who hath called you unto his kingdom and glory. To the end he may stablish your hearts unblameable in holiness before God, even our Father, at the coming of our Lord Jesus Christ with all his saints. (1 Thess. 2:12–13a)

For God hath not called us unto uncleanness, but unto holiness. (1 Thess. 4:7)

According as he hath chosen us in him before the foundation of the world, that we should be holy and without blame before him in love. (Eph. 1:4)

Sanctify yourselves therefore, and be ye holy: for I am the LORD your God. (Lev. 20:7)

9   For laying aside the commandment of God, ye hold the tradition of men... And he said unto them, Full well ye reject the commandment of God, that ye may keep your own tradition... Making the word of God of none effect through your tradition. (Mark 7:8a, 9, 13a)

Beware lest any man spoil you through philosophy and vain deceit, after the tradition of men, after the rudiments of the world, and not after Christ. (Col. 2:8)

Then Peter and the other apostles answered and said, We ought to obey God rather than men. (Acts 5:29)

10   I am the Lord your God, which have separated you from other people... And ye shall be holy unto me: for I the Lord am holy, and have severed you from other people, that ye should be mine. (Lev. 20:2ba, 26)

Wherefore come out from among them, and be ye separate, saith the Lord, and touch not the unclean thing; and I will receive you. (2 Cor. 6:17)

11   (Jesus said) And he that sent me is with me: the Father hath not left me alone; for I do always those things that please him. (John 8:29)

Apart from Christ Himself, an incredible example is Enoch.

And Enoch walked with God: and he was not; for God took him. (Gen. 5:24)

By faith Enoch was translated that he should not see death; and was not found, because God had translated him: for before his translation he had this testimony, that he pleased God. (Heb. 11:5)

12   That he no longer should live the rest of his time in the flesh to the lusts of men, but to the will of God. (1 Pet. 4:2)

That the righteousness of the law might be fulfilled in us, who walk not after the flesh, but after the Spirit. (Rom. 8:4)

This I say then, Walk in the Spirit, and ye shall not fulfil the lust of the flesh... If we live in the Spirit, let us also walk in the Spirit. (Gal. 5:16, 25)

13   Not as though I had already attained, either were already perfect: but I follow after, if that I may apprehend that for which also I am apprehended of Christ Jesus. Brethren, I count not myself to have apprehended: but this one thing I do, forgetting those things which are behind, and reaching forth unto those

things which are before, I press toward the mark for the prize of the high calling of God in Christ Jesus. (Phil. 3:12–14)

14 If we say that we have no sin, we deceive ourselves, and the truth is not in us... If we say that we have not sinned, we make him a liar, and his word is not in us. (1 John 1:8, 10)

15 Be ye angry, and sin not: let not the sun go down upon your wrath: Neither give place to the devil. Let him that stole steal no more: but rather let him labour, working with his hands the thing which is good, that he may have to give to him that needeth. Let no corrupt communication proceed out of your mouth, but that which is good to the use of edifying, that it may minister grace unto the hearers. And grieve not the holy Spirit of God, whereby ye are sealed unto the day of redemption. Let all bitterness, and wrath, and anger, and clamour, and evil speaking, be put away from you, with all malice... But fornication, and all uncleanness, or covetousness, let it not be once Neither filthiness, nor foolish talking, nor jesting, which are not convenient: but rather giving of thanks. (Eph. 4:26–31, 5:3–4)

Cleanse ourselves from filthiness of the flesh and perfect holiness. (2 Cor. 7:1)

16 For whom he did foreknow, he also did predestinate to be conformed to the image of his Son, that he might be the firstborn among many brethren. (Rom. 8:29)

17 Blessed is the man that...his delight is in the law of the LORD; and in his law doth he meditate day and night. And he shall be like a tree planted by the rivers of water, that bringeth forth his fruit in his season; his leaf also shall not wither; and whatsoever he doeth shall prosper. (Ps. 1:1a, 2–3)

The fear of the LORD is a fountain of life, to depart from the snares of death. (Prov. 14:27)

Every good gift and every perfect gift is from above, and cometh down from the Father of lights, with whom is no variableness, neither shadow of turning. (James 1:17)

But the wisdom that is from above is first pure, then peaceable, gentle, and easy to be intreated, full of mercy and good fruits, without partiality, and without hypocrisy. And the fruit of righteousness is sown in peace of them that make peace. (James 3:17–18)

18 But the fruit of the Spirit is love, joy, peace, longsuffering, gentleness, goodness, faith, Meekness, temperance: against such there is no law. (Gal. 5:22–23)

19 This book of the law shall not depart out of thy mouth; but thou shalt meditate therein day and night, that thou mayest observe to do according to all that is written therein: for then thou shalt make thy way prosperous, and then thou shalt have good success. (Josh. 1:8)

20 Blessed are the undefiled in the way, who walk in the law of the LORD. Blessed are they that keep his testimonies, and that seek him with the whole heart. (Ps. 119:1–2)

And the work of righteousness shall be peace; and the effect of righteousness quietness and assurance for ever. (Isa. 32:17)

I will greatly rejoice in the LORD, my soul shall be joyful in my God; for he hath clothed me with the garments of salvation, he hath covered me with the robe of righteousness, as a bridegroom decketh himself with ornaments, and as a bride adorneth herself with her jewels. (Isa. 61:10)

For the kingdom of God is not meat and drink; but righteousness, and peace, and joy in the Holy Ghost. (Rom. 14:17)

[21] Blessed are they which do hunger and thirst after righteousness: for they shall be filled... Blessed are the pure in heart: for they shall see God. (Matt. 5:6, 8)

Thou wilt shew me the path of life: in thy presence is fulness of joy; at thy right hand there are pleasures for evermore. (Ps. 16:11)

Now unto him that is able to keep you from falling, and to present you faultless before the presence of his glory with exceeding joy, To the only wise God our Saviour. (Jude 1:24–25a)

What Is a Wrong Path
of Holiness?

On a hillside near the shore of the Sea of Galilee, Jesus preached His most famous message: the Sermon on the Mount. Filling three chapters of Matthew's Gospel, it is His longest recorded sermon in the Bible. Part of the thrust of the message is the contrast it draws with the religious ideas of the Pharisees.

Pharisees and Legalism

Christians and non-Christians complain about people acting "holier than thou" and "legalistic." Indeed, "legalism" destroys loving and joyful spiritual attitudes.[1] This wrong approach to our Christian life path *is* addressed in God's Word directly and repeatedly through the religious sect of the Pharisees, *the epitome of legalism* and the lightning rod of God's condemnation.

The Pharisees fervently believed in separation. Even the word *Pharisee* comes from an Aramaic word meaning *separated one* or *separatist*.[2] Anyone that advocates separation from the evils of this world[3] is by definition a separatist. However, multiple references in all four Gospels, the book of Acts, and the Epistles, condemn the Pharisees' doctrine, attitudes, and practice. *So Pharisee has come to mean separatist in an ungodly sense. And Pharisees are the Bible's major example of legalism.*

During Jesus's ministry, Pharisees vehemently opposed him.[4] However, after His death, various Pharisees professed themselves believers and became Christians. Among them were some who felt that all male believers must be circumcised.[5] Such circumcision was the first step in obeying the Jewish law.[6] So, in the early church, this same legalistic Pharisaical group became known as "the circumcision."[7]

Today, no one completely fulfills the mold of the Pharisee. However, Christ warned of the "leaven of the Pharisees,"[8] which is not grounded on faith and service to God in love.[9] Instead, it is rooted in the flesh and is rightly called "self-righteousness."[10] By means of the many New Testament passages about the Pharisees and those promoting circumcision, we can understand the errors of legalism.

Specific Errors of Pharisees and Legalism

Pharisees wrongly handle the Word of God by adding their own traditions to it. In their mind, those traditions equal biblical doctrine.[11] They follow those traditions while ignoring or neglecting important scriptural doctrines about obedience to God, judgment, mercy, and faith.[12] Such additions may displace or set aside biblical truth.[13] Or worse, the additions may contradict biblical truth.[14]

An example of legalistic logic was their rule about the Sabbath. Based on Bible verses to do no work on the Sabbath,[15] Pharisees twisted the idea to mean not even helping people on the Sabbath.[16] Moreover, they sought to use their rule as a reason to oppose Jesus.[17]

Pharisees believe that all true Christians must add good works to grace for salvation.[18] Paul, in Galatians, explained how they wanted to turn the believers from righteousness by faith to righteousness by works.[19] Of course, this is totally wrong and contrary to salvation without works.[20]

Pharisees are proud of their position and self-righteous traditions.[21] Since they believe they are the only ones who understand all the laws of righteousness, this makes them feel superior.[22] Such an attitude has a "form of godliness"[23] but is *not* based on faith and service to God in love. Proud of their own ways, they seek to make personal followers instead of pointing people to God.[24]

Pharisees are more concerned about how people view and honor them instead of how God sees them. Their motivation is the praise of men and not the praise of God.[25]

As merciless judges, Pharisees freely condemn others, even the faithful and godly. Legalists may criticize others who sincerely praise and honor Jesus.[26] *Judging others is a central attitude of the self-righteous.*[27] Their judgment usually is based on man's tradition and not on biblical truth.[28] Beyond condemning sinners, the self-righteous may actually persecute the innocent.[29] This attitude of condemnation does not leave room for showing mercy.[30] It is uncaring for souls.[31] Having unrepentant hearts themselves,[32] they reject evidence of repentance in others and do not want to associate with them.[33]

Pharisees do not recognize the work of God. Separatists want evidence of God's working, even after they actually have seen God's working.[34] Jesus cast out demons, and the Pharisees accused Him of doing it in the power of the devil.[35] Christ's healing on the Sabbath was particularly condemned.[36]

Pharisees lack love.[37] They do not love God.[38] And they do not love those in need.[39]

Pharisees are hypocrites, separating heart attitude from external conduct. We are told to "beware the leaven of the Pharisees," which is hypocrisy,[40] because true godliness comes from the heart.[41] They are actors, whose actions are calculated to look good[42] but whose heart sometimes hides secret sin.[43] For all their effort at looking good, some of their sins are obvious: they are covetous,[44] amassing wealth at the expense of the poor.[45]

By intimidating and criticizing, Pharisees seek to turn individuals, churches, and fellowships to their ideas.[46] The circumcision crowd demanded that new believers become circumcised according to the Law of Moses.[47] They even contended with the disciples over circumcision and the Law,[48] intimidating and bullying godly men into ungodly separation.[49] Being unruly and deceivers, they push their doctrine, undermining Christian growth.[50] Their doctrine and ways have greatly hindered the testimony of the gospel.[51]

Pharisees need to be confronted in love with doctrinal truth. We must beware of the legalistic doctrine of the Pharisees as it can spread and corrupt the testimony of true righteousness by faith.[52] We should be an open testimony to those who put confidence in fleshly works.[53]

Are We Legalistic in Our Christian Walk?

As believers we should ask ourselves, "Am I thinking and acting like a Pharisee?" Am I trusting in good works or my own righteousness for salvation? Do I have an attitude of criticism and condemnation toward others? Am I prideful and more concerned how people view me than how God sees me? Am I a hypocrite and insincere in my Christian walk? Do I cause trouble in the church?

Legalists are proud of the path they have chosen and freely condemn others. They point their toes at men's ideas instead of God and His word.

So what is the key to true holiness?

Notes

1. But now we are delivered from the law, that being dead wherein we were held; that we should serve in newness of spirit, and not in the oldness of the letter. (Rom. 7:6)

     Who also hath made us able ministers of the new testament, not of the letter, but of the spirit for the letter killeth, but the spirit giveth life. (2 Cor. 3:6)

2. Colin Brown, *The New International Dictionary of New Testament Theology*, Vol. 2 (Grand Rapids: Zondervan, 1976), 810.

3. The world cannot hate you; but me it hateth, because I testify of it, that the works thereof are evil. (John 7:7)

     I pray not that thou shouldest take them out of the world, but that thou shouldest keep them from the evil. (John 17:15)

     Who gave himself for our sins, that he might deliver us from this present evil world, according to the will of God and our Father. (Gal. 1:4)

4. And the chief priests and scribes stood and vehemently accused him. (Luke 23:10)

5. And the apostles and brethren that were in Judaea heard that the Gentiles had also received the word of God. And when Peter was come up to Jerusalem, they that were of the circumcision contended with him. (Acts 11:1–2)

     And certain men which came down from Judaea taught the brethren, and said, Except ye be circumcised after the manner of Moses, ye cannot be saved. (Act 15:1)

6. For circumcision verily profiteth, if thou keep the law: but if thou be a breaker of the law, thy circumcision is made uncircumcision. (Rom. 2:25)

     For as many as are of the works of the law are under the curse: for it is written, Cursed is every one that continueth not in all things which are written in the book of the law to do them. But that no man is justified by the law in the sight of God, it is evident: for, The just shall live by faith. And the law is not of faith: but, The man that doeth them shall live in them. (Gal. 3:10–12)

7. But there rose up certain of the sect of the Pharisees which believed, saying, That it was needful to circumcise them, and to command them to keep the law of Moses. (Acts 15:5)

     And they of the circumcision which believed were astonished, as many as came with Peter, because that on the Gentiles also was poured out the gift of the Holy Ghost. (Acts 10:45)

     And when Peter was come up to Jerusalem, they that were of the circumcision contended with him. (Acts 11:2)

For before that certain came from James, he did eat with the Gentiles: but when they were come, he withdrew and separated himself, fearing them which were of the circumcision. (Gal. 2:12)

8   Then Jesus said unto them, Take heed and beware of the leaven of the Pharisees and of the Sadducees... Then understood they how that he bade them not beware of the leaven of bread, but of the doctrine of the Pharisees and of the Sadducees. (Matt. 16:6, 12)

9   For in Jesus Christ neither circumcision availeth anything, nor uncircumcision; but faith which worketh by love. (Gal. 5:6)

Remembering without ceasing your work of faith, and labour of love, and patience of hope in our Lord Jesus Christ, in the sight of God and our Father. (1 Thess. 1:3)

I thank my God, making mention of thee always in my prayers, Hearing of thy love and faith, which thou hast toward the Lord Jesus, and toward all saints. (Phil. 1:4–5)

For God is not unrighteous to forget your work and labour of love, which ye have shewed toward his name, in that ye have ministered to the saints, and do minister. (Heb. 6:10)

10   For they being ignorant of God's righteousness and going about to establish their own righteousness, have not submitted themselves unto the righteousness of God. (Rom. 10:3)

11   Ye hypocrites, well did Esaias prophesy of you, saying, This people draweth nigh unto me with their mouth, and honoureth me with their lips; but their heart is far from me. But in vain they do worship me, teaching for doctrines the commandments of men. (Matt. 15:7–9)

12   Woe unto you, scribes and Pharisees, hypocrites! for ye pay tithe of mint and anise and cummin, and have omitted the weightier matters of the law, judgment, mercy, and faith: these ought ye to have done, and not to leave the other undone. Ye blind guides, which strain at a gnat, and swallow a camel. (Matt. 23:23–24)

13   Woe unto you, ye blind guides, which say, Whosoever shall swear by the temple, it is nothing; but whosoever shall swear by the gold of the temple, he is a debtor! Ye fools and blind: for whether is greater, the gold, or the temple that sanctifieth the gold? And, Whosoever shall swear by the altar, it is nothing; but whosoever sweareth by the gift that is upon it, he is guilty. Ye fools and blind: for whether is greater, the gift, or the altar that sanctifieth the gift? Whoso therefore shall swear by the altar, sweareth by it, and by all things thereon. And whoso shall swear by the temple, sweareth by it, and by him that dwelleth therein. And he that shall swear by heaven, sweareth by the throne of God, and by him that sitteth thereon. (Matt. 23:16–22)

14   Every word of God is pure... Add thou not unto his words, lest he reprove thee, and thou be found a liar. (Prov. 30:5a, 6)

But he answered and said unto them, Why do ye also transgress the commandment of God by your tradition? For God commanded, saying, Honour thy father and mother: and, He that curseth father or mother, let him die the death. But ye say, Whosoever shall say to his father or his mother, It is a gift, by whatsoever thou mightest be profited by me; And honour not his father or his mother, he shall be free. Thus have ye made the commandment of God of none effect by your tradition. (Matt. 15:3–6)

15 Remember the sabbath day, to keep it holy. (Exod. 20:8)

But the seventh day is the sabbath of the Lord thy God: in it thou shalt not do any work, thou, nor thy son, nor thy daughter, nor thy manservant, nor thy maidservant, nor thine ox, nor thine ass, nor any of thy cattle, nor thy stranger that is within thy gates; that thy manservant and thy maidservant may rest as well as thou. (Deut. 5:14)

16 And the ruler of the synagogue answered with indignation, because that Jesus had healed on the sabbath day, and said unto the people, There are six days in which men ought to work: in them therefore come and be healed, and not on the sabbath day. (Luke 13:14)

And the scribes and Pharisees watched him, whether he would heal on the sabbath day; that they might find an accusation against him. (Luke 6:7)

17 And, behold, there was a man which had his hand withered. And they asked him, saying, Is it lawful to heal on the sabbath days? that they might accuse him... Then saith he to the man, Stretch forth thine hand. And he stretched it forth; and it was restored whole, like as the other. Then the Pharisees went out, and held a council against him, how they might destroy him. (Matt. 12:10, 13–14)

18 And certain men which came down from Judea taught the brethren, and said, Except ye be circumcised after the manner of Moses, ye cannot be saved. When therefore Paul and Barnabas had no small dissension and disputation with them, they determined that Paul and Barnabas, and certain other of them, should go up to Jerusalem unto the apostles and elders about this question... But there rose up certain of the sect of the Pharisees which believed, saying, That is was needful to circumcise them, and to command them to keep the Law of Moses. (Acts 15:1–2, 5)

Thou seest, brother, how many thousands of Jews there are which believe; and they are all zealous of the law. (Acts 21:20b)

19 Therefore by the deeds of the law there shall no flesh be justified in his sight: for by the law is the knowledge of sin. But now the righteousness of God without the law is manifested, being witnessed by the law and the prophets; Even the righteousness of God which is by faith of Jesus Christ unto all and upon all them that believe: for there is no difference. (Rom. 3:20–22)

Behold, I Paul say unto you, that if ye be circumcised, Christ shall profit you nothing. For I testify again to every man that is circumcised, that he is a debtor to do the whole law. Christ is become of no effect unto you, whosoever of you are justified by the law; ye are fallen from grace. For we through the Spirit wait for the hope of righteousness by faith. For in Jesus Christ neither circumcision availeth any thing, nor uncircumcision; but faith which worketh by love. Ye did run well; who did hinder you that ye should not obey the truth? This persuasion cometh not of him that calleth you. A little leaven leaveneth the whole lump. (Gal. 5:2–9)

Yea doubtless, and I count all things but loss for the excellency of the knowledge of Christ Jesus my Lord: for whom I have suffered the loss of all things, and do count them but dung, that I may win Christ, And be found in him, not having mine own righteousness, which is of the law, but that which is through the faith of Christ, the righteousness which is of God by faith. (Phil. 3:8–9)

20 Therefore we conclude that a man is justified by faith without the deeds of the law… Seeing it is one God, which shall justify the circumcision by faith, and uncircumcision through faith. (Rom. 3:28, 30)

What shall we say then? That the Gentiles, which followed not after righteousness, have attained to righteousness, even the righteousness which is of faith. But Israel, which followed after the law of righteousness, hath not attained to the law of righteousness. Wherefore? Because they sought it not by faith, but as it were by the works of the law. For they stumbled at that stumbling stone. (Rom. 9:30–32)

Knowing that a man is not justified by the works of the law, but by the faith of Jesus Christ, even we have believed in Jesus Christ, that we might be justified by the faith of Christ, and not by the works of the law: for by the works of the law shall no flesh be justified. (Gal. 2:16)

But that no man is justified by the law in the sight of God, it is evident: for, The just shall live by faith. And the law is not of faith: but, The man that doeth them shall live in them. Christ hath redeemed us from the curse of the law, being made a curse for us: for it is written, Cursed is every one that hangeth on a tree. (Gal. 3:11–13)

For by grace are ye saved through faith; and that not of yourselves: it is the gift of God: Not of works, lest any man should boast. (Eph. 2:8–9)

21 And he [Jesus] spake this parable unto certain which trusted in themselves that they were righteous, and despised others: Two men went up into the temple to pray; the one a Pharisee, and the other a publican. The Pharisee stood and prayed thus with himself, God, I thank thee, that I am not as other men are, extortioners, unjust, adulterers, or even as this publican. I fast twice in the week, I give tithes of all that I possess. (Luke 18:9–12)

22 But when he [John the Baptist] saw many of the Pharisees and Sadducees come to his baptism, he said unto them, O generation of vipers, who hath warned you to flee from the wrath to come? Bring forth therefore fruits meet for repentance: And think not to say within yourselves, We have Abraham to our

father: for I say unto you, that God is able of these stones to raise up children unto Abraham. (Matt. 3:7–9)

And he spake this parable unto certain which trusted in themselves that they were righteous, and despised others: Two men went up into the temple to pray; the one a Pharisee, and the other a publican. The Pharisee stood and prayed thus with himself, God, I thank thee, that I am not as other men are, extortioners, unjust, adulterers, or even as this publican. I fast twice in the week, I give tithes of all that I possess. And the publican, standing afar off, would not lift up so much as his eyes unto heaven, but smote upon his breast, saying, God be merciful to me a sinner. I tell you, this man went down to his house justified rather than the other: for every one that exalteth himself shall be abased; and he that humbleth himself shall be exalted. (Luke 18:9–14)

Then came the officers to the chief priests and Pharisees; and they said unto them, Why have ye not brought him? The officers answered, Never man spake like this man. Then answered them the Pharisees, Are ye also deceived? Have any of the rulers or of the Pharisees believed on him? But this people who knoweth not the law are cursed. (John 7:45–49)

Then they reviled him, and said, Thou art his [Jesus'] disciple; but we are Moses' disciples. We know that God spake unto Moses: as for this fellow, we know not from whence he is... Thou wast altogether born in sins, and dost thou teach us? And they cast him out. (John 9:28–29, 34)

23 Having a form of godliness, but denying the power thereof: such turn away. (2 Tim. 3:5)

24 Woe unto you, scribes and Pharisees, hypocrites! for ye compass sea and land to make one proselyte, and when he is made, ye make him twofold more the child of hell than yourselves. (Matt. 23:15)

25 Then spake Jesus to the multitude, and to his disciples, Saying, The scribes and the Pharisees sit in Moses' seat... But all their works they do for to be seen of men... And love the uppermost rooms at feasts, and the chief seats in the synagogues, And greetings in the markets, and to be called of men, Rabbi, Rabbi. (Matt. 23:1–2, 5a, 6–7)

For they loved the praise of men more than the praise of God. (John 12:43)

26 And, behold, a woman in the city, which was a sinner, when she knew that Jesus sat at meat in the Pharisee's house, brought an alabaster box of ointment, And stood at his feet behind him weeping, and began to wash his feet with tears, and did wipe them with the hairs of her head, and kissed his feet, and anointed them with the ointment. Now when the Pharisee which had bidden him saw it, he spake within himself, saying, This man, if he were a prophet, would have known who and what manner of woman this is that toucheth him: for she is a sinner. (Luke 7:37–39)

And when he was come nigh, even now at the descent of the mount of Olives, the whole multitude of the disciples began to rejoice and praise God with a loud voice for all the mighty works that they had seen; Saying, Blessed be the King that cometh in the name of the Lord: peace in heaven, and glory in the highest. And some of the Pharisees from among the multitude said unto him, Master, rebuke thy disciples. (Luke 19:37–39)

27 Two men went up into the temple to pray; the one a Pharisee, and the other a publican. The Pharisee stood and prayed thus with himself, God, I thank thee, that I am not as other men are, extortioners, unjust, adulterers, or even as this publican. I fast twice in the week, I give tithes of all that I possess. (Luke 18:10–12)

28 At that time Jesus went on the sabbath day through the corn; and his disciples were an hungred, and began to pluck the ears of corn, and to eat. But when the Pharisees saw it, they said unto him, Behold, thy disciples do that which is not lawful to do upon the sabbath day. But he said unto them… But if ye had known what this meaneth, I will have mercy, and not sacrifice, ye would not have condemned the guiltless. (Matt. 12:1–3a, 7)

Then came to Jesus scribes and Pharisees, which were of Jerusalem, saying, why do thy disciples transgress the tradition of the elders? For they wash not their hands when they eat bread. (Matt. 15:1–2)

29 Woe unto you, scribes and Pharisees, hypocrites! Because ye build the tombs of the prophets, and garnish the sepulchres of the righteous, and say, If we had been in the days of our fathers, we would not have been partakers with them in the blood of the prophets. Wherefore ye be witnesses unto yourselves, that ye are the children of them which killed the prophets. (Matt. 23:29–31)

Much people of the Jews therefore knew that he was there: and they came not for Jesus' sake only, but that they might see Lazarus also, whom he had raised from the dead. But the chief priests consulted that they might put Lazarus also to death; because that by reason of him many of the Jews went away, and believed on Jesus. (John 12:9–11)

Who both killed the Lord Jesus, and their own prophets, and have persecuted us; and they please not God, and are contrary to all men. (1 Thess. 2:15)

30 And it came to pass, as Jesus sat at meat in the house, behold, many publicans and sinners came and sat down with him and his disciples. And when the Pharisees saw it, they said unto his disciples, Why eateth your Master with publicans and sinners? (Matt. 9:10–11)

31 But woe unto you, scribes and Pharisees, hypocrites! for ye shut up the kingdom of heaven against men: for ye neither go in yourselves, neither suffer ye them that are entering to go in. (Matt. 23:13)

32 In those days came John the Baptist, preaching in the wilderness of Judaea, And saying, Repent ye: for the kingdom of heaven is at hand… Then went out to him Jerusalem, and all Judaea, and all the region round about Jordan, and were baptized of him in Jordan, confessing their sins. But when he saw many of the Pharisees and Sadducees come to his baptism, he said unto them, O generation of vipers, who hath warned you to flee from the wrath to come? (Matt. 3:1–2, 5–7)

For John came unto you in the way of righteousness, and ye believed him not: but the publicans and the harlots believed him: and ye, when ye had seen it, repented not afterward, that ye might believe him. (Matt. 21:32)

And all the people that heard him, and the publicans, justified God, being baptized with the baptism of John. But the Pharisees and lawyers rejected the counsel of God against themselves, being not baptized of him. (Luke 7:29–30)

33 And one of the Pharisees desired him that he would eat with him. And he went into the Pharisee's house, and sat down to meat. And, behold, a woman in the city, which was a sinner, when she knew that Jesus sat at meat in the Pharisee's house, brought an alabaster box of ointment, And stood at his feet behind him weeping, and began to wash his feet with tears, and did wipe them with the hairs of her head, and kissed his feet, and anointed them with the ointment. Now when the Pharisee which had bidden him saw it, he spake within himself, saying, This man, if he were a prophet, would have known who and what manner of woman this is that toucheth him: for she is a sinner… And he turned to the woman, and said unto Simon, Seest thou this woman? I entered into thine house, thou gavest me no water for my feet: but she hath washed my feet with tears, and wiped them with the hairs of her head. Thou gavest me no kiss: but this woman since the time I came in hath not ceased to kiss my feet. My head with oil thou didst not anoint: but this woman hath anointed my feet with ointment. Wherefore I say unto thee, her sins, which are many, are forgiven; for she loved much: but to whom little is forgiven, the same loveth little. And he said unto her, Thy sins are forgiven. (Luke 7:36–39, 44–48)

34 And he was casting out a devil, and it was dumb. And it came to pass, when the devil was gone out, the dumb spake; and the people wondered. But some of them said, He casteth out devils through Beelzebub the chief of the devils. And others tempting him, sought of him a sign from heaven. (Luke 11:14–16)

35 But the Pharisees said, He casteth out devils through the prince of the devils. (Matt. 9:34)

But when the Pharisees heard it, they said, this fellow doth not cast out devils, but by Beelzebub the prince of the devils. (Matt. 12:24)

36 And he entered again into the synagogue; and there was a man there which had a withered hand. And they watched him, whether he would heal him on the Sabbath day; that they might accuse him. (Mark 3:1–2)

Then again the Pharisees also asked him how he had received his sight. He said unto them, He put clay upon mine eyes, and I washed, and do see. Therefore said some of the Pharisees, this man is not of God, because he keepeth not the Sabbath day. Others said, how can a man that is a sinner do such miracles? And there was a division among them. (John 9:15–16)

37 This people draweth nigh unto me with their mouth, and honoureth me with their lips; but their heart is far from me. (Matt. 15:8)

But woe unto you, Pharisees! For ye tithe mint and rue and all manner of herbs, and pass over judgment and the love of God: these out ye to have done, and not to leave the other undone. (Luke 11:42)

38 But I know you, that ye have not the love of God in you. (John 5:42)

39 But their scribes and Pharisees murmured against his disciples, saying, why do ye eat and drink with publicans and sinners? And Jesus answering, said unto them, they that are whole need not a physician; but they that are sick. I came not to call the righteous, but sinners to repentance. (Luke 5:30–32)

40 Beware ye of the leaven of the Pharisees, which is hypocrisy. (Luke 12:1a)

41 For he is not a Jew, which is one outwardly; neither is that circumcision, which is outward in the flesh: But he is a Jew, which is one inwardly; and circumcision is that of the heart, in the spirit, and not in the letter; whose praise is not of men, but of God. (Rom. 2:28–29)

42 But all their works they do for to be seen of men: they make broad their phylacteries, and enlarge the borders of their garments. (Matt. 23:5)

43 Woe unto you, scribes and Pharisees, hypocrites! for ye make clean the outside of the cup and of the platter, but within they are full of extortion and excess... Woe unto you, scribes and Pharisees, hypocrites! for ye are like unto whited sepulchres, which indeed appear beautiful outward, but are within full of dead men's bones, and of all uncleanness. Even so ye also outwardly appear righteous unto men, but within ye are full of hypocrisy and iniquity. (Matt. 23:25, 27–28)

44 And the Pharisees also, who were covetous, heard all these things: and they derided him. (Luke 16:14)

45 Woe unto you, scribes and Pharisees, hypocrites! for ye devour widows' houses, and for a pretence make long prayer: therefore ye shall receive the greater damnation. (Matt. 23:14)

46 Thou seest, brother, how many thousands of Jews there are which believe; and they are all zealous of the law. (Acts 21:20b)

47 But there rose up certain of the sect of the Pharisees which believed, saying, That it was needful to circumcise them, and to command them to keep the law of Moses. (Acts 15:5)

48 And when Peter was come up to Jerusalem, they that were of the circumcision contended with him. (Acts 11:2)

And certain men which came down from Judaea taught the brethren, and said, Except ye be circumcised after the manner of Moses, ye cannot be saved. When therefore Paul and Barnabas had no small dissension and disputation with them, they determined that Paul and Barnabas, and certain other of them, should go up to Jerusalem unto the apostles and elders about this question. (Acts 15:1–2)

49 But when Peter was come to Antioch, I withstood him to the face, because he was to be blamed. For before that certain came from James, he did eat with the Gentiles: but when they were come, he withdrew and separated himself, fearing them which were of the circumcision. And the other Jews dissembled

likewise with him; insomuch that Barnabas also was carried away with their dissimulation. (Gal. 2:11–13)

50 For there are many unruly and vain talkers and deceivers, specially they of the circumcision: Whose mouths must be stopped, who subvert whole houses, teaching things which they ought not, for filthy lucre's sake... Wherefore rebuke them sharply, that they may be sound in the faith; Not giving heed to Jewish fables, and commandments of men, that turn from the truth. (Titus 1:10–11, 13b–14)

51 Woe to you, teachers of the law and Pharisees, you hypocrites! You shut the door of the kingdom of heaven in people's faces. You yourselves do not enter, nor will you let those enter who are trying to... Woe to you, teachers of the law and Pharisees, you hypocrites! You travel over land and sea to win a single convert, and when you have succeeded, you make them twice as much a child of hell as you are. (Matt. 23:13, 15).

52 Then Jesus said unto them, Take heed and beware of the leaven of the Pharisees and of the Sadducees... How is it that ye do not understand that I spake it not to you concerning bread, that ye should beware of the leaven of the Pharisees and of the Sadducees? Then understood they how that he bade them not beware of the leaven of bread, but of the doctrine of the Pharisees and of the Sadducees. (Matt. 16:6, 11–12)

He [Jesus] began to say unto his disciples first of all, Beware ye of the leaven of the Pharisees, which is hypocrisy. (Luke 12:1b)

Your glorying is not good. Know ye not that a little leaven leaveneth the whole lump? Purge out therefore the old leaven, that ye may be a new lump, as ye are unleavened. For even Christ our Passover is sacrificed for us: Therefore let us keep the feast, not with old leaven, neither with the leaven of malice and wickedness: but with the unleavened bread of sincerity and truth. (1 Cor. 5:6–8)

For in Jesus Christ neither circumcision availeth anything, nor uncircumcision; but faith which worketh by love Ye did run well; who did hinder you that ye should not obey the truth? This persuasion cometh not of him that calleth you. A little leaven leaveneth the whole lump. I have confidence in you through the Lord, that ye will be none otherwise minded: but he that troubleth you shall bear his judgment, whosoever he be. (Gal. 5:6–10)

53 Beware of dogs, beware of evil workers, beware of the concision. For we are the circumcision, which worship God in the spirit, and rejoice in Christ Jesus, and have no confidence in the flesh. (Phil. 3:2–3)

What Is the Key to
True Holiness?

A woman briefly stepped out of her house. When she turned to go back inside, she saw fire coming from several windows. Braving the raging flames, she ran to her baby's room. She pulled her child from his crib and wrapped him in a blanket. Moments later, with burns on her face and arms and clothes smoking, she carried her child to safety. Love carried her heart beyond bravery to a willing sacrifice of herself.

Love

God is love.[1] It is as much a part of His nature as His holiness, and it existed between the Father and Son before the world began.[2] Like holiness, we understand love by Who He is and what He does. The plan of God is to bring us into Christ, into the perfect, eternal fullness of His love[3] and never to be separated from it.[4]

God showed a compassion for our needs and a desire for our good, even to the point of sacrificing Himself in the Person of Jesus Christ.[5] That sacrifice not only saves us from eternal damnation but makes us children of the Father[6] and part of the beloved bride of Christ.[7] We are called to that love relationship with God and called to demonstrating His love toward others[8] in all its beauty, fullness, and sacrifice.[9]

Love's Relation to Holiness

So how does love relate to holiness? We grow in holiness as we grow in obedience to the Lord's commands, which include His command to love.[10] *True holiness is trust and obedience to the Lord out of love. Love is the central attitude and motivation for holiness.*[11]

Our walk in this life cannot be an arbitrary balance between holiness and love. They are *not* two different ends of a spectrum of behavioral choices. They are combined in God, and He has called us to *both*.[12]

This basic command to love others is repeatedly emphasized in the Word of God.[13] Scripture binds together our love for God with showing love toward others.[14] It is impossible to live holy and to despise or hate others.[15] Love is the premier testimony of Christ's disciples,[16] which encourages and helps build the church.[17]

Wrong Directions of Love

The command to love does not refer to everything in this world. While showing compassion and service to others, we are not to love the sinful attitudes and actions of this world.[18] Moreover, if God grants us wealth in this world, we are not to love it.[19]

Self-Love

What about self-love, self-esteem, self-worth, and positive identity? The scripture refers to such love when it declares, "Love thy neighbor as yourself."[20] Every normal person seeks the basics for themselves: food, clothing, shelter, periodic rest, relief from suffering. So we are to help others with their needs.[21] But godly self-love never leads to selfishness because, while we care for our basic needs, our focus is God and service to others.[22]

Our personal sense of self-worth comes from being the objects of God's love and His acceptance of us through Christ.[23] He first loved us and by grace through faith made us His children.[24] What an incredible position.[25] We call the Sovereign God of the universe

"Father"![26] Moreover, I "forgive myself" because God has.[27] I find myself significant because God has found me significant.[28] We are His creation doing His work.[29]

The error in the modern emphasis on self-love, self-esteem, and self-worth is "self."[30] A proper understanding of self-love is only found as a servant of God and in our focus on Him.[31] We seek to be more Christlike;[32] and that emphasis makes us a better person. Self-esteem and self-worth put on meekness and humility as we grow in the image of Jesus.[33]

True obedience to God comes from the heart,[34]
loving Him and loving others.[35]
Love is the key, the attitude, and the motivation to true holiness.

But is it possible to love others without violating
our love to God and His command to be holy? Is it
possible in this world to combine such love toward
God and others and be holy at the same time?
Yes! The scripture shows us _One_ Who did it and did it best of all.

Notes

1   But thou, O Lord, art a God full of compassion, and gracious, longsuffering, and plenteous in mercy and truth. (Ps. 86:15)

   He that loveth not knoweth not God; for God is love... And we have known and believed the love that God hath to us. God is love; and he that dwelleth in love dwelleth in God, and God in him. (1 John 4:8, 16)

2   I in them, and thou in me, that they may be made perfect in one; and that the world may know that thou hast sent me, and hast loved them, as thou hast loved me. Father, I will that they also, whom thou hast given me, be with me where I am; that they may behold my glory, which thou hast given me: for thou lovedst me before the foundation of the world. (John 17:23–24)

3   Neither pray I for these alone, but for them also which shall believe on me through their word; That they all may be one; as thou, Father, art in me, and I in thee, that they also may be one in us: that the world may believe that thou hast sent me. And the glory which thou gavest me I have given them; that they may be one, even as we are one:... And I have declared unto them thy name, and will declare it: that the love wherewith thou hast loved me may be in them, and I in them. (John 17:20–22, 26)

   But God, who is rich in mercy, for his great love wherewith he loved us, Even when we were dead in sins, hath quickened us together with Christ, (by grace ye are saved;) And hath raised us up together, and made us sit together in heavenly places in Christ Jesus: That in the ages to come he might shew the exceeding riches of his grace in his kindness toward us through Christ Jesus. (Eph. 2:4–7)

   That Christ may dwell in your hearts by faith; that ye, being rooted and grounded in love, May be able to comprehend with all saints what is the breadth, and length, and depth, and height; And to know the love of Christ, which passeth knowledge, that ye might be filled with all the fulness of God. (Eph. 3:17–19)

4   For I am persuaded, that neither death, nor life, nor angels, nor principalities, nor powers, nor things present, nor things to come, Nor height, nor depth, nor any other creature, shall be able to separate us from the love of God, which is in Christ Jesus our Lord. (Rom. 8:38–39)

5   For God so loved the world, that he gave his only begotten Son, that whosoever believeth in him should not perish, but have everlasting life. (John 3:16)

   In this was manifested the love of God toward us, because that God sent his only begotten Son into the world, that we might live through him. (1 John 4:9)

   I am crucified with Christ: nevertheless I live; yet not I, but Christ liveth in me: and the life which I now live in the flesh I live by the faith of the Son of God, who loved me, and gave himself for me. (Gal. 2:20)

6   For ye have not received the spirit of bondage again to fear; but ye have received the Spirit of adoption, whereby we cry, Abba, Father. (Rom. 8:15)

   And will be a Father unto you, and ye shall be my sons and daughters, saith the Lord Almighty. (2 Cor. 6:18)

   And because ye are sons, God hath sent forth the Spirit of his Son into your hearts, crying, Abba, Father. (Gal. 4:6)

7   Husbands, love your wives, even as Christ also loved the church, and gave himself for it... For we are members of his body, of his flesh, and of his bones... This is a great mystery: but I speak concerning Christ and the church. (Eph. 5:25, 30, 32)

   And there came unto me one of the seven...saying, Come hither, I will shew thee the bride, the Lamb's wife. (Rev. 21:9)

8   And thou shalt love the Lord thy God with all thy heart, and with all thy soul, and with all thy mind, and with all thy strength: this is the first commandment. And the second is like, namely this, Thou shalt love thy neighbour as thyself. There is none other commandment greater than these. (Mark 12:30–31)

   On these two commandments hang all the law and the prophets. (Matt. 22:40)

9   Hereby perceive we the love of God, because he laid down his life for us: and we ought to lay down our lives for the brethren. But whoso hath this world's good, and seeth his brother have need, and shutteth up his bowels of compassion from him, how dwelleth the love of God in him? (1 John 3:16–17)

10 But take diligent heed to do the commandment and the law, which Moses the servant of the Lord charged you, to love the Lord your God, and to walk in all his ways, and to keep his commandments, and to cleave unto him, and to serve him with all your heart and with all your soul. (Josh. 22:5)

   By this we know that we love the children of God, when we love God, and keep his commandments. For this is the love of God, that we keep his commandments: and his commandments are not grievous. (1 John 5:2–3)

   Owe no man any thing, but to love one another: for he that loveth another hath fulfilled the law. (Rom. 13:8)

   And beside this, giving all diligence, add to your faith virtue; and to virtue knowledge; And to knowledge temperance; and to temperance patience; and to patience godliness; And to godliness brotherly kindness; and to brotherly kindness charity [love]. For if these things be in you, and abound, they make you that ye shall neither be barren nor unfruitful in the knowledge of our Lord Jesus Christ. (2 Pet. 1:5–8)

11 Now the end of the commandment is charity out of a pure heart, and of a good conscience, and of faith unfeigned. (1 Tim. 1:5)

   He that hath my commandments, and keepeth them, he it is that loveth me: and he that loveth me shall be loved of my Father, and I will love him, and will manifest myself to him... Jesus answered and said unto him, If a man love me, he will keep my words: and my Father will love him, and we will come unto him, and make our abode with him. (John 14:21, 23)

Love worketh no ill to his neighbour: therefore love is the fulfilling of the law. (Rom. 13:10)

For all the law is fulfilled in one word, even in this; Thou shalt love thy neighbour as thyself. (Gal. 5:14)

But whoso keepeth his word, in him verily is the love of God perfected: hereby know we that we are in him. (1 John 2:5)

And the Lord make you to increase and abound in love one toward another, and toward all men, even as we do toward you: To the end he may stablish your hearts unblameable in holiness before God, even our Father, at the coming of our Lord Jesus Christ with all his saints. (1 Thess. 3:12–13)

[12] Let all your things be done with charity [love]. (1 Cor. 16:14)

And above all these things put on charity [love], which is the bond of perfectness. (Col. 3:14)

I thank my God, making mention of thee always in my prayers, Hearing of thy love and faith, which thou hast toward the Lord Jesus, and toward all saints. (Phil. 4–5)

[13] A new commandment I give unto you, That ye love one another; as I have loved you, that ye also love one another. By this shall all men know that ye are my disciples, if ye have love one to another. (John 13:34–35)

This is my commandment, That ye love one another, as I have loved you. Greater love hath no man than this, that a man lay down his life for his friends. Ye are my friends, if ye do whatsoever I command you... These things I command you, that ye love one another. (John 15:12–14, 17)

[14] In this the children of God are manifest, and the children of the devil: whosoever doeth not righteousness is not of God, neither he that loveth not his brother. For this is the message that ye heard from the beginning, that we should love one another... We know that we have passed from death unto life, because we love the brethren. He that loveth not his brother abideth in death. Whosoever hateth his brother is a murderer: and ye know that no murderer hath eternal life abiding in him. Hereby perceive we the love of God, because he laid down his life for us: and we ought to lay down our lives for the brethren. But whoso hath this world's good, and seeth his brother have need, and shutteth up his bowels of compassion from him, how dwelleth the love of God in him? (1 John 3:10–11, 14–17)

Beloved, if God so loved us, we ought also to love one another. No man hath seen God at any time. If we love one another, God dwelleth in us, and his love is perfected in us... If a man say, I love God, and hateth his brother, he is a liar: for he that loveth not his brother whom he hath seen, how can he love God whom he hath not seen? And this commandment have we from him, That he who loveth God love his brother also... Whosoever believeth that Jesus is the

Christ is born of God: and every one that loveth him that begat loveth him also that is begotten of him. (1 John 4:11–12, 20–5:1)

And now I beseech thee, lady, not as though I wrote a new commandment unto thee, but that which we had from the beginning, that we love one another. And this is love, that we walk after his commandments. (2 John 1:5–6a)

15 He that saith, I know him, and keepeth not his commandments, is a liar, and the truth is not in him. But whoso keepeth his word, in him verily is the love of God perfected: hereby know we that we are in him... He that saith he is in the light, and hateth his brother, is in darkness even until now... But he that hateth his brother is in darkness, and walketh in darkness, and knoweth not whither he goeth, because that darkness hath blinded his eyes. (1 John 2:4–5, 9, 11)

We know that we have passed from death unto life, because we love the brethren. He that loveth not his brother abideth in death. Whosoever hateth his brother is a murderer: and ye know that no murderer hath eternal life abiding in him. (1 John 3:14–15)

Beloved, let us love one another: for love is of God; and every one that loveth is born of God, and knoweth God. He that loveth not knoweth not God; for God is love... And we have known and believed the love that God hath to us. God is love; and he that dwelleth in love dwelleth in God, and God in him. (1 John 4:7–8, 16)

As we have therefore opportunity, let us do good unto all men, especially unto them who are of the household of faith. (Gal. 6:10)

16 A new commandment I give unto you, That ye love one another; as I have loved you, that ye also love one another. By this shall all men know that ye are my disciples, if ye have love one to another. (John 13:34–35)

17 But speaking the truth in love, may grow up into him in all things, which is the head, even Christ: From whom the whole body fitly joined together and compacted by that which every joint supplieth, according to the effectual working in the measure of every part, maketh increase of the body unto the edifying of itself in love. (Eph. 4:15–16)

But as touching brotherly love ye need not that I write unto you: for ye yourselves are taught of God to love one another. (1 Thess. 4:9)

We are bound to thank God always for you, brethren, as it is meet, because that your faith groweth exceedingly, and the charity of every one of you all toward each other aboundeth. (2 Thess. 1:3)

For we have great joy and consolation in thy love, because the bowels of the saints are refreshed by thee, brother. (Phil. 7)

For God is not unrighteous to forget your work and labour of love, which ye have shewed toward his name, in that ye have ministered to the saints, and do minister. (Heb. 6:10)

Hereby perceive we the love of God, because he laid down his life for us: and we ought to lay down our lives for the brethren. But whoso hath this world's good, and seeth his brother have need, and shutteth up his bowels of compassion from him, how dwelleth the love of God in him? My little children, let us not love in word, neither in tongue; but in deed and in truth. (1 John 3:16–18)

18 Love not the world, neither the things that are in the world. If any man love the world, the love of the Father is not in him. (1 John 2:15)

19 No servant can serve two masters: for either he will hate the one, and love the other; or else he will hold to the one, and despise the other. Ye cannot serve God and mammon. And the Pharisees also, who were covetous, heard all these things: and they derided him. (Luke 16:13–14)

For the love of money is the root of all evil: which while some coveted after, they have erred from the faith, and pierced themselves through with many sorrows. But thou, O man of God, flee these things; and follow after righteousness, godliness, faith, love, patience, meekness. (1 Tim. 6:10–11)

20 And the second is like unto it, Thou shalt love thy neighbour as thyself. (Matt. 22:39)

21 And sold their possessions and goods, and parted them to all men, as every man had need. (Acts 2:45)

But he, willing to justify himself, said unto Jesus, And who is my neighbour? And Jesus answering said, A certain man went down from Jerusalem to Jericho, and fell among thieves, which stripped him of his raiment, and wounded him, and departed, leaving him half dead. And by chance there came down a certain priest that way: and when he saw him, he passed by on the other side. And likewise a Levite, when he was at the place, came and looked on him, and passed by on the other side. But a certain Samaritan, as he journeyed, came where he was: and when he saw him, he had compassion on him, And went to him, and bound up his wounds, pouring in oil and wine, and set him on his own beast, and brought him to an inn, and took care of him. And on the morrow when he departed, he took out two pence, and gave them to the host, and said unto him, Take care of him; and whatsoever thou spendest more, when I come again, I will repay thee. Which now of these three, thinkest thou, was neighbour unto him that fell among the thieves? And he said, He that shewed mercy on him. Then said Jesus unto him, Go, and do thou likewise. (Luke 10:29–37)

If thine enemy be hungry, give him bread to eat; and if he be thirsty, give him water to drink. (Prov. 25:21)

And he shall set the sheep on his right hand, but the goats on the left. Then shall the King say unto them on his right hand, Come, ye blessed of my Father, inherit the kingdom prepared for you from the foundation of the world: For I was an hungred, and ye gave me meat: I was thirsty, and ye gave me drink: I was a stranger, and ye took me in: Naked, and ye clothed me: I was sick, and ye visited me: I was in prison, and ye came unto me. Then shall the righteous answer him, saying, Lord, when saw we thee an hungred, and fed thee? or thirsty, and gave thee drink? When saw we thee a stranger, and took thee in? or naked, and clothed thee? Or when saw we thee sick, or in prison, and came unto thee? And the King shall answer and say unto them, Verily I say unto you,

Inasmuch as ye have done it unto one of the least of these my brethren, ye have done it unto me. (Matt. 25:33–40)

22 And now, Israel, what doth the Lord thy God require of thee, but to fear the Lord thy God, to walk in all his ways, and to love him, and to serve the Lord thy God with all thy heart and with all thy soul. (Deut. 10:12)

For, brethren, ye have been called unto liberty; only use not liberty for an occasion to the flesh, but by love serve one another. (Gal. 5:13)

For we preach not ourselves, but Christ Jesus the Lord; and ourselves your servants for Jesus' sake. (2 Cor. 4:5)

23 Even when we were dead in sins, hath quickened us together with Christ, (by grace ye are saved;) And hath raised us up together, and made us sit together in heavenly places in Christ Jesus: That in the ages to come he might shew the exceeding riches of his grace in his kindness toward us through Christ Jesus. (Eph. 2:5–7)

24 According as he hath chosen us in him before the foundation of the world, that we should be holy and without blame before him in love: Having predestinated us unto the adoption of children by Jesus Christ to himself, according to the good pleasure of his will, To the praise of the glory of his grace, wherein he hath made us accepted in the beloved. In whom we have redemption through his blood, the forgiveness of sins, according to the riches of his grace. (Eph. 1:4–7)

For by grace are ye saved through faith; and that not of yourselves: it is the gift of God: Not of works, lest any man should boast. (Eph. 2:8–9)

Who hath saved us, and called us with an holy calling, not according to our works, but according to his own purpose and grace, which was given us in Christ Jesus before the world began. (2 Tim. 1:9)

25 Behold, what manner of love the Father hath bestowed upon us, that we should be called the sons of God: therefore the world knoweth us not, because it knew him not. (1 John 3:1)

26 For ye have not received the spirit of bondage again to fear; but ye have received the Spirit of adoption, whereby we cry, Abba, Father. (Rom. 8:15)

And because ye are sons, God hath sent forth the Spirit of his Son into your hearts, crying, Abba, Father. (Gal. 4:6)

Grace to you, and peace, from God our Father and the Lord Jesus Christ. (Phil. 1:3)

27 In whom we have redemption through his blood, the forgiveness of sins, according to the riches of his grace. (Eph. 1:7)

Who hath delivered us from the power of darkness, and hath translated us into the kingdom of his dear Son: 14 In whom we have redemption through his blood, even the forgiveness of sins. (Col. 1:13–14)

And you, being dead in your sins and the uncircumcision of your flesh, hath he quickened together with him, having forgiven you all trespasses; Blotting out the handwriting of ordinances that was against us, which was contrary to us, and took it out of the way, nailing it to his cross. (Col. 2:13–14)

[28] Now therefore ye are no more strangers and foreigners, but fellow citizens with the saints, and of the household of God; And are built upon the foundation of the apostles and prophets, Jesus Christ himself being the chief corner stone; In whom all the building fitly framed together groweth unto an holy temple in the Lord: In whom ye also are builded together for an habitation of God through the Spirit. (Eph. 2:19–22)

Now our Lord Jesus Christ himself, and God, even our Father, which hath loved us, and hath given us everlasting consolation and good hope through grace, Comfort your hearts, and stablish you in every good word and work. (2 Thess. 2:16–17)

Who gave himself for us, that he might redeem us from all iniquity, and purify unto himself a peculiar people, zealous of good works. (Titus 2:14)

[29] Therefore if any man be in Christ, he is a new creature: old things are passed away; behold, all things are become new. And all things are of God, who hath reconciled us to himself by Jesus Christ, and hath given to us the ministry of reconciliation; To wit, that God was in Christ, reconciling the world unto himself, not imputing their trespasses unto them; and hath committed unto us the word of reconciliation. Now then we are ambassadors for Christ, as though God did beseech you by us: we pray you in Christ's stead, be ye reconciled to God. (2 Cor. 5:17–20)

For we are his workmanship, created in Christ Jesus unto good works, which God hath before ordained that we should walk in them. (Eph. 2:10)

Lie not one to another, seeing that ye have put off the old man with his deeds; And have put on the new man, which is renewed in knowledge after the image of him that created him. (Col. 3:9–10)

[30] Mortify therefore your members which are upon the earth; fornication, uncleanness, inordinate affection, evil concupiscence, and covetousness, which is idolatry: For which things' sake the wrath of God cometh on the children of disobedience. (Col. 3:5–6)

But put ye on the Lord Jesus Christ, and make not provision for the flesh, to fulfil the lusts thereof. (Rom. 13:14)

[31] By love serve one another. (Gal. 5:13b)

As we have therefore opportunity, let us do good unto all men, especially unto them who are of the household of faith. (Gal. 6:10)

Ye shall walk after the Lord your God, and fear him, and keep his commandments, and obey his voice, and ye shall serve him, and cleave unto him. (Deut. 13:4)

Then saith Jesus unto him, Get thee hence, Satan: for it is written, Thou shalt worship the Lord thy God, and him only shalt thou serve. (Matt. 4:10)

[32] And this I pray, that your love may abound yet more and more in knowledge and in all judgment; That ye may approve things that are excellent; that ye may be sincere and without offence till the day of Christ; Being filled with the fruits

of righteousness, which are by Jesus Christ, unto the glory and praise of God. (Phil. 1:9–11)

Be ye therefore followers of God, as dear children; And walk in love, as Christ also hath loved us, and hath given himself for us an offering and a sacrifice to God for a sweet smelling savour. (Eph. 5:1–2)

Till we all come in the unity of the faith, and of the knowledge of the Son of God, unto a perfect man, unto the measure of the stature of the fulness of Christ. (Eph. 4:13)

³³ I therefore, the prisoner of the Lord, beseech you that ye walk worthy of the vocation wherewith ye are called, With all lowliness and meekness, with longsuffering, forbearing one another in love. (Eph. 4:1–2)

Let nothing be done through strife or vainglory; but in lowliness of mind let each esteem other better than themselves... Let this mind be in you, which was also in Christ Jesus. (Phil. 2:3, 5)

To speak evil of no man, to be no brawlers, but gentle, shewing all meekness unto all men. (Titus 3:2)

³⁴ This day the Lord thy God hath commanded thee to do these statutes and judgments: thou shalt therefore keep and do them with all thine heart, and with all thy soul. (Deut. 26:16)

Keep thy heart with all diligence; for out of it are the issues of life. (Prov. 4:23)

³⁵ Master, which is the great commandment in the law? Jesus said unto him, Thou shalt love the Lord thy God with all thy heart, and with all thy soul, and with all thy mind. This is the first and great commandment. And the second is like unto it, Thou shalt love thy neighbour as thyself. On these two commandments hang all the law and the prophets. (Matt. 22:36–40)

Now the end of the commandment is charity [love] out of a pure heart, and of a good conscience, and of faith unfeigned. (1 Tim. 1:5)

Who Did It Best?

Arriving at a large construction site, I saw no clear path through the dangerous piles of debris and constantly moving equipment. Ted had invited me to his office to discuss some business. I knew the directions to the construction site. However, when I asked him for the specific path within the site to his office, he said, "Meet me at the gate and follow me through."

A short time later, he found me at the entry. "Come with me," Ted beckoned with a tilt of his head and sweep of his arm. His tone and gestures spoke authority. Flooded with relief that he would personally guide me, my mind never considered disagreement.

"Stay close and listen to me," he commanded. "This place is even more dangerous than it looks. But I can walk you safely through." And he did.

Jesus Our Guide

Through pitfalls and dangers, confusion and turmoil, Jesus is the one to lead us in this life.[1] He is part of the Triune God, by Whom all was created.[2] He came to earth, born of a virgin, lived among us,[3] and taught us.[4] He showed us how to walk through His world. He is the one we must follow.[5]

His Holy Walk of Faith *in* and Not *of* the World

In His earthly ministry, Jesus showed faith. Many understand faith to mean belief in the unknown. However, Christian faith means dependent trust and obedience toward God.[6] Christ manifested continuous trust.[7] Moreover, He was obedient in every word He spoke[8] and every action He displayed.[9] In fact, His walk and all that He did on the earth was so perfectly obedient that He received the public commendation of the Father.[10] He totally surrendered His will and way to the Father,[11] even unto death.[12]

So how should we understand Christ's relation to this sinful world as He walked among us? The words *in* and *of* help us understand. A scuba diver dons his wet suit, mask, fins, and oxygen tank. Slipping into the water, he swims alongside the fish that are *of* the water. The diver is *in* the water with them but does not take on all the life ways of the fish. Walking this earth, Christ was *in* the world, surrounded by worldly influences and living in the midst of evil.[13] He was not *of* the world, never manifested worldliness, never partook of the sin of this world.[14] He never compromised His life or message,[15] living a life of perfect holiness.[16]

His Love-Walk among Sinners and Unbelievers

Jesus showed many acts of compassion, giving testimony to Who He was.[17] His love was clear to those who saw Him.[18] Pharisees believed that showing such compassion to the disobedient and sinful compromises righteous conduct.[19] However, scripture tells us that our righteous God abounds in mercy, grace, and loving-kindness.[20] Christ, the very image of the invisible God,[21] perfectly joined holiness and love while interacting with a sinful world. Our own demonstrations of love, especially to fellow believers, broadcast to all that we follow Christ.[22]

The Commands to Follow Him

Jesus desires that we follow Him and not participate with the evil in this world.[23] He never surrendered to fleshly desires,[24] just as we are *not to do*.[25] Refusing the world's ways,[26] He displayed our proper walk.[27] And He resisted the devil,[28] as we are commanded *to do*.[29] So believers are called *out* of the world[30] while continuing to walk *in* the world. Our progressive sanctification in this life is a walk that becomes less and less *of* the world.[31] However, we are not just passing time *in* the world; we are here to be witnesses to those still *of* the world.[32]

How Did He Do It?

While being holy and loving at the same time, how did Jesus walk with sinners and believers who sinned? Some feel they cannot show God's overflowing love with all its mercy, grace, forgiveness, long-suffering, gentleness, goodness, and meekness. They believe such love would compromise their obedience to God or such love would be an acceptance of other's sin. Others think that to walk in such obedience, and even to speak of God's holiness, will blunt the love they want to show. But Christ did both.

How?
How do we walk in obedience and in separation unto God and at the same time show love toward individuals or groups of people who are disobedient and compromised by sin or wrong doctrine?

Notes

1   Take my yoke upon you, and learn of me; for I am meek and lowly in heart: and ye shall find rest unto your souls. For my yoke is easy, and my burden is light. (Matt. 11:29–30)

I am the good shepherd: the good shepherd giveth his life for the sheep… I am the good shepherd, and know my sheep, and am known of mine. (John 10:11, 14)

The Lord is my shepherd; I shall not want. He maketh me to lie down in green pastures: he leadeth me beside the still waters. He restoreth my soul: he leadeth me in the paths of righteousness for his name's sake. Yea, though I walk through the valley of the shadow of death, I will fear no evil: for thou art with me; thy rod and thy staff they comfort me… Surely goodness and mercy shall follow me all the days of my life. (Ps. 23:1–4, 6a)

2   In the beginning was the Word, and the Word was with God, and the Word was God. The same was in the beginning with God. All things were made by him; and without him was not any thing made that was made. (John 1:1–3)

For by him [God's dear Son] were all things created, that are in heaven, and that are in earth, visible and invisible, whether they be thrones, or dominions, or principalities, or powers: all things were created by him, and for him: And he is before all things, and by him all things consist. (Col. 1:16–17)

3   Therefore the Lord himself shall give you a sign; Behold, a virgin shall conceive, and bear a son, and shall call his name Immanuel. (Isa. 7:14)

But while he thought on these things, behold, the angel of the Lord appeared unto him in a dream, saying, Joseph, thou son of David, fear not to take unto thee Mary thy wife: for that which is conceived in her is of the Holy Ghost. And she shall bring forth a son, and thou shalt call his name Jesus: for he shall save his people from their sins. Now all this was done, that it might be fulfilled which was spoken of the Lord by the prophet, saying, Behold, a virgin shall be with child, and shall bring forth a son, and they shall call his name Emmanuel, which being interpreted is, God with us. (Matt. 1:20–23)

Hereby know ye the Spirit of God: Every spirit that confesseth that Jesus Christ is come in the flesh is of God. (1 John 4:2)

4   And they went into Capernaum; and straightway on the sabbath day he entered into the synagogue, and taught. And they were astonished at his doctrine: for he taught them as one that had authority, and not as the scribes. (Mark 1:21–22)

And he went forth again by the sea side; and all the multitude resorted unto him, and he taught them. (Mark 2:13)

And Jesus, when he came out, saw much people, and was moved with compassion toward them, because they were as sheep not having a shepherd: and he began to teach them many things. (Mark 6:34)

And he arose from thence, and cometh into the coasts of Judaea by the farther side of Jordan: and the people resort unto him again; and, as he was wont, he taught them again. (Mark 10:1)

5   And when he had called the people unto him with his disciples also, he said unto them, Whosoever will come after me, let him deny himself, and take up his cross, and follow me. (Mark 8:34)

And he said to them all, If any man will come after me, let him deny himself, and take up his cross daily, and follow me. (Luke 9:23)

Then spake Jesus again unto them, saying, I am the light of the world: he that followeth me shall not walk in darkness, but shall have the light of life. (John 8:12)

He that saith he abideth in him ought himself also so to walk, even as he walked. (1 John 2:6)

6   And Samuel said, Hath the LORD as great delight in burnt offerings and sacrifices, as in obeying the voice of the LORD? Behold, to obey is better than sacrifice, and to hearken than the fat of rams. (1 Sam. 15:22)

Cause me to hear thy lovingkindness in the morning; for in thee do I trust: cause me to know the way wherein I should walk; for I lift up my soul unto thee. (Ps. 143:8)

Trust in the Lord with all thine heart; and lean not unto thine own understanding. In all thy ways acknowledge him [obeying Him], and he shall direct thy paths. (Prov. 3:5–6)

Trust ye in the LORD for ever: for in the LORD JEHOVAH is everlasting strength. (Isa. 26:4)

7   And I knew that thou hearest me always: but because of the people which stand by I said it, that they may believe that thou hast sent me. (John 11:42)

8   For he whom God hath sent speaketh the words of God: for God giveth not the Spirit by measure unto him. (John 3:34)

For I have given unto them the words which thou [God the Father] gavest me. (John 17:8a)

9   Jesus saith unto them, My meat is to do the will of him that sent me, and to finish his work. (John 4:34)

But I have greater witness than that of John: for the works which the Father hath given me to finish, the same works that I do, bear witness of me, that the Father hath sent me. (John 5:36)

I have glorified thee on the earth: I have finished the work which thou gavest me to do. (John 17:4)

10   And lo a voice from heaven, saying, This is my beloved Son, in whom I am well pleased. (Matt. 3:17) (Mark 1:11 and Luke 3:22 are parallel passages.)

While he yet spake, behold, a bright cloud overshadowed them: and behold a voice out of the cloud, which said, This is my beloved Son, in whom I am well pleased; hear ye him. (Matt. 17:5)

For he received from God the Father honour and glory, when there came such a voice to him from the excellent glory, This is my beloved Son, in whom I am well pleased. (2 Pet. 1:17)

11 Saying, Father,…not my will, but thine, be done. (Luke 22:42)

12 He humbled himself, and became obedient unto death, even the death of the cross. (Phil. 2:8b)

13 And when the people were gathered thick together, he began to say, This is an evil generation: they seek a sign; and there shall no sign be given it, but the sign of Jonas the prophet. (Luke 11:29)

And this is the condemnation, that light is come into the world, and men loved darkness rather than light, because their deeds were evil. (John 3:19)

The world cannot hate you; but me it hateth, because I testify of it, that the works thereof are evil. (John 7:7)

For all that is in the world, the lust of the flesh, and the lust of the eyes, and the pride of life, is not of the Father, but is of the world. (1 John 2:16)

14 Who did no sin, neither was guile found in his mouth. (1 Pet. 2:22)

For he hath made him to be sin for us, who knew no sin; that we might be made the righteousness of God in him. (2 Cor. 5:21)

15 Which of you convinceth me of sin? And if I say the truth, why do ye not believe me? (John 8:46)

Pilate therefore went forth again, and saith unto them, Behold, I bring him forth to you, that ye may know that I find no fault in him. (John 19:4)

Then said Pilate to the chief priests and to the people, I find no fault in this man… Said unto them, Ye have brought this man unto me, as one that perverteth the people: and, behold, I, having examined him before you, have found no fault in this man touching those things whereof ye accuse him. (Luke 23:4, 14)

16 For of a truth against thy holy child Jesus, whom thou hast anointed, both Herod, and Pontius Pilate, with the Gentiles, and the people of Israel, were gathered together… By stretching forth thine hand to heal; and that signs and wonders may be done by the name of thy holy child Jesus. (Acts 4:27, 30)

But this man, because he continueth ever, hath an unchangeable priesthood. Wherefore he is able also to save them to the uttermost that come unto God by him, seeing he ever liveth to make intercession for them. For such an high priest became us, who is holy, harmless, undefiled, separate from sinners, and made higher than the heavens. (Heb. 7:24–26)

17 And Jesus went forth, and saw a great multitude, and was moved with compassion toward them, and he healed their sick. (Matt. 14:14)

But I have greater witness than that of John: for the works which the Father hath given me to finish, the same works that I do, bear witness of me, that the Father hath sent me. (John 5:36)

Jesus answered them, I told you, and ye believed not: the works that I do in my Father's name, they bear witness of me... If I do not the works of my Father, believe me not. But if I do, though ye believe not me, believe the works: that ye may know, and believe, that the Father is in me, and I in him. (John 10:25, 37–38)

Believest thou not that I am in the Father, and the Father in me? the words that I speak unto you I speak not of myself: but the Father that dwelleth in me, he doeth the works. Believe me that I am in the Father, and the Father in me: or else believe me for the very works' sake. (John 14:10–11)

18 And Jesus went about all Galilee, teaching in their synagogues, and preaching the gospel of the kingdom, and healing all manner of sickness and all manner of disease among the people. And his fame went throughout all Syria. (Matt. 4:23–24a)

And were beyond measure astonished, saying, He hath done all things well: he maketh both the deaf to hear, and the dumb to speak. (Mark 7:37)

But so much the more went there a fame abroad of him: and great multitudes came together to hear, and to be healed by him of their infirmities. (Luke 5:15)

And he came down with them, and stood in the plain, and the company of his disciples, and a great multitude of people out of all Judaea and Jerusalem, and from the sea coast of Tyre and Sidon, which came to hear him, and to be healed of their diseases. (Luke 6:17)

And when he was come nigh, even now at the descent of the mount of Olives, the whole multitude of the disciples began to rejoice and praise God with a loud voice for all the mighty works that they had seen. (Luke 19:37)

19 And it came to pass, as Jesus sat at meat in the house, behold, many publicans and sinners came and sat down with him and his disciples. And when the Pharisees saw it, they said unto his disciples, Why eateth your Master with publicans and sinners? But when Jesus heard that, he said unto them, They that be whole need not a physician, but they that are sick. But go ye and learn what that meaneth, I will have mercy, and not sacrifice: for I am not come to call the righteous, but sinners to repentance. (Matt. 9:10–13)

20 We have thought of thy lovingkindness, O God, in the midst of thy temple. According to thy name, O God, so is thy praise unto the ends of the earth: thy right hand is full of righteousness. (Ps. 48:9–10)

But the mercy of the LORD is from everlasting to everlasting upon them that fear him, and his righteousness unto children's children. (Ps. 103:17)

Gracious is the LORD, and righteous; yea, our God is merciful. (Ps. 116:5)

For his merciful kindness is great toward us: and the truth of the LORD endureth for ever. Praise ye the LORD. (Ps. 117:2)

The LORD is gracious, and full of compassion; slow to anger, and of great mercy. The LORD is good to all: and his tender mercies are over all his works… The LORD is righteous in all his ways, and holy in all his works. (Ps. 145:8–9, 17)

He that followeth after righteousness and mercy findeth life, righteousness, and honour. (Prov. 21:21)

21 God, who at sundry times and in divers manners spake in time past unto the fathers by the prophets, Hath in these last days spoken unto us by his Son, whom he hath appointed heir of all things, by whom also he made the worlds; Who being the brightness of his glory, and the express image of his person, and upholding all things by the word of his power, when he had by himself purged our sins, sat down on the right hand of the Majesty on high. (Heb. 1:1–3)

22 A new commandment I give unto you, That ye love one another; as I have loved you, that ye also love one another. By this shall all men know that ye are my disciples, if ye have love one to another. (John 13:34–35)

23 And now I am no more in the world, but these are in the world, and I come to thee… While I was with them in the world, I kept them in thy name… And now come I to thee; and these things I speak in the world…they are not of the world, even as I am not of the world. I pray not that thou shouldest take them out of the world, but that thou shouldest keep them from the evil… As thou hast sent me into the world, even so have I also sent them into the world. (John 17:11a, 12a, 13a, 14b–15, 18)

As ye have therefore received Christ Jesus the Lord, so walk ye in him. (Col. 2:6)

24 For in that he himself hath suffered being tempted, he is able to succour them that are tempted. (Heb. 2:18)

For we have not an high priest which cannot be touched with the feeling of our infirmities; but was in all points tempted like as we are, yet without sin. (Heb. 4:15)

25 But put ye on the Lord Jesus Christ, and make not provision for the flesh, to fulfil the lusts thereof. (Rom. 13:14)

26 And because I tell you the truth, ye believe me not. Which of you convinceth me of sin? And if I say the truth, why do ye not believe me? (John 8:45–46)

27 I beseech you therefore, brethren, by the mercies of God, that ye present your bodies a living sacrifice, holy, acceptable unto God, which is your reasonable service. And be not conformed to this world: but be ye transformed by the renewing of your mind, that ye may prove what is that good, and acceptable, and perfect, will of God. (Rom. 12:1–2)

He that saith he abideth in him ought himself also so to walk, even as he walked. (1 John 2:6)

28 Jesus fasted forty days and nights, then resisted the temptations of the Devil by the word of God. (Matt. 4; Mark 1; Luke 4)

29 Submit yourselves therefore to God. Resist the devil, and he will flee from you. (James 4:7)

30 If ye were of the world, the world would love his own: but because ye are not of the world, but I have chosen you out of the world, therefore the world hateth you. (John 15:19)

I have manifested thy name unto the men which thou gavest me out of the world: thine they were, and thou gavest them me; and they have kept thy word. (John 17:6)

Wherefore come out from among them, and be ye separate, saith the Lord, and touch not the unclean thing; and I will receive you. (1 Cor. 6:17)

31 He that saith he abideth in Him ought himself also so to walk, even as he walked. (1 John 2:6)

That ye would walk worthy of God, who hath called you unto his kingdom and glory.(1 Thess. 2:12)

Let us walk honestly, as in the day; and not in rioting and drunkenness, not in chambering and wantonness, not in strife and envying. (Rom. 13:13)

For we are his workmanship, created in Christ Jesus unto good works, which God hath before ordained that we should walk in them. (Eph. 2:10)

I therefore, the prisoner of the Lord, beseech you that ye walk worthy of the vocation wherewith ye are called… This I say therefore, and testify in the Lord, that ye henceforth walk not as other Gentiles walk, in the vanity of their mind. (Eph. 4:1, 17)

For ye were sometimes darkness, but now are ye light in the Lord: walk as children of light. (Eph. 5:8)

That ye might walk worthy of the Lord unto all pleasing, being fruitful in every good work, and increasing in the knowledge of God. (Col. 1:10)

32 Then spake Jesus again unto them, saying, I am the light of the world: he that followeth me shall not walk in darkness, but shall have the light of life. (John 8:12)

As long as I am in the world, I am the light of the world. (John 9:5)

Ye are the light of the world. A city that is set on an hill cannot be hid. (Matt. 5:14)

That ye may be blameless and harmless, the sons of God, without rebuke, in the midst of a crooked and perverse nation, among whom ye shine as lights in the world. (Phil. 2:15)

Walking
the Path

How? Faith and Virtue

Without acting worldly on the one hand or like a legalistic Pharisee on the other, how can we walk pleasing to God? Further, how can we relate to individuals, or churches, or organizations, or movements that walk contrary to God's truth and commands? Also, how can we understand a God-pleasing path for our feet without a deluge of words? A flood of commentary can drown us and leave us more confused.

Decades ago, I hurried up and down hospital corridors as a doctor in training. Each year new doctors coming into our program had to be oriented by those of us further along. While the chief doctor had the ultimate responsibility for the patient, all of us under him performed many tasks for patient care. We devised a simple, humorous principle for our job: "Make the chief look good." When the chief looked good, it was because the patient was doing well. And we were doing everything necessary for the patient's progress: history, physical, lab tests, procedures, records, orders, consults, literature research, dressing changes…whatever.

Seriously, instead of overwhelming commentary, we can seek simple phrases that convey core values. The Word of God abounds in such straightforward principles. For example, Jesus's answers to those who questioned Him were both profound and elegantly simple, striking to the heart of the issue. The topics touched on in these chapters have brought huge debates among some believers. However, reviewing God's Word and following Jesus's example, some simple principles can light the way and direct us in our walk with the Lord.

The *application* of these principles may be simple, or complex, or even very difficult. Thankfully, as believers, we have the Spirit and the Word to guide us in applying them in the wisest way for a given situation. So we will look at the principles from God's Word and leave specific applications to believers led by the Holy Spirit. Let Him apply the Word in the context of our own lives and our own culture.

The Path of Biblical Principles

In 2 Peter, the apostle gives us an outline of key words that define our Christian growth. He lays out a logical sequence of characteristics in which we need to mature within our own lives as well as our interaction with others. They are not a progression in the sense that we learn a hundred percent of one before we go on to the next. For example, we begin with virtue, then grow in knowledge, even while developing in virtue and maturing in it for the rest of our lives. *The further down Peter's list we are progressing while still growing in the previous levels, the greater the spiritual maturity we show.*

> And beside this, giving all diligence, add to your faith virtue; and to virtue knowledge; And to knowledge temperance; and to temperance patience; and to patience godliness; And to godliness brotherly kindness; and to brotherly kindness charity. (2 Pet. 1:5–7)

Faith is the beginning, then

1) Virtue
   2) Knowledge
      3) Temperance (Self-Control)
         4) Patience (Endurance)
            5) Godliness
               6) Brotherly Kindness
                  7) Charity (Love)

Faith the Beginning

Peter starts with faith as the basis for what follows. He is addressing believers who have entered the family of God by grace through faith.[1] Whatever age or situation we are in our lives on the day we are born again, we are pointing our toes to the Lord and taking the first step on the *right* path, the God-pleasing path. And in our faith-walk of dependent trust and obedience to the Lord, Peter says our next step is virtue.

Virtue: Walking Worthy by Putting Off and Putting On

One day, little Tommy's father sat next to him on a bench and carefully explained, "I know that Joe's father allows him to do certain things that I don't allow you to do. But you are my son, and in our family, I want you to act differently." On the street where Tommy and Joe lived, everyone knew they had fathers with different standards.

We are God's children.[2] In His family we are a new creation with a changed heart.[3] We are neither children of the devil, nor part of the world.[4] Wherever we live, the Lord calls us to walk worthy of Him,[5] in His holiness, with His virtue.[6] God knows our heart,[7] so our walk must be sincere.[8] Such sincerity is in contrast to the conduct of Pharisees who are hypocritical in their outward show of virtue.[9]

Decisions

With a new heart, our desires for life have changed.[10] Many desires in our life are altered immediately when we are born again. However, other habits and tendencies can be a struggle for years to come.[11] The paths that we walk have opportunities for right choices and for wrong ones.[12] So our growth in virtue becomes a constant work of faith decisions to put off the old fleshly deeds and to put on Christlike behavior.[13]

The scripture declares plainly the things we should take out of our lives: drunkenness, immoral behavior, strife, envying,[14] anger, wrath, malice, blasphemy, filthy speech, lying.[15] Things to put on include mercy, kindness, humbleness, meekness and long-suffering, patience, forgiveness, and love.[16] And we must put on virtue even in our thought life.[17]

Talking to Our Father

Life is not easy and can be very complicated. Sometimes we become discouraged[18] or fail to do what is right.[19] God already knows everything,[20] but He still wants us to pray to Him about our problems and desires.[21] While the Lord is continually working in and through us to His glory,[22] He desires to work through our faith,[23] which is exceedingly precious in His sight.[24] And prayer is an act of faith, showing both dependent trust[25] and obedience.[26]

Famous pictures come to us from the time of President John F. Kennedy in the early 1960s. As president of the United States, his time and workplace were extremely guarded. Only high government officials could come into his office. The pictures show his son and daughter freely walking up to his desk. In a loving home, every child freely goes to their parents about their needs. Before the all-wise, sovereign God of the universe, we are children, *His* children.[27] We call out to our *Father*,[28] and our prayer comes to His very throne room,[29] to a Father whose great grace and love for us is beyond our comprehension.[30]

In acknowledgement of Who He is and what He has done, we should start each prayer time with thanksgiving and worship.[31] Moreover, a daily walk with God is a daily turning to Him[32] for forgiveness, for comfort, for guidance, and for provision.[33]

Witnessing

God wants the whole earth to hear His word,[34] especially about Jesus.[35] He calls us to tell the world the Good News.[36] He honors those who talk unashamed of Him,[37] who freely confess Jesus Christ,[38] and who testify to what He has done in us and can do in others.[39] Moreover, our faithful conduct before our Heavenly Father constantly witnesses to those around us, both saved and unsaved.[40]

Relating only to those in our own believer fellowship is not how we understand Christ's life in the world among believers and unbelievers.[41] Instead, reaching out in love toward others is basic to the Christian walk[42] and also a witness.[43] Jesus constantly showed compassion, which was a testimony to His words.[44] He commanded His disciples to do the same.[45]

Our words and actions must be a humble acknowledgment that we are totally unworthy sinners[46] who found in Christ forgiveness, mercy, grace, and the free gift of eternal life.[47] We did not receive all this due to our own righteousness or virtue, so we cannot boast in ourselves.[48] Our testimony points others to Jesus and not ourselves.[49] On the other hand, we see that Pharisees boast in their own self-righteousness.[50]

We may reach out, fellowshipping for testimony as, for example, Christ did with both Pharisees[51] and publicans.[52] The Pharisees criticized Him for such fellowship with "publicans and sinners."[53] Jesus explained that it was part of His ministry.[54] However, when reaching out to others, we must be faithful to our testimony,[55] maintaining our integrity,[56] and not doing it for social or financial gain.[57] Jesus did not commit or join Himself to those to whom He was witnessing.[58] He spoke the word and conducted Himself without compromise.[59]

Persecution

As we listen to our Heavenly Father and not the world,[60] people notice.[61] Consequently, some will abandon us,[62] or even persecute us,[63] because our conduct is a testimony[64] and rebuke to their sinful ways.[65] Scripture tells us to expect persecution[66] and to endure it.[67] The unsaved are against us because our feet are on a different path.[68] Persecution may come from family,[69] friends,[70] the world,[71] or even religious Pharisees.[72] While legalistic Pharisees claim to be on the same path as we, they judge us because their toes are not really pointed to God's Word.[73]

Growing in virtue, we work to humbly keep our toes pointed
to the Lord, and we become more focused on what our
Father thinks of us, rather than what others think of us.
As we "put off" and "put on," our life becomes a testimony to
others that we are God's children, which may bring persecution.

Children naturally grow in their knowledge and
understanding of their parents' expectations.
Likewise, God calls us to grow in
knowledge of Him and His ways.

Notes

1 Simon Peter, a servant and an apostle of Jesus Christ, to them that have obtained like precious faith with us through the righteousness of God and our Saviour Jesus Christ: Grace and peace be multiplied unto you through the knowledge of God, and of Jesus our Lord, According as his divine power hath given unto us all things that pertain unto life and godliness, through the knowledge of him that hath called us to glory and virtue. (2 Pet. 1:1–3)

2 The Spirit itself beareth witness with our spirit, that we are the children of God. (Rom. 8:16)

    For ye are all the children of God by faith in Christ Jesus. (Gal. 3:26)

    Be ye therefore followers of God, dear children. (Eph. 5:1)

3 And hope maketh not ashamed; because the love of God is shed abroad in our hearts by the Holy Ghost which is given unto us. (Rom. 5:5)

    Who hath also sealed, and give the earnest of the Spirit in our hearts. (2 Cor. 1:22)

    For God, who commanded the light to shine out of darkness, hath shined in our hearts, to give the light of the knowledge of the glory of God in the face of Jesus Christ. (2 Cor. 4:6)

    Therefore if any man be in Christ, he is a new creature: old things are passed away; behold, all things are become new. (2 Cor. 5:17)

    And because ye are sons, God hath sent forth the Spirit of his Son into your hearts, crying, Abba, Father. (Gal. 4:6)

4 Wherein in time past ye walked according to the course of this world, according to the prince of the power of the air, the spirit that now worketh in the children of disobedience: Among whom also we all had our conversation in times past in the lusts of our flesh, fulfilling the desires of the flesh and of the mind; and were by nature the children of wrath, even as others. (Eph. 2:2–3)

    For ye were sometimes darkness, but now are ye light in the Lord: walk as children of light: (For the fruit of the Spirit is in all goodness and righteousness and truth;) Proving what is acceptable unto the Lord. (Eph. 5:8–10)

    Ye are all the children of light, and the children of the day: we are not of the night, nor of darkness. (1 Thess. 5:5)

5 That ye would walk worthy of God, who hath called you unto his kingdom and glory. (1 Thess. 2:12)

6 But the fruit of the Spirit is love, joy, peace, longsuffering, gentleness, goodness, faith, Meekness, temperance: against such there is no law… If we live in the Spirit, let us also walk in the Spirit. (Gal. 5:22–23, 25)

    But as he which hath called you is holy, so be ye holy in all manner of conversation; Because it is written, Be ye holy; for I am holy. (1 Pet. 1:15–16)

According as his divine power hath given unto us all things that pertain unto life and godliness, through the knowledge of him that hath called us to glory and virtue. (2 Pet. 1:3)

7 But the LORD said unto Samuel, Look not on his countenance, or on the height of his stature; because I have refused him: for the LORD seeth not as man seeth; for man looketh on the outward appearance, but the LORD looketh on the heart. (1 Sam. 16:7)

Let the words of my mouth, and the meditation of my heart, be acceptable in thy sight, O LORD, my strength, and my redeemer. (Ps. 19:14)

Shall not God search this out? for he knoweth the secrets of the heart. (Ps. 44:21)

I the LORD search the heart, I try the reins, even to give every man according to his ways, and according to the fruit of his doings. (Jer. 17:10)

8 Who shall ascend into the hill of the LORD? or who shall stand in his holy place? He that hath clean hands, and a pure heart; who hath not lifted up his soul unto vanity, nor sworn deceitfully. He shall receive the blessing from the LORD, and righteousness from the God of his salvation. (Ps. 24:3–5)

Let integrity and uprightness preserve me; for I wait on thee. (Ps. 25:21)

The mouth of the righteous speaketh wisdom, and his tongue talketh of judgment. The law of his God is in his heart; none of his steps shall slide. (Ps. 37:30–31)

If I regard iniquity in my heart, the Lord will not hear me. (Ps. 66:18)

Keep thy heart with all diligence; for out of it are the issues of life. (Prov. 4:23)

The just man walketh in his integrity: his children are blessed after him. (Prov. 20:7)

If thou sayest, Behold, we knew it not; doth not he that pondereth the heart consider it? and he that keepeth thy soul, doth not he know it? and shall not he render to every man according to his works? (Prov. 24:12)

Blessed are the pure in heart: for they shall see God. (Matt. 5:8)

But that on the good ground are they, which in an honest and good heart, having heard the word, keep it, and bring forth fruit with patience. (Luke 8:15)

That ye may approve things that are excellent; that ye may be sincere and without offence till the day of Christ. (Phil. 1:10)

Now the end of the commandment is charity out of a pure heart, and of a good conscience, and of faith unfeigned. (1 Tim. 1:5)

For the word of God is quick, and powerful, and sharper than any two edged sword, piercing even to the dividing asunder of soul and spirit, and of the joints and marrow, and is a discerner of the thoughts and intents of the heart. (Heb. 4:12)

Pray for us: for we trust we have a good conscience, in all things willing to live honestly. (Heb. 13:18)

[9] Ye hypocrites, well did Esaias prophesy of you, saying, This people draweth nigh unto me with their mouth, and honoureth me with their lips; but their heart is far from me... Then came his disciples, and said unto him, Knowest thou that the Pharisees were offended, after they heard this saying? (Matt. 15:7–8, 12)

But woe unto you, scribes and Pharisees, hypocrites! for ye shut up the kingdom of heaven against men: for ye neither go in yourselves, neither suffer ye them that are entering to go in. Woe unto you, scribes and Pharisees, hypocrites! for ye devour widows' houses, and for a pretence make long prayer: therefore ye shall receive the greater damnation. Woe unto you, scribes and Pharisees, hypocrites! for ye compass sea and land to make one proselyte, and when he is made, ye make him twofold more the child of hell than yourselves... Woe unto you, scribes and Pharisees, hypocrites! for ye pay tithe of mint and anise and cummin, and have omitted the weightier matters of the law, judgment, mercy, and faith: these ought ye to have done, and not to leave the other undone... Woe unto you, scribes and Pharisees, hypocrites! for ye make clean the outside of the cup and of the platter, but within they are full of extortion and excess... Woe unto you, scribes and Pharisees, hypocrites! for ye are like unto whited sepulchers, which indeed appear beautiful outward, but are within full of dead men's bones, and of all uncleanness... Woe unto you, scribes and Pharisees, hypocrites! because ye build the tombs of the prophets, and garnish the sepulchers of the righteous, And say, If we had been in the days of our fathers, we would not have been partakers with them in the blood of the prophets. Wherefore ye be witnesses unto yourselves, that ye are the children of them which killed the prophets. Fill ye up then the measure of your fathers. Ye serpents, ye generation of vipers, how can ye escape the damnation of hell? (Matt. 23:13–15, 23, 25, 27, 29–33)

[10] What fruit had ye then in those things whereof ye are now ashamed? for the end of those things is death. (Rom. 6:21)

Yea doubtless, and I count all things but loss for the excellency of the knowledge of Christ Jesus my Lord: for whom I have suffered the loss of all things, and do count them but dung, that I may win Christ... Brethren, I count not myself to have apprehended: but this one thing I do, forgetting those things which are behind, and reaching forth unto those things which are before, I press toward the mark for the prize of the high calling of God in Christ Jesus. (Phil. 3:8, 13–14)

Wherefore seeing we also are compassed about with so great a cloud of witnesses, let us lay aside every weight, and the sin which doth so easily beset us, and let us run with patience the race that is set before us, Looking unto Jesus the author and finisher of our faith; who for the joy that was set before him endured the cross, despising the shame, and is set down at the right hand of the throne of God. (Heb. 12:1–2)

How much more shall the blood of Christ, who through the eternal Spirit offered himself without spot to God, purge your conscience from dead works to serve the living God? (Heb. 9:14)

11 For we know that the law is spiritual: but I am carnal, sold under sin. For that which I do I allow not: for what I would, that do I not; but what I hate, that do I. If then I do that which I would not, I consent unto the law that it is good. Now then it is no more I that do it, but sin that dwelleth in me. For I know that in me (that is, in my flesh,) dwelleth no good thing: for to will is present with me; but how to perform that which is good I find not. For the good that I would I do not: but the evil which I would not, that I do. Now if I do that I would not, it is no more I that do it, but sin that dwelleth in me. I find then a law, that, when I would do good, evil is present with me. For I delight in the law of God after the inward man: But I see another law in my members, warring against the law of my mind, and bringing me into captivity to the law of sin which is in my members. O wretched man that I am! who shall deliver me from the body of this death? I thank God through Jesus Christ our Lord. So then with the mind I myself serve the law of God; but with the flesh the law of sin. (Rom. 7:14–25)

12 Blessed are they that keep his testimonies, and that seek him with the whole heart. They also do no iniquity: they walk in his ways. Thou hast commanded us to keep thy precepts diligently. O that my ways were directed to keep thy statutes!... Wherewithal shall a young man cleanse his way? by taking heed thereto according to thy word... I have chosen the way of truth: thy judgments have I laid before me... Incline my heart unto thy testimonies, and not to covetousness... I thought on my ways, and turned my feet unto thy testimonies... I have refrained my feet from every evil way, that I might keep thy word... I have inclined mine heart to perform thy statutes always, even unto the end... Order my steps in thy word: and let not any iniquity have dominion over me... I have kept thy precepts and thy testimonies: for all my ways are before thee... Let thine hand help me; for I have chosen thy precepts. (Ps. 119:2–5, 9, 30, 36, 59, 101, 112, 133, 168, 173)

Be ye therefore followers of God, as dear children. (Eph. 5:1)

See that none render evil for evil unto any man; but ever follow that which is good, both among yourselves, and to all men. (1 Thess. 5:15)

13 Ponder the path of thy feet, and let all thy ways be established. Turn not to the right hand nor to the left: remove thy foot from evil. (Prov. 4:26–27)

That ye put off concerning the former conversation the old man, which is corrupt according to the deceitful lusts... And that ye put on the new man, which after God is created in righteousness and true holiness. (Eph. 4:22, 24)

But put ye on the Lord Jesus Christ, and make not provision for the flesh, to fulfil the lusts thereof. (Rom. 13:14)

This is a faithful saying, and these things I will that thou affirm constantly, that they which have believed in God might be careful to maintain good works. These things are good and profitable unto men. (Titus 3:8)

14 The night is far spent, the day is at hand: let us therefore cast off the works of darkness, and let us put on the armour of light. Let us walk honestly, as in the day; not in rioting and drunkenness, not in chambering and wantonness, not in strife and envying. (Rom. 13:12–13)

15 Now the works of the flesh are manifest, which are these; Adultery, fornication, uncleanness, lasciviousness, Idolatry, witchcraft, hatred, variance, emulations, wrath, strife, seditions, heresies, envyings, murders, drunkenness, revellings, and such like: of the which I tell you before, as I have also told you in time past, that they which do such things shall not inherit the kingdom of God. (Gal. 5:19–21)

But now ye also put off all these; anger, wrath, malice, blasphemy, filthy communication out of your mouth. Lie not one to another, seeing that ye have put off the old man with his deeds; And have put on the new man, which is renewed in knowledge after the image of him that created him. (Col. 3:8–10)

16 But the fruit of the Spirit is love, joy, peace, longsuffering, gentleness, goodness, faith, Meekness, temperance: against such there is no law. (Gal. 5:22–23)

Put on therefore, as the elect of God, holy and beloved, bowels of mercies, kindness, humbleness of mind, meekness, longsuffering; Forbearing one another, and forgiving one another, if any man have a quarrel against any: even as Christ forgave you, so also do ye. And above all these things put on charity, which is the bond of perfectness. (Col. 3:12–14)

17 Finally, brethren, whatsoever things are true, whatsoever things are honest, whatsoever things are just, whatsoever things are pure, whatsoever things are lovely, whatsoever things are of good report; if there be any virtue, and if there be any praise, think on these things. (Phil. 4:8)

18 O my God, my soul is cast down within me… Why art thou cast down, O my soul? and why art thou disquieted within me? hope thou in God: for I shall yet praise him, who is the health of my countenance, and my God. (Ps. 42:6a, 11)

19 For that which I do I allow not: for what I would, that do I not; but what I hate, that do I. If then I do that which I would not, I consent unto the law that it is good. Now then it is no more I that do it, but sin that dwelleth in me. For I know that in me (that is, in my flesh,) dwelleth no good thing: for to will is present with me; but how to perform that which is good I find not. For the good that I would I do not: but the evil which I would not, that I do. Now if I do that I would not, it is no more I that do it, but sin that dwelleth in me. I find then a law, that, when I would do good, evil is present with me. For I delight in the law of God after the inward man: But I see another law in my members, warring against the law of my mind, and bringing me into captivity to the law of sin which is in my members. O wretched man that I am! Who shall deliver me from the body of this death? I thank God through Jesus Christ our Lord. So

then with the mind I myself serve the law of God; but with the flesh the law of sin. (Rom. 7:15–25)

20 Great is our Lord, and of great power: his understanding is infinite. (Ps. 147:5)

For if our heart condemn us, God is greater than our heart, and knoweth all things. (1 John 3:20)

21 And call upon me in the day of trouble: I will deliver thee, and thou shalt glorify me. (Ps. 50:15)

Cast thy burden upon the LORD, and he shall sustain thee: he shall never suffer the righteous to be moved. (Ps. 55:22)

Come unto me, all ye that labour and are heavy laden, and I will give you rest. Take my yoke upon you, and learn of me; for I am meek and lowly in heart: and ye shall find rest unto your souls. For my yoke is easy, and my burden is light. (Matt. 11:28–30)

Pray without ceasing. (1 Thess. 5:17)

22 For our light affliction, which is but for a moment, worketh for us a far more exceeding and eternal weight of glory. (2 Cor. 4:17)

For we are his workmanship, created in Christ Jesus unto good works, which God hath before ordained that we should walk in them. (Eph. 2:10)

Being filled with the fruits of righteousness, which are by Jesus Christ, unto the glory and praise of God. (Phil. 1:11)

Who hath saved us, and called us with an holy calling, not according to our works, but according to his own purpose and grace, which was given us in Christ Jesus before the world began. (2 Tim. 1:9)

23 Trust in the LORD with all thine heart; and lean not unto thine own understanding. In all thy ways acknowledge him, and he shall direct thy paths. (Prov. 3:5–6)

For therein is the righteousness of God revealed from faith to faith: as it is written, The just shall live by faith. (Rom. 1:17)

Therefore being justified by faith, we have peace with God through our Lord Jesus Christ: By whom also we have access by faith into this grace wherein we stand, and rejoice in hope of the glory of God. (Rom. 5:1–2)

Now to him that is of power to stablish you according to my gospel, and the preaching of Jesus Christ, according to the revelation of the mystery, which was kept secret since the world began, But now is made manifest, and by the scriptures of the prophets, according to the commandment of the everlasting God, made known to all nations for the obedience of faith. (Rom. 16:25–26)

For we walk by faith, not by sight. (2 Cor. 5:7)

I am crucified with Christ: nevertheless I live; yet not I, but Christ liveth in me: and the life which I now live in the flesh I live by the faith of the Son of God, who loved me, and gave himself for me. (Gal. 2:20)

But without faith it is impossible to please him: for he that cometh to God must believe that he is, and that he is a rewarder of them that diligently seek him. (Heb. 11:6)

For whatsoever is born of God overcometh the world: and this is the victory that overcometh the world, even our faith. (1 John 5:4)

24 That the trial of your faith, being much more precious than of gold that perisheth, though it be tried with fire, might be found unto praise and honour and glory at the appearing of Jesus Christ. (1 Pet. 1:7)

25 Wait on the LORD: be of good courage, and he shall strengthen thine heart: wait, I say, on the LORD. (Ps. 27:14)

26 But this thing commanded I them, saying, Obey my voice, and I will be your God, and ye shall be my people: and walk ye in all the ways that I have commanded you, that it may be well unto you. (Jer. 7:23)

27 For ye are all the children of God by faith in Christ Jesus. (Gal. 3:26)

Behold, what manner of love the Father hath bestowed upon us, that we should be called the sons of God: therefore the world knoweth us not, because it knew him not. Beloved, now are we the sons of God, and it doth not yet appear what we shall be: but we know that, when he shall appear, we shall be like him; for we shall see him as he is. (1 John 3:1–2)

28 And because ye are sons, God hath sent forth the Spirit of his Son into your hearts, crying, Abba, Father. Wherefore thou art no more a servant, but a son; and if a son, then an heir of God through Christ. (Gal. 4:6–7)

29 In my distress I called upon the LORD, and cried unto my God: he heard my voice out of his temple, and my cry came before him, even into his ears. (Ps. 18:6)

I love the LORD, because he hath heard my voice and my supplications. Because he hath inclined his ear unto me, therefore will I call upon him as long as I live… Gracious is the LORD, and righteous; yea, our God is merciful… For thou hast delivered my soul from death, mine eyes from tears, and my feet from falling… I will offer to thee the sacrifice of thanksgiving, and will call upon the name of the LORD. (Ps. 116:1–2, 5, 8, 17)

And another angel came and stood at the altar, having a golden censer; and there was given unto him much incense, that he should offer it with the prayers of all saints upon the golden altar which was before the throne. And the smoke of the incense, which came with the prayers of the saints, ascended up before God out of the angel's hand. (Rev. 8:3–4)

30 But as it is written, Eye hath not seen, nor ear heard, neither have entered into the heart of man, the things which God hath prepared for them that love him. (1 Cor. 2:9)

According as he hath chosen us in him before the foundation of the world, that we should be holy and without blame before him in love. (Eph. 1:4)

Behold, what manner of love the Father hath bestowed upon us, that we should be called the sons of God: therefore the world knoweth us not, because it knew him not. Beloved, now are we the sons of God, and it doth not yet appear what we shall be: but we know that, when he shall appear, we shall be like him;

for we shall see him as he is. And every man that hath this hope in him purifieth himself, even as he is pure. (1 John 3:1–3)

³¹ I will call upon the LORD, who is worthy to be praised. (Ps. 18:3a)

O give thanks unto the LORD; call upon his name: make known his deeds among the people. (Ps. 105:1)

I will offer to thee the sacrifice of thanksgiving, and will call upon the name of the LORD. (Ps. 116:17)

³² So will I sing praise unto thy name for ever, that I may daily perform my vows. (Ps. 61:8)

³³ Hear me when I call, O God of my righteousness: thou hast enlarged me when I was in distress; have mercy upon me, and hear my prayer. (Ps. 4:1)

My voice shalt thou hear in the morning, O LORD; in the morning will I direct my prayer unto thee, and will look up. (Ps. 5:3)

Hear, O LORD, and have mercy upon me: LORD, be thou my helper. (Ps. 30:10)

Have mercy upon me, O God, according to thy lovingkindness: according unto the multitude of thy tender mercies blot out my transgressions. (Ps. 51:1)

Be merciful unto me, O Lord: for I cry unto thee daily… For thou, Lord, art good, and ready to forgive; and plenteous in mercy unto all them that call upon thee… In the day of my trouble I will call upon thee: for thou wilt answer me. (Ps. 86:3, 5, 7)

Mine eye mourneth by reason of affliction; LORD, I have called daily upon thee, I have stretched out my hands unto thee. (Ps. 88:9)

The LORD is merciful and gracious, slow to anger, and plenteous in mercy… For as the heaven is high above the earth, so great is his mercy toward them that fear him… But the mercy of the LORD is from everlasting to everlasting upon them that fear him, and his righteousness unto children's children. (Ps. 103:8, 11, 17)

I called upon the LORD in distress: the LORD answered me, and set me in a large place. (Ps. 118:5)

Look thou upon me, and be merciful unto me, as thou usest to do unto those that love thy name. (Ps. 119:132)

Cause me to hear thy lovingkindness in the morning; for in thee do I trust: cause me to know the way wherein I should walk; for I lift up my soul unto thee. (Ps. 143:8)

The LORD taketh pleasure in them that fear him, in those that hope in his mercy. (Ps. 147:11)

Blessed is the man that heareth me, watching daily at my gates, waiting at the posts of my doors. (Prov. 8:34)

Give us this day our daily bread. (Matt. 6:11)

And he said to them all, If any man will come after me, let him deny himself, and take up his cross daily, and follow me. (Luke 9:23)

But my God shall supply all your need according to his riches in glory by Christ Jesus. (Phil. 4:19)

Behold, we count them happy which endure. Ye have heard of the patience of Job, and have seen the end of the Lord; that the Lord is very pitiful, and of tender mercy. (James 5:11)

34 Give ear, O ye heavens, and I will speak; and hear, O earth, the words of my mouth. My doctrine shall drop as the rain, my speech shall distil as the dew, as the small rain upon the tender herb, and as the showers upon the grass: Because I will publish the name of the Lord: ascribe ye greatness unto our God. He is the Rock, his work is perfect: for all his ways are judgment: a God of truth and without iniquity, just and right is he. (Deut. 32:1–4)

Declare his glory among the heathen; his marvelous works among all nations. For great is the Lord, and greatly to be praised: he also is to be feared above all gods. For all the gods of the people are idols: but the Lord made the heavens. Glory and honour are in his presence; strength and gladness are in his place. Give unto the Lord, ye kindreds of the people, give unto the Lord glory and strength. Give unto the Lord the glory due unto his name: bring an offering, and come before him: worship the Lord in the beauty of holiness. Fear before him, all the earth: the world also shall be stable, that it be not moved. Let the heavens be glad, and let the earth rejoice: and let men say among the nations, The Lord reigneth. (1 Chron. 16:24–31)

Come near, ye nations, to hear; and hearken, ye people: let the earth hear, and all that is therein; the world, and all things that come forth of it. (Isa. 34:1)

Hear this, all ye people; give ear, all ye inhabitants of the world: Both low and high, rich and poor,... They that trust in their wealth, and boast themselves in the multitude of their riches; None of them can by any means redeem his brother, nor give to God a ransom for him: (For the redemption of their soul is precious, and it ceaseth for ever:) That he should still live for ever, and not see corruption. (Ps. 49:1–2, 6–9)

Look unto me, and be ye saved, all the ends of the earth: for I am God, and there is none else. (Isa. 45:22)

35 And said unto them, Thus it is written, and thus it behoved Christ to suffer, and to rise from the dead the third day: And that repentance and remission of sins should be preached in his name among all nations, beginning at Jerusalem. (Luke 24:46–47)

To him give all the prophets witness, that through his name whosoever believeth in him shall receive remission of sins. (Acts 10:43)

36 Go ye therefore, and teach all nations, baptizing them in the name of the Father, and of the Son, and of the Holy Ghost: Teaching them to observe all things whatsoever I have commanded you: and, lo, I am with you always, even unto the end of the world. Amen. (Matt. 28:19–20)

And he said unto them, Go ye into all the world, and preach the gospel to every creature. (Mark 16:15)

And how shall they preach, except they be sent? as it is written, How beautiful are the feet of them that preach the gospel of peace, and bring glad tidings of good things! (Rom. 10:15)

37 For I am not ashamed of the gospel of Christ: for it is the power of god unto salvation to every one that believeth; to the Jew first, and also to the Greek. (Rom. 1:16)

Be not thou therefore ashamed of the testimony of our Lord, nor of me his prisoner: but be thou partaker of the afflictions of the gospel according to the power of God. (2 Tim. 1:8)

38 Whosoever therefore shall confess me before men, him will I confess also before my Father which is in heaven. (Matt. 10:32)

Also I say unto you, Whosoever shall confess me before men, him shall the Son of man also confess before the angels of God. (Luke 12:8)

39 For I am not ashamed of the gospel of Christ: for it is the power of God unto salvation to every one that believeth; to the Jew first, and also to the Greek. (Rom. 1:16)

40 Ye are the light of the world. A city that is set on an hill cannot be hid. Neither do men light a candle, and put it under a bushel, but on a candlestick; and it giveth light unto all that are in the house. Let your light so shine before men, that they may see your good works, and glorify your Father which is in heaven. (Matt. 5:14–16)

Now thanks be unto God, which always causeth us to triumph in Christ, and maketh manifest the savour of his knowledge by us in every place. For we are unto God a sweet savour of Christ, in them that are saved, and in them that perish: To the one we are the savour of death unto death; and to the other the savour of life unto life. And who is sufficient for these things? (2 Cor. 2:14–16)

Let no man despise thy youth; but be thou an example of the believers, in word, in conversation, in charity, in spirit, in faith, in purity. (1 Tim. 4:12)

41 And John answered him, saying, Master, we saw one casting out devils in thy name, and he followeth not us: and we forbad him, because he followeth not us. But Jesus said, Forbid him not: for there is no man which shall do a miracle in my name, that can lightly speak evil of me. For he that is not against us is on our part. (Mark 9:38–40)

And John answered and said, Master, we saw one casting out devils in thy name; and we forbad him, because he followeth not with us. And Jesus said unto him, Forbid him not: for he that is not against us is for us. (Luke 9:49–50)

And Jesus entered and passed through Jericho. And, behold, there was a man named Zacchaeus, which was the chief among the publicans, and he was rich. And he sought to see Jesus who he was; and could not for the press, because he was little of stature. And he ran before, and climbed up into a sycamore tree to see him: for he was to pass that way. And when Jesus came to the place, he looked up, and saw him, and said unto him, Zacchaeus, make haste, and come down; for today I must abide at thy house. And he made haste, and came down, and received him joyfully. And when they saw it, they all murmured, saying, That he was gone to be guest with a man that is a sinner. (Luke 19:1–7)

42 And the second is like unto it, Thou shalt love thy neighbour as thyself. (Matt. 22:39)

And the second is like, namely this, Thou shalt love thy neighbour as thyself. There is none other commandment greater than these... And to love him with all the heart, and with all the understanding, and with all the soul, and with all the strength, and to love his neighbour as himself, is more than all whole burnt offerings and sacrifices. (Mark 12:31, 33)

For this, Thou shalt not commit adultery, Thou shalt not kill, Thou shalt not steal, Thou shalt not bear false witness, Thou shalt not covet; and if there be any other commandment, it is briefly comprehended in this saying, namely, Thou shalt love thy neighbour as thyself. Love worketh no ill to his neighbour: therefore love is the fulfilling of the law. (Rom. 13:9–10)

For all the law is fulfilled in one word, even in this; Thou shalt love thy neighbour as thyself. (Gal. 5:14)

If ye fulfil the royal law according to the scripture, Thou shalt love thy neighbour as thyself, ye do well. (James 2:8)

43 A new commandment I give unto you, That ye love one another; as I have loved you, that ye also love one another. By this shall all men know that ye are my disciples, if ye have love one to another. (John 13:34–35)

44 But I have greater witness than that of John: for the works which the Father hath given me to finish, the same works that I do, bear witness of me, that the Father hath sent me. (John 5:36)

Jesus answered them, I told you, and ye believed not: the works that I do in my Father's name, they bear witness of me... But if I do, though ye believe not me, believe the works: that ye may know, and believe, that the Father is in me, and I in him. (John 10:25, 38)

Believe me that I am in the Father, and the Father in me: or else believe me for the very works' sake. (John 14:11)

Now when he was in Jerusalem at the passover, in the feast day, many believed in his name, when they saw the miracles which he did. (John 2:23)

45 And he sent them to preach the kingdom of God, and to heal the sick. (Luke 9:2)

46 And you hath he quickened, who were dead in trespasses and sins; Wherein in time past ye walked according to the course of this world, according to the prince of the power of the air, the spirit that now worketh in the children of disobedience: Among whom also we all had our conversation in times past in the lusts of our flesh, fulfilling the desires of the flesh and of the mind; and were by nature the children of wrath, even as others. (Eph. 2:1–3)

And you, that were sometime alienated and enemies in your mind by wicked works, yet now hath he reconciled. (Col. 1:21)

And you, being dead in your sins and the uncircumcision of your flesh, hath he quickened together with him, having forgiven you all trespasses. (Col. 2:13)

For all have sinned, and come short of the glory of God. (Rom. 3:23)

47 That whosoever believeth in him should not perish, but have eternal life. For God so loved the world, that he gave his only begotten Son, that whosoever believeth in him should not perish, but have everlasting life. (John 3:15–16)

For the wages of sin is death; but the gift of God is eternal life through Jesus Christ our Lord. (Rom. 6:23)

For by grace are ye saved through faith; and that not of yourselves: it is the gift of God: Not of works, lest any man should boast. (Eph. 2:8–9)

But after that the kindness and love of God our Saviour toward man appeared, Not by works of righteousness which we have done, but according to his mercy he saved us, by the washing of regeneration, and renewing of the Holy Ghost; Which he shed on us abundantly through Jesus Christ our Saviour; That being justified by his grace, we should be made heirs according to the hope of eternal life. (Titus 3:4–7)

48 For all have sinned, and come short of the glory of God; Being justified freely by his grace through the redemption that is in Christ Jesus: Whom God hath set forth to be a propitiation through faith in his blood, to declare his righteousness for the remission of sins that are past, through the forbearance of God; To declare, I say, at this time his righteousness: that he might be just, and the justifier of him which believeth in Jesus. Where is boasting then? It is excluded. By what law? Of works? Nay: but by the law of faith. Therefore we conclude that a man is justified by faith without the deeds of the law. (Rom. 3:23–28)

But God, who is rich in mercy, for his great love wherewith he loved us, Even when we were dead in sins, hath quickened us together with Christ, (by grace ye are saved;) And hath raised us up together, and made us sit together in heavenly places in Christ Jesus: That in the ages to come he might shew the exceeding riches of his grace in his kindness toward us through Christ Jesus. For by grace are ye saved through faith; and that not of yourselves: it is the gift of God: Not of works, lest any man should boast. (Eph. 2:4–9)

49 And I, brethren, when I came to you, came not with excellency of speech or of wisdom, declaring unto you the testimony of God. For I determined not to know any thing among you, save Jesus Christ, and him crucified. And I was with you in weakness, and in fear, and in much trembling. And my speech and my preaching was not with enticing words of man's wisdom, but in demonstration of the Spirit and of power: That your faith should not stand in the wisdom of men, but in the power of God. (1 Cor. 2:1–5)

For I delivered unto you first of all that which I also received, how that Christ died for our sins according to the scriptures; And that he was buried, and that he rose again the third day according to the scriptures. (1 Cor. 15:3–4)

But God forbid that I should glory, save in the cross of our Lord Jesus Christ, by whom the world is crucified unto me, and I unto the world. (Gal. 6:14)

50 And he spake this parable unto certain which trusted in themselves that they were righteous, and despised others: Two men went up into the temple to pray; the one a Pharisee, and the other a publican. The Pharisee stood and prayed thus with himself, God, I thank thee, that I am not as other men are, extortioners, unjust, adulterers, or even as this publican. I fast twice in the week, I give tithes of all that I possess. And the publican, standing afar off, would not lift up so much as his eyes unto heaven, but smote upon his breast, saying, God be merciful to me a sinner. I tell you, this man went down to his house justified rather than the other: for every one that exalteth himself shall be abased; and he that humbleth himself shall be exalted. (Luke 18:9–14)

51 And one of the Pharisees desired him that he would eat with him. And he went into the Pharisee's house, and sat down to meat. (Luke 7:36)

52 And it came to pass, as Jesus sat at meat in the house, behold, many publicans and sinners came and sat down with him and his disciples. And when the Pharisees saw it, they said unto his disciples, Why eateth your Master with publicans and sinners? (Matt. 9:10–11)

And Levi made him a great feast in his own house: and there was a great company of publicans and of others that sat down with them. But their scribes and Pharisees murmured against his disciples, saying, Why do ye eat and drink with publicans and sinners? (Luke 5:29–30)

53 Note that the Pharisee's phrase "publicans and sinners" was their term for worthless, compromised, morally corrupt, and evil people. Pharisees considered themselves morally superior to the publicans and sinners and would never associate with them.

54 And when the scribes and Pharisees saw him eat with publicans and sinners, they said unto his disciples, how is it that he eateth and drinketh with publicans and sinners? When Jesus heard it, he saith unto them, they that are whole have no need of the physician, but they that are sick: I came not to call the righteous, but sinners to repentance. (Mark 2:16–17)

55 Nebuchadnezzar spake and said unto them, Is it true, O Shadrach, Meshach, and Abednego, do not ye serve my gods, nor worship the golden image which I have set up?… Shadrach, Meshach, and Abednego, answered and said to the king, O Nebuchadnezzar, we are not careful to answer thee in this matter. If it be so, our God whom we serve is able to deliver us from the burning fiery furnace, and he will deliver us out of thine hand, O king. But if not, be it known unto thee, O king, that we will not serve thy gods, nor worship the golden image which thou hast set up. (Dan. 3:14, 16–18)

His lord said unto him, well done, thou good and faithful servant: thou hast been faithful over a few things, I will make thee ruler over many things: enter thou into the joy of thy lord. (Matt. 25:21)

And the Lord said, who then is that faithful and wise steward, whom his lord shall make ruler over his household, to give them their portion of meat in due season? (Luke 12:42)

If therefore ye have not been faithful in the unrighteous mammon, who will commit to your trust the true riches? (Luke 16:11)

Moreover it is required in stewards, that a man be found faithful. (1 Cor. 4:2)

Fear none of those things which thou shalt suffer: behold, the devil shall cast some of you into prison, that ye may be tried; and ye shall have tribulation ten days: be thou faithful unto death, and I will give thee a crown of life. (Rev. 2:10)

56 The LORD shall judge the people: judge me, O LORD, according to my righteousness, and according to mine integrity that is in me. (Ps. 7:8)

Let integrity and uprightness preserve me; for I wait on thee. (Ps. 25:21)

Judge me, O LORD; for I have walked in mine integrity: I have trusted also in the LORD; therefore I shall not slide. (Ps. 26:1)

The integrity of the upright shall guide them: but the perverseness of transgressors shall destroy them. (Prov. 11:3)

The just man walketh in his integrity: his children are blessed after him. (Prov. 20:7)

For our rejoicing is this, the testimony of our conscience, that in simplicity and godly sincerity, not with fleshly wisdom, but by the grace of God, we have had our conversation in the world, and more abundantly to you-ward. (2 Cor. 1:12)

For we are not as many, which corrupt the word of God: but as of sincerity, but as of God, in the sight of God speak we in Christ. (2 Cor. 2:17)

In all things shewing thyself a pattern of good works: in doctrine shewing uncorruptness, gravity, sincerity. (Titus 2:7)

That ye may approve things that are excellent; that ye may be sincere and without offence till the day of Christ. (Phil. 1:10)

Do all things without murmurings and disputings: That ye may be blameless and harmless, the sons of God, without rebuke, in the midst of a crooked and perverse nation, among whom ye shine as lights in the world; Holding forth the word of life. (Phil. 2:14–16a)

57 He that is faithful in that which is least is faithful also in much: and he that is unjust in the least is unjust also in much. If therefore ye have not been faithful in the unrighteous mammon, who will commit to your trust the true riches? And if ye have not been faithful in that which is another man's, who shall give you that which is your own? (Luke 16:10–12)

For what is a man advantaged, if he gain the whole world, and lose himself, or be cast away? (Luke 9:25)

Behold, the third time I am ready to come to you; and I will not be burdensome to you: for I seek not yours, but you: for the children ought not to lay up for the parents, but the parents for the children. And I will very gladly spend and be spent for you; though the more abundantly I love you, the less I be loved. But be it so, I did not burden you: nevertheless, being crafty, I caught you with guile. Did I make a gain of you by any of them whom I sent unto you? I desired Titus, and with him I sent a brother. Did Titus make a gain of you? walked we not in the same spirit? walked we not in the same steps? (2 Cor. 12:14–18)

Then Balak the son of Zippor, king of Moab, arose and warred against Israel, and sent and called Balaam the son of Beor to curse you: But I would not hearken unto Balaam; therefore he blessed you still: so I delivered you out of his hand. (Josh. 24:9–10)

Which have forsaken the right way, and are gone astray, following the way of Balaam the son of Bosor, who loved the wages of unrighteousness. (2 Pet. 2:15)

Woe unto them! for they have gone in the way of Cain, and ran greedily after the error of Balaam for reward, and perished in the gainsaying of Core. (Jude 1:11)

58 Now when he was in Jerusalem at the passover, in the feast day, many believed in his name, when they saw the miracles which he did. But Jesus did not commit himself unto them, because he knew all men, And needed not that any should testify of man: for he knew what was in man. (John 2:23–25)

59 Which of you convinceth me of sin? And if I say the truth, why do ye not believe me? (John 8:46)

For he hath made him to be sin for us, who knew no sin; that we might be made the righteousness of God in him. (2 Cor. 5:21)

60 Blessed is the man that walketh not in the counsel of the ungodly, nor standeth in the way of sinners, nor sitteth in the seat of the scornful. But his delight is in the law of the Lord; and in his law doth he meditate day and night. And he shall be like a tree planted by the rivers of water, that bringeth forth his fruit in his season; his leaf also shall not wither; and whatsoever he doeth shall prosper. (Ps. 1:1–3)

This book of the law shall not depart out of thy mouth; but thou shalt meditate therein day and night, that thou mayest observe to do according to all that is written therein: for then thou shalt make thy way prosperous, and then thou shalt have good success. (Josh. 1:8)

61 That ye may be blameless and harmless, the sons of God, without rebuke, in the midst of a crooked and perverse nation, among whom ye shine as lights in the world. (Phil. 2:15)

62 They went out from us, but they were not of us; for if they had been of us, they would no doubt have continued with us: but they went out, that they might be made manifest that they were not all of us. (1 John 2:19)

63 An unjust man is an abomination to the just: and he that is upright in the way is abomination to the wicked. (Prov. 29:27)

Blessed are ye, when men shall revile you, and persecute you, and shall say all manner of evil against you falsely, for my sake. (Matt. 5:11)

Remember the word that I said unto you, The servant is not greater than his lord. If they have persecuted me, they will also persecute you; if they have kept my saying, they will keep yours also. (John 15:20)

64 If ye know that he is righteous, ye know that every one that doeth righteousness is born of him. (1 John 2:29)

Now thanks be unto God, which always causeth us to triumph in Christ, and maketh manifest the savour of his knowledge by us in every place. For we are unto God a sweet savour of Christ, in them that are saved, and in them that perish. (2 Cor. 2:14–15)

65 Proving what is acceptable unto the Lord. And have no fellowship with the unfruitful works of darkness, but rather reprove them. (Eph. 5:10–11)

66 But he shall receive an hundred fold now in this time, houses, and brethren, and sisters, and mothers, and children, and lands, with persecutions; and in the world to come eternal life. (Mark 10:30)

Yea, and all that will live godly in Christ Jesus shall suffer persecution. (2 Tim. 3:12)

67 The proud have had me greatly in derision: yet have I not declined from thy law... The bands of the wicked have robbed me: but I have not forgotten thy law. (Ps. 119:51, 61)

Hearken unto me, ye that know righteousness, the people in whose heart is my law; fear ye not the reproach of men, neither be ye afraid of their revilings. For the moth shall eat them up like a garment, and the worm shall eat them like wool: but my righteousness shall be for ever, and my salvation from generation to generation... I, even I, am he that comforteth you: who art thou, that thou shouldest be afraid of a man that shall die, and of the son of man which shall be made as grass. (Isa. 51:7–8, 12)

Blessed are they which are persecuted for righteousness' sake: for theirs is the kingdom of heaven. Blessed are ye, when men shall revile you, and persecute you, and shall say all manner of evil against you falsely, for my sake. Rejoice, and be exceeding glad: for great is your reward in heaven: for so persecuted they the prophets which were before you. (Matt. 5:10–12)

Remember the word that I said unto you, The servant is not greater than his lord. If they have persecuted me, they will also persecute you; if they have kept my saying, they will keep yours also. (John 15:20)

These things I have spoken unto you, that in me ye might have peace. In the world ye shall have tribulation: but be of good cheer; I have overcome the world. (John 16:33)

But and if ye suffer for righteousness' sake, happy are ye: and be not afraid of their terror, neither be troubled. (1 Pet. 3:14)

My brethren, count it all joy when ye fall into divers temptations; Knowing this, that the trying of your faith worketh patience. But let patience have her perfectwork, that ye may be perfect and entire, wanting nothing. (James 1:2–4)

68 My son, walk not thou in the way with them; refrain thy foot from their path. (Prov. 1:15)

The way of the wicked is an abomination unto the LORD: but he loveth him that followeth after righteousness... The way of life is above to the wise, that he may depart from hell beneath. (Prov. 15:9, 24)

I thought on my ways, and turned my feet unto thy testimonies... I have refrained my feet from every evil way, that I might keep thy word. (Ps. 119:59, 101)

Shew me thy ways, O LORD; teach me thy paths. (Ps. 25:4)

He restoreth my soul: he leadeth me in the paths of righteousness for his name's sake. (Ps. 23:3)

69 And the brother shall deliver up the brother to death, and the father the child: and the children shall rise up against their parents, and cause them to be put to death... And a man's foes shall be they of his own household. (Matt. 10:21, 36)

70 Yea, mine own familiar friend, in whom I trusted, which did eat of my bread, hath lifted up his heel against me. (Ps. 41:9)

71 If the world hate you, ye know that it hated me before it hated you. If ye were of the world, the world would love his own: but because ye are not of the world, but I have chosen you out of the world, therefore the world hateth you. (John 15:18–19)

72 And the scribes and Pharisees watched him, whether he would heal on the sabbath day; that they might find an accusation against him. (Luke 6:7)

And the Pharisees went forth, and straight way took counsel with the Herodians against him, how they might destroy him. (Mark 3:6)

Remember the word that I said unto you, The servant is not greater than his lord. If they have persecuted me, they will also persecute you; if they have kept my saying, they will keep yours also. (John 15:20)

73 Ye hypocrites, well did Esaias prophesy of you, saying, This people draweth nigh unto me with their mouth, and honoureth me with their lips; but their heart is far from me. But in vain they do worship me, teaching for doctrines the commandments of men. (Matt. 15:7–9)

How? Knowledge

When my wife and I moved to Brazil, we first settled in a large city called Manaus. This centuries-old location on the merging of the Amazon and Negro Rivers has a confusing pattern of streets. So one of the first things we bought beside food was a map. The more streets we learned, the easier we transported our family from one place to the other. When discussing destinations with colleagues and friends, the map settled any disagreements.

Knowledge: Growing in Understanding of God and His Word

All the teaching and stories of the Bible were written for us[1] like a road map of streets we may travel. We learn the scriptures[2] so we can apply them in the circumstances of life[3] and grow in our own conduct.[4] Moreover, knowing God's Word[5] means growing in the grace and knowledge of Jesus Christ[6] and His walk.[7] We understand more about the Lord, His purposes, the path we are walking, and the paths we should not take.

We mature in Scripture so that we can understand right doctrine, as the authority of Scripture,[8] the virgin birth of Jesus,[9] the deity of Christ,[10] His sinless life,[11] His blood atonement for sin,[12] His literal bodily resurrection,[13] His physical return to the earth,[14] salvation by grace through faith.[15] We also mature in Scripture so that we can understand how to walk by faith,[16] to follow Christ,[17] to grow in holiness,[18] and to grow in love toward others.[19]

Increasing in the wisdom of Scripture[20] gives us a better insight into the slavery of sin[21] and its consequences,[22] like our Manaus map documented streets to use and streets to avoid. When others gave us street directions, we checked what they said against the map of the city. Some in Manaus gave us bad directions. Understanding God's Word helps us to see clearly the lies of men[23] and to stand fast,[24] especially in the last days, when false prophets and wrong doctrine will abound.[25]

Knowledge of the Word equips us in our life and witness to others.[26]

To use the sharp sword of the Word wisely, we must add self-control to knowledge.

Notes

1 Now all these things happened unto them for ensamples: and they are written for our admonition, upon whom the ends of the world are come. (1 Cor. 10:11)

2 Study to shew thyself approved unto God, a workman that needeth not to be ashamed, rightly dividing the word of truth. (2 Tim. 2:15)

3 Cause me to hear thy lovingkindness in the morning; for in thee do I trust: cause me to know the way wherein I should walk; for I lift up my soul unto thee... Teach me to do thy will; for thou art my God: thy spirit is good; lead me into the land of uprightness. (Ps. 143:8, 10)

4 All scripture is given by inspiration of God, and is profitable for doctrine, for reproof, for correction, for instruction in righteousness: That the man of God may be perfect, throughly furnished unto all good works. (2 Tim. 3:16–17)

   That ye might walk worthy of the Lord unto all pleasing, being fruitful in every good work, and increasing in the knowledge of God. (Col. 1:10)

5 Shew me thy ways, O Lord; teach me thy paths. Lead me in thy truth, and teach me. (Ps. 25:4–5a)

   Teach me good judgment and knowledge: for I have believed thy commandments... Thou art good, and doest good; teach me thy statutes... Thy hands have made me and fashioned me: give me understanding, that I may learn thy commandments. (Ps. 119:66, 68, 73)

6 Take my yoke upon you, and learn of me; for I am meek and lowly in heart: and ye shall find rest unto your souls. (Matt. 11:29)

   Grace and peace be multiplied unto you through the knowledge of God, and of Jesus our Lord. (2 Pet. 1:2)

   But grow in grace, and in the knowledge of our Lord and Saviour Jesus Christ. To him be glory both now and for ever. Amen. (2 Pet. 3:18)

7 Then spake Jesus again unto them, saying, I am the light of the world: he that followeth me shall not walk in darkness, but shall have the light of life. (John 8:12)

   But as God hath distributed to every man, as the Lord hath called every one, so let him walk. And so ordain I in all churches. (1 Cor. 7:17)

   For we are his workmanship, created in Christ Jesus unto good works, which God hath before ordained that we should walk in them. (Eph. 2:10)

   As ye have therefore received Christ Jesus the Lord, so walk ye in him. (Col. 2:6)

   But if we walk in the light, as he is in the light, we have fellowship one with another, and the blood of Jesus Christ his Son cleanseth us from all sin. (1 John 1:7)

He that saith he abideth in him ought himself also so to walk, even as he walked. (1 John 2:6)

8 All scripture is given by inspiration of God, and is profitable for doctrine, for reproof, for correction, for instruction in righteousness: That the man of God may be perfect, throughly furnished unto all good works. (2 Tim. 3:16–17)

9 Behold, a virgin shall be with child, and shall bring forth a son, and they shall call his name Emmanuel, which being interpreted is, God with us. (Matt. 1:23)

To a virgin espoused to a man whose name was Joseph, of the house of David; and the virgin's name was Mary. (Luke 1:27)

10 In the beginning was the Word, and the Word was with God, and the Word was God. The same was in the beginning with God. All things were made by him; and without him was not any thing made that was made. (John 1:1–3)

Who is the image of the invisible God, the firstborn of every creature: For by him were all things created, that are in heaven, and that are in earth, visible and invisible, whether they be thrones, or dominions, or principalities, or powers: all things were created by him, and for him: 17 And he is before all things, and by him all things consist. (Col. 1:15–17)

11 For he hath made him to be sin for us, who knew no sin; that we might be made the righteousness of God in him. (2 Cor. 5:21)

12 Much more then, being now justified by his blood, we shall be saved from wrath through him. (Rom. 5:9)

In whom we have redemption through his blood, the forgiveness of sins, according to the riches of his grace. (Eph. 1:7)

13 To whom also he shewed himself alive after his passion by many infallible proofs, being seen of them forty days, and speaking of the things pertaining to the kingdom of God. (Acts 1:3)

And with great power gave the apostles witness of the resurrection of the Lord Jesus: and great grace was upon them all. (Acts 4:33)

I am he that liveth, and was dead; and, behold, I am alive for evermore, Amen; and have the keys of hell and of death. (Rev. 1:18)

14 Which also said, Ye men of Galilee, why stand ye gazing up into heaven? this same Jesus, which is taken up from you into heaven, shall so come in like manner as ye have seen him go into heaven. (Acts 1:11)

For the Son of man shall come in the glory of his Father with his angels; and then he shall reward every man according to his works. (Matt. 16:27)

When the Son of man shall come in his glory, and all the holy angels with him, then shall he sit upon the throne of his glory. (Matt. 25:31)

15 For by grace are ye saved through faith; and that not of yourselves: it is the gift of God: Not of works, lest any man should boast. (Eph. 2:8–9)

16 For therein is the righteousness of God revealed from faith to faith: as it is written, The just shall live by faith. (Rom. 1:17)

I am crucified with Christ: nevertheless I live; yet not I, but Christ liveth in me: and the life which I now live in the flesh I live by the faith of the Son of God, who loved me, and gave himself for me. (Gal. 2:20)

17 For even hereunto were ye called: because Christ also suffered for us, leaving us an example, that ye should follow his steps. (1 Pet. 2:21)

18 I speak after the manner of men because of the infirmity of your flesh: for as ye have yielded your members servants to uncleanness and to iniquity unto iniquity; even so now yield your members servants to righteousness unto holiness. (Rom. 6:19)

For God hath not called us unto uncleanness, but unto holiness. (1 Thess. 4:7)

19 A new commandment I give unto you, That ye love one another; as I have loved you, that ye also love one another. By this shall all men know that ye are my disciples, if ye have love one to another. (John 13:34–35)

And this I pray, that your love may abound yet more and more in knowledge and in all judgment. (Phil. 1:9)

And the Lord make you to increase and abound in love one toward another, and toward all men, even as we do toward you. (1 Thess. 3:12)

20 A wise man will hear, and will increase learning; and a man of understanding shall attain unto wise counsels:... The fear of the Lord is the beginning of knowledge: but fools despise wisdom and instruction. (Prov. 1:5, 7)

Who is a wise man and endued with knowledge among you? let him shew out of a good conversation his works with meekness of wisdom. (James 3:13)

21 But now, after that ye have known God, or rather are known of God, how turn ye again to the weak and beggarly elements, whereunto ye desire again to be in bondage? (Gal. 4:9)

Stand fast therefore in the liberty wherewith Christ hath made us free, and be not entangled again with the yoke of bondage. (Gal. 5:1)

Know ye not, that to whom ye yield yourselves servants to obey, his servants ye are to whom ye obey; whether of sin unto death, or of obedience unto righteousness? (Rom. 6:16)

While they promise them liberty, they themselves are the servants of corruption: for of whom a man is overcome, of the same is he brought in bondage. (2 Pet. 2:19)

22 There is a way that seemeth right unto a man, but the end thereof are the ways of death. (Prov. 16:25)

What fruit had ye then in those things whereof ye are now ashamed? For the end of those things is death. (Rom. 6:21)

23 That we henceforth be no more children, tossed to and fro, and carried about with every wind of doctrine, by the sleight of men, and cunning craftiness, whereby they lie in wait to deceive. (Eph. 4:14)

Holding fast the faithful word as he hath been taught, that he may be able by sound doctrine both to exhort and to convince the gainsayers. They profess that they know God; but in works they deny him, being abominable, and disobedient, and unto every good work reprobate. (Titus 1:9, 16)

Be not carried about with divers and strange doctrines. For it is a good thing that the heart be established with grace; not with meats, which have not profited them that have been occupied therein. (Heb. 13:9)

But there were false prophets also among the people, even as there shall be false teachers among you, who privily shall bring in damnable heresies, even denying the Lord that bought them, and bring upon themselves swift destruction. And many shall follow their pernicious ways; by reason of whom the way of truth shall be evil spoken of. And through covetousness shall they with feigned words make merchandise of you: whose judgment now of a long time lingereth not, and their damnation slumbereth not. (2 Pet. 2:1–3)

For many deceivers are entered into the world, who confess not that Jesus Christ is come in the flesh. This is a deceiver and an antichrist. (2 John 7)

For there are certain men crept in unawares, who were before of old ordained to this condemnation, ungodly men, turning the grace of our God into lasciviousness, and denying the only Lord God, and our Lord Jesus Christ. Likewise also these filthy dreamers defile the flesh, despise dominion, and speak evil of dignities. But these speak evil of those things which they know not: but what they know naturally, as brute beasts, in those things they corrupt themselves. These are murmurers, complainers, walking after their own lusts; and their mouth speaketh great swelling words, having men's persons in admiration because of advantage. How that they told you there should be mockers in the last time, who should walk after their own ungodly lusts. These be they who separate themselves, sensual, having not the Spirit. (Jude 4, 8, 10, 16, 18–19)

24 For they that are such serve not our Lord Jesus Christ, but their own belly; and by good words and fair speeches deceive the hearts of the simple. (Rom. 16:18)

Wherefore take unto you the whole armour of God, that ye may be able to withstand in the evil day, and having done all, to stand. Stand therefore, having your loins girt about with truth, and having on the breastplate of righteousness. (Eph. 6:13–14)

Therefore, brethren, stand fast, and hold the traditions which ye have been taught, whether by word, or our epistle. (2 Thess. 2:15)

Watch ye, stand fast in the faith, quit you like men, be strong. (1 Cor. 16:13)

25 Now the Spirit speaketh expressly, that in the latter times some shall depart from the faith, giving heed to seducing spirits, and doctrines of devils; Speaking lies in hypocrisy; having their conscience seared with a hot iron. (1 Tim. 4:1–2)

This know also, that in the last days perilous times shall come. For men shall be lovers of their own selves, covetous, boasters, proud, blasphemers, disobedient to parents, unthankful, unholy, Without natural affection, trucebreakers, false accusers, incontinent, fierce, despisers of those that are good, Traitors, heady, high minded, lovers of pleasures more than lovers of God; Having a form of godliness, but denying the power thereof: from such turn away. (2 Tim. 3:1–5)

Knowing this first, that there shall come in the last days scoffers, walking after their own lusts, And saying, Where is the promise of his coming? for since the fathers fell asleep, all things continue as they were from the beginning of the creation. (2 Pet. 3:3–4)

And because iniquity shall abound, the love of many shall wax cold. (Matt. 24:12)

26 For the word of God is quick, and powerful, and sharper than any two edged sword, piercing even to the dividing asunder of soul and spirit, and of the joints and marrow, and is a discerner of the thoughts and intents of the heart. (Heb. 4:12)

How? Self-Control

Every four years, the Soccer World Cup is held to determine the best team among all the countries of the world. Brazil leads the world with five wins, though it should be six. One year they fielded an all-star team that was favored to win the coveted prize. Leading up to the final matches, the confident players set aside self-discipline and partied instead of practicing. The next day, they played the one team they should have beaten easily. They lost and went home in disgrace.

Self-Control: Self-Discipline and Assessing Instead of Condemning Others

Self-Control in Virtue and Knowledge

Self-control means self-discipline in *daily* applying God's Word to our own feet and path,[1] *daily* praying[2] and studying God's Word,[3] *daily* working on virtue in our life,[4] *daily* keeping our bodies in God's service.[5] With self-control, we turn away from doing wrong and, instead, train ourselves to do right.[6] Such self-discipline is acceptable in general society[7] and important for Christian leadership.[8] Like all our Christian walk, self-control is dependent on God's grace and help.[9]

As we grow in knowledge, we must watch that we do not use it in a fleshly or prideful way.[10] One of those wrong tendencies is to judge and condemn others, like a legalistic Pharisee.[11]

Assessing Instead of Condemning

Soon after we arrived in a town called Santo Antonia in Brazil, a man came knocking on our door saying his wife was *passando mal*, which literally means "passing badly." Struggling to understand his excited unschooled Portuguese, we simply followed him to his riverfront shack. His wife had just delivered a baby and was hemorrhaging. With the few medical supplies we had available at the time, we stopped the bleeding, and she survived.

A few nights later a young woman came to the house saying her mother was *passando mal* in the head. We rushed to the house, thinking stroke or seizure and wondering how we could help. The mother had a simple headache and asked if we had a pill for it, as the little pharmacy store was closed. We learned that *passando mal* means anything from a simple headache to a troubling illness to being at the point of death.

In the Bible, we are called to "judge" many different situations. However, the word *judge*, like *passando mal*, contains a whole range of meaning: from simple assessment or understanding[12] to making a decision,[13] all the way to condemnation.[14]

Three Institutions that God Ordained to Judge on the Earth

God has ordained three institutions to judge and punish people on the earth: the family, the church, and the government. In the family, parents are called upon to rule over their children.[15] While the goal of parents is to train their children,[16] they have the right before God to punish them.[17]

The church is commanded to judge or pass sentence among its members, sometimes even to the point of expelling them from fellowship as believers.[18] The goal of church discipline is twofold: to help members understand what is right[19] so they can repent and can be received back into fellowship[20] and also to purify the membership of those who will not repent.[21]

Civil government has the divine authority to judge, even to the death penalty.[22] So the three institutions have the right of passing judgment and rendering some form of punishment.

Individual Christians Assess and Do Not Condemn Others

Each believer can "judge" in the sense of understanding others and assessing their behavior, for by the fruit of people's lives, we will know them.[23] A person's mouth and actions will eventually reflect what is in his heart, which is the source of the issues of life.[24]

As *individual* believers, we are commanded not to pass sentence on others.[25] Such condemnation of others is often accomplished by gossip,[26] which is wrong.[27] Moreover, what we condemn in others, we may be doing ourselves.[28] Our personal walk should be showing mercy,[29] forgiveness,[30] love,[31] and overcoming evil with good.[32]

Our personal condemnation should be of sin in our own lives.[33]

We Can Be Fooled but God Knows

When we see the fruit, we can still be deceived,[34] as people try to fool us into thinking that they are looking to God.[35] Only the Lord knows with absolute certainty and judges the heart.[36] He has reserved all judgment to Himself and is the One Who will judge His people.[37] All vengeance, even upon believers, belongs to Him.[38] He will judge the world[39] and decree ultimate condemnation.[40]

With self-control, we daily train ourselves to turn from the wrong ways to the right. Also, we use the Word of God with self-control to assess and understand others. *Personal* condemnation should only be against the sin in our own lives.

However, people and situations can cause us problems. What is the proper attitude about those problems in our life path?

Notes

1   Concerning the works of men, by the word of thy lips I have kept me from the paths of the destroyer. Hold up my goings in thy paths, that my footsteps slip not. (Ps. 17:4–5)

Teach me thy way, O LORD, and lead me in a plain path, because of mine enemies. (Ps. 27:11)

I thought on my ways, and turned my feet unto thy testimonies... I have refrained my feet from every evil way, that I might keep thy word... Thy word is a lamp unto my feet, and a light unto my path... I have inclined mine heart to perform thy statutes alway, even unto the end. (Ps. 119:59, 101, 105, 112)

Enter not into the path of the wicked, and go not in the way of evil men... Ponder the path of thy feet, and let all thy ways be established. Turn not to the right hand nor to the left: remove thy foot from evil. (Prov. 4:14, 26–27)

He that is slow to anger is better than the mighty; and he that ruleth his spirit than he that taketh a city. (Prov. 16:32)

Know ye not that they which run in a race run all, but one receiveth the prize? So run, that ye may obtain. And every man that striveth for the mastery is temperate in all things. Now they do it to obtain a corruptible crown; but we an incorruptible. I therefore so run, not as uncertainly; so fight I, not as one that beateth the air: But I keep under my body, and bring it into subjection: lest that by any means, when I have preached to others, I myself should be a castaway. (1 Cor. 9:24–27)

See then that ye walk circumspectly, not as fools, but as wise. (Eph. 5:150)

Not as though I had already attained, either were already perfect: but I follow after, if that I may apprehend that for which also I am apprehended of Christ Jesus. Brethren, I count not myself to have apprehended: but this one thing I do, forgetting those things which are behind, and reaching forth unto those things which are before, I press toward the mark for the prize of the high calling of God in Christ Jesus. (Phil. 3:12–14)

And make straight paths for your feet, lest that which is lame be turned out of the way; but let it rather be healed. (Heb. 12:13)

2   Give us this day our daily bread. (Matt. 6:11)

My voice shalt thou hear in the morning, O LORD; in the morning will I direct my prayer unto thee, and will look up. (Ps. 5:3)

Evening, and morning, and at noon, will I pray, and cry aloud: and he shall hear my voice. (Ps. 55:17)

For my soul is full of troubles: and my life draweth nigh unto the grave. (Ps. 88:3)

Cause me to hear thy lovingkindness in the morning; for in thee do I trust: cause me to know the way wherein I should walk; for I lift up my soul unto thee. (Ps. 143:8)

3 My hands also will I lift up unto thy commandments, which I have loved; and I will meditate in thy statutes. (Ps. 119:48)

Blessed is the man that heareth me, watching daily at my gates, waiting at the posts of my doors. (Prov. 8:34)

These were more noble than those in Thessalonica, in that they received the word with all readiness of mind, and searched the scriptures daily, whether those things were so. (Acts 17:11)

4 Therefore we are buried with him by baptism into death: that like as Christ was raised up from the dead by the glory of the Father, even so we also should walk in newness of life. (Rom. 6:4)

Let us walk honestly, as in the day; not in rioting and drunkenness, not in chambering and wantonness, not in strife and envying. (Rom. 13:13)

But have renounced the hidden things of dishonesty, not walking in craftiness, nor handling the word of God deceitfully; but by manifestation of the truth commending ourselves to every man's conscience in the sight of God. (2 Cor. 4:2)

For ye were sometimes darkness, but now are ye light in the Lord: walk as children of light. (Eph. 5:8)

That ye might walk worthy of the Lord unto all pleasing, being fruitful in every good work, and increasing in the knowledge of God. (Col. 1:10)

Furthermore then we beseech you, brethren, and exhort you by the Lord Jesus, that as ye have received of us how ye ought to walk and to please God, so ye would abound more and more. (1 Thess. 4:1)

Wherefore seeing we also are compassed about with so great a cloud of witnesses, let us lay aside every weight, and the sin which doth so easily beset us, and let us run with patience the race that is set before us, Looking unto Jesus the author and finisher of our faith; who for the joy that was set before him endured the cross, despising the shame, and is set down at the right hand of the throne of God. (Heb. 12:1–2)

5 And he said to them all, If any man will come after me, let him deny himself, and take up his cross daily, and follow me. (Luke 9:23)

Let not sin therefore reign in your mortal body, that ye should obey it in the lusts thereof. Neither yield ye your members as instruments of unrighteousness unto sin: but yield yourselves unto God, as those that are alive from the dead, and your members as instruments of righteousness unto God… Know ye not, that to whom ye yield yourselves servants to obey, his servants ye are to whom ye obey; whether of sin unto death, or of obedience unto righteousness? But God be thanked, that ye were the servants of sin, but ye have obeyed from the heart that form of doctrine which was delivered you. (Rom. 6:12–13, 16–17)

⁶ And herein do I exercise myself, to have always a conscience void to offence toward God, and toward men. (Acts 24:16)

But I keep under my body, and bring it into subjection: lest that by any means, when I have preached to others, I myself should be a castaway. (1 Cor. 9:27)

But strong meat belongeth to them that are of full age, even those who by reason of use have their senses exercised to discern both good and evil. (Heb. 5:14)

⁷ Meekness, temperance [self-control]: against such there is no law. (Gal. 5:23)

⁸ This is a true saying, if a man desire the office of a bishop, he desireth a good work. A bishop then must be blameless, the husband of one wife, vigilant, sober, of good behaviour, given to hospitality, apt to teach; Not given to wine, no striker, not greedy of filthy lucre; but patient, not a brawler, not covetous; One that ruleth well his own house, having his children in subjection with all gravity; (For if a man know not how to rule his own house, how shall he take care of the church of God?) Not a novice, lest being lifted up with pride he fall into the condemnation of the devil. Moreover he must have a good report of them which are without; lest he fall into reproach and the snare of the devil Likewise must the deacons be grave, not double tongued, not given to much wine, not greedy of filthy lucre; Holding the mystery of the faith in a pure conscience. And let these also first be proved; then let them use the office of a deacon, being found blameless. Even so must their wives be grave, not slanderers, sober, faithful in all things. Let the deacons be the husbands of one wife, ruling their children and their own houses well. (1 Tim. 3:1–12)

For this cause left I thee in Crete, that thou shouldest set in order the things that are wanting, and ordain elders in every city, as I had appointed thee: If any be blameless, the husband of one wife, having faithful children not accused of riot or unruly. For a bishop must be blameless, as the steward of God; not self willed, not soon angry, not given to wine, no striker, not given to filthy lucre; But a lover of hospitality, a lover of good men, sober, just, holy, temperate; Holding fast the faithful word as he hath been taught, that he may be able by sound doctrine both to exhort and to convince the gainsayers. (Titus 1:5–9)

That the aged men be sober, grave, temperate, sound in faith, in charity, in patience... Young men likewise exhort to be sober minded... Teaching us that, denying ungodliness and worldly lusts, we should live soberly, righteously, and godly, in this present world. (Titus 2:2, 6, 12)

⁹ Set a watch, O LORD, before my mouth; keep the door of my lips. Incline not my heart to any evil thing, to practise wicked works with men that work iniquity: and let me not eat of their dainties. (Ps. 141:3–4)

¹⁰ Now as touching things offered unto idols, we know that we all have knowledge. Knowledge puffeth up, but charity edifieth... For if any man see thee which hast knowledge sit at meat in the idol's temple, shall not the conscience of him which is weak be emboldened to eat those things which are offered to idols; And

through thy knowledge shall the weak brother perish, for whom Christ died? (1 Cor. 8:1, 10–11)

And though I have the gift of prophecy, and understand all mysteries, and all knowledge; and though I have all faith, so that I could remove mountains, and have not charity [love], I am nothing. (1 Cor. 13:2)

11 Judge not, that ye be not judged. For with what judgment ye judge, ye shall be judged: and with what measure ye mete, it shall be measured to you again. (Matt. 7:1–2)

Judge not, and ye shall not be judged: condemn not, and ye shall not be condemned: forgive, and ye shall be forgiven. (Luke 6:37)

Therefore thou art inexcusable, O man, whosoever thou art that judgest: for wherein thou judgest another, thou condemnest thyself; for thou that judgest doest the same things. But we are sure that the judgment of God is according to truth against them which commit such things. And thinkest thou this, O man, that judgest them which do such things, and doest the same, that thou shalt escape the judgment of God? (Rom. 2:1–3)

12 And shall not uncircumcision which is by nature, if it fulfil the law, judge thee, who by the letter and circumcision dost transgress the law? (Rom. 2:27)

I speak as to wise men; judge ye what I say. (1 Cor. 10:15)

For the love of Christ constraineth us; because we thus judge, that if one died for all, then were all dead. (2 Cor. 5:14)

13 Judge not according to the appearance, but judge righteous judgment. (John 7:24)

But Peter and John answered and said unto them, Whether it be right in the sight of God to hearken unto you more than unto God, judge ye. (Acts 4:19)

Through faith also Sara herself received strength to conceive seed, and was delivered of a child when she was past age, because she judged him faithful who had promised. (Heb. 11:11)

14 Now will I shortly pour out my fury upon thee, and accomplish mine anger upon thee: and I will judge thee according to thy ways, and will recompense thee for all thine abominations. (Ezek. 7:8)

And they cried with a loud voice, saying, How long, O Lord, holy and true, dost thou not judge and avenge our blood on them that dwell on the earth? (Rev. 6:10)

And I saw heaven opened, and behold a white horse; and he that sat upon him was called Faithful and True, and in righteousness he doth judge and make war. (Rev. 19:11)

15 Children, obey your parents in the Lord: for this is right. Honour thy father and mother; (which is the first commandment with promise. (Eph. 6:1–2)

Children, obey your parents in all things: for this is well pleasing unto the Lord. (Col. 3:20)

A bishop then must be... One that ruleth well his own house, having his children in subjection with all gravity; 5 (For if a man know not how to rule his own house, how shall he take care of the church of God?)… Let the deacons be the husbands of one wife, ruling their children and their own houses well. (1 Tim. 3:2a, 4–5, 12)

16 And ye shall teach them your children, speaking of them when thou sittest in thine house, and when thou walkest by the way, when thou liest down, and when thou risest up. (Deut. 11:19)

And he said unto them, Set your hearts unto all the words which I testify among you this day, which ye shall command your children to observe to do, all the words of this law. (Deut. 32:46)

Train up a child in the way he should go: and when he is old, he will not depart from it. (Prov. 22:6)

17 Withhold not correction from the child: for if thou beatest him with the rod, he shall not die. (Prov. 23:13)

Foolishness is bound in the heart of a child; but the rod of correction shall drive it far from him. (Prov. 22:15)

The rod and reproof give wisdom: but a child left to himself bringeth his mother to shame. (Prov. 29:15)

But if ye be without chastisement, whereof all are partakers, then are ye bastards, and not sons. (Heb. 12:8)

18 Moreover if thy brother shall trespass against thee, go and tell him his fault between thee and him alone: if he shall hear thee, thou hast gained thy brother. But if he will not hear thee, then take with thee one or two more, that in the mouth of two or three witnesses every word may be established. And if he shall neglect to hear them, tell it unto the church: but if he neglect to hear the church, let him be unto thee as an heathen man and a publican. (Matt. 18:15–17)

A man that is an heretick after the first and second admonition reject. (Titus 3:10)

19 It is reported commonly that there is fornication among you, and such fornication as is not so much as named among the Gentiles, that one should have his father's wife. And ye are puffed up, and have not rather mourned, that he that hath done this deed might be taken away from among you. For I verily, as absent in body, but present in spirit, have judged already, as though I were present, concerning him that hath so done this deed, In the name of our Lord Jesus Christ, when ye are gathered together, and my spirit, with the power of our Lord Jesus Christ, To deliver such an one unto Satan for the destruction of the flesh, that the spirit may be saved in the day of the Lord Jesus. Your glorying is not good. Know ye not that a little leaven leaveneth the whole lump? Purge out therefore the old leaven, that ye may be a new lump, as ye are unleavened. For even Christ our passover is sacrificed for us:… I wrote unto you in an epistle not to company with fornicators:… But now I have written unto you not to keep company, if any man that is called a brother be a fornicator, or covetous, or an idolater, or a railer, or a drunkard, or an extortioner; with such an one no

not to eat... Therefore put away from among yourselves that wicked person. (1 Cor. 5:1–7, 9, 11, 13b)

20 Sufficient to such a man is this punishment, which was inflicted of many. So that contrariwise ye ought rather to forgive him, and comfort him, lest perhaps such a one should be swallowed up with overmuch sorrow. Wherefore I beseech you that ye would confirm your love toward him... To whom ye forgive any thing, I forgive also: for if I forgave any thing, to whom I forgave it, for your sakes forgave I it in the person of Christ. (2 Cor. 2:6–8, 10)

21 It is reported commonly that there is fornication among you, and such fornication as is not so much as named among the Gentiles, that one should have his father's wife. And ye are puffed up, and have not rather mourned, that he that hath done this deed might be taken away from among you... Your glorying is not good. Know ye not that a little leaven leaveneth the whole lump? Purge out therefore the old leaven, that ye may be a new lump, as ye are unleavened. For even Christ our passover is sacrificed for us: Therefore let us keep the feast, not with old leaven, neither with the leaven of malice and wickedness; but with the unleavened bread of sincerity and truth. I wrote unto you in an epistle not to company with fornicators: Yet not altogether with the fornicators of this world, or with the covetous, or extortioners, or with idolaters; for then must ye needs go out of the world. But now I have written unto you not to keep company, if any man that is called a brother be a fornicator, or covetous, or an idolater, or a railer, or a drunkard, or an extortioner; with such an one no not to eat. For what have I to do to judge them also that are without? do not ye judge them that are within? But them that are without God judgeth. Therefore put away from among yourselves that wicked person. (1 Cor. 5:1–2, 6–13)

Unto the angel of the church of Ephesus write; These things saith he that holdeth the seven stars in his right hand, who walketh in the midst of the seven golden candlesticks; I know thy works, and thy labour, and thy patience, and how thou canst not bear them which are evil: and thou hast tried them which say they are apostles, and are not, and hast found them liars. (Rev. 2:1–2)

22 Whoso sheddeth man's blood, by man shall his blood be shed: for in the image of God made he man. (Gen. 9:6)

Let every soul be subject unto the higher powers. For there is no power but of God: the powers that be are ordained of God. Whosoever therefore resisteth the power, resisteth the ordinance of God: and they that resist shall receive to themselves damnation. For rulers are not a terror to good works, but to the evil. Wilt thou then not be afraid of the power? do that which is good, and thou shalt have praise of the same: For he is the minister of God to thee for good. But if thou do that which is evil, be afraid; for hebeareth not the sword in vain: for he is the minister of God, a revenger to execute wrath upon him that doeth evil. (Rom. 13:1–4)

Or unto governors, as unto them that are sent by him for the punishment of evildoers, and for the praise of them that do well. (1 Pet. 2:14)

23 Even so every good tree bringeth forth good fruit; but a corrupt tree bringeth forth evil fruit. A good tree cannot bring forth evil fruit, neither can a corrupt tree bring forth good fruit... Wherefore by their fruits ye shall know them. (Matt. 7:17–18, 20)

Either make the tree good, and his fruit good; or else make the tree corrupt, and his fruit corrupt: for the tree is known by his fruit. (Matt. 12:33)

24 Keep thy heart with all diligence; for out of it are the issues of life. (Prov. 4:23)

The heart of the wise teacheth his mouth, and addeth learning to his lips. (Prov. 16:23)

He that is of a proud heart stirreth up strife. (Prov. 28:25a)

O generation of vipers, how can ye, being evil, speak good things? for out of the abundance of the heart the mouth speaketh. A good man out of the good treasure of the heart bringeth forth good things: and an evil man out of the evil treasure bringeth forth evil things. (Matt. 12:34–35)

This people draweth nigh unto me with their mouth, and honoureth me with their lips; but their heart is far from me... But those things which proceed out of the mouth come forth from the heart; and they defile the man. For out of the heart proceed evil thoughts, murders, adulteries, fornications, thefts, false witness, blasphemies. (Matt. 15:8, 18–19)

For a good tree bringeth not forth corrupt fruit; neither doth a corrupt tree bring forth good fruit. For every tree is known by his own fruit. For of thorns men do not gather figs, nor of a bramble bush gather they grapes. A good man out of the good treasure of his heart bringeth forth that which is good; and an evil man out of the evil treasure of his heart bringeth forth that which is evil: for of the abundance of the heart his mouth speaketh. (Luke 6:43–45)

25 Judge not, that ye be not judged. For with what judgment ye judge, ye shall be judged: and with what measure ye mete, it shall be measured to you again. And why beholdest thou the mote that is in thy brother's eye, but considerest not the beam that is in thine own eye? Or how wilt thou say to thy brother, Let me pull out the mote out of thine eye; and, behold, a beam is in thine own eye? Thou hypocrite, first cast out the beam out of thine own eye; and then shalt thou see clearly to cast out the mote out of thy brother's eye. (Matt. 7:1–5)

Be ye therefore merciful, as your Father also is merciful. Judge not, and ye shall not be judged: condemn not, and ye shall not be condemned: forgive, and ye shall be forgiven: Give, and it shall be given unto you; good measure, pressed down, and shaken together, and running over, shall men give into your bosom. For with the same measure that ye mete withal it shall be measured to you again. (Luke 6:36–38)

But why dost thou judge thy brother? or why dost thou set at nought thy brother? for we shall all stand before the judgment seat of Christ... Let us not therefore judge one another any more: but judge this rather, that no man put a stumbling block or an occasion to fall in his brother's way. (Rom. 14:10, 13)

26 He that covereth a transgression seeketh love; but he that repeateth a matter separateth very friends. (Prov. 17:9)

Let all bitterness, and wrath, and anger, and clamour, and evil speaking, be put away from you, with all malice. (Eph. 4:31)

But now ye also put off all these; anger, wrath, malice, blasphemy, filthy communication out of your mouth. (Col. 3:8)

To speak evil of no man, to be no brawlers, but gentle, shewing all meekness unto all men. (Titus 3:2)

Speak not evil one of another, brethren. He that speaketh evil of his brother, and judgeth his brother, speaketh evil of the law, and judgeth the law: but if thou judge the law, thou art not a doer of the law, but a judge. There is one lawgiver, who is able to save and to destroy: who art thou that judgest another? (James 4:11–12)

27 To speak evil of no man, to be no brawlers, but gentle, shewing all meekness unto all men. (Titus 3:2)

28 Therefore thou art inexcusable, O man, whosoever thou art that judgest: for wherein thou judgest another, thou condemnest thyself; for thou that judgest doest the same things. (Rom. 2:1)

29 Let not mercy and truth forsake thee: bind them about thy neck; write them upon the table of thine heart (Prov. 3:3)

He hath shewed thee, O man, what is good; and what doth the Lord require of thee, but to do justly, and to love mercy, and to walk humbly with thy God? (Micah 6:8)

Blessed are the merciful: for they shall obtain mercy. (Matt. 5:7)

But the wisdom that is from above is first pure, then peaceable, gentle, and easy to be intreated, full of mercy and good fruits, without partiality, and without hypocrisy. (James 3:17)

30 And forgive us our debts, as we forgive our debtors... For if ye forgive men their trespasses, your heavenly Father will also forgive you: But if ye forgive not men their trespasses, neither will your Father forgive your trespasses. (Matt. 6:12, 14–15)

31 Thou shalt not avenge, nor bear any grudge against the children of thy people, but thou shalt love thy neighbour as thyself: I am the Lord. (Lev. 19:18)

Hatred stirreth up strifes: but love covereth all sins. (Prov. 10:12)

A new commandment I give unto you, That ye love one another; as I have loved you, that ye also love one another. By this shall all men know that ye are my disciples, if ye have love one to another. (John 13:34–35)

This is my commandment, That ye love one another, as I have loved you. Greater love hath no man than this, that a man lay down his life for his friends... These things I command you, that ye love one another. (John 15:12–13, 17)

Owe no man any thing, but to love one another: for he that loveth another hath fulfilled the law. For this, Thou shalt not commit adultery, Thou shalt not kill, Thou shalt not steal, Thou shalt not bear false witness, Thou shalt not covet; and if there be any other commandment, it is briefly comprehended in this saying, namely, Thou shalt love thy neighbour as thyself. Love worketh no ill to his neighbour: therefore love is the fulfilling of the law. (Rom. 13:8–10)

And walk in love, as Christ also hath loved us, and hath given himself for us an offering and a sacrifice to God for a sweet smelling savour. (Eph. 5:2)

We know that we have passed from death unto life, because we love the brethren. He that loveth not his brother abideth in death. (1 John 3:14)

32 Bless them which persecute you: bless, and curse not. Rejoice with them that do rejoice, and weep with them that weep. Be of the same mind one toward another. Mind not high things, but condescend to men of low estate. Be not wise in your own conceits. Recompense to no man evil for evil. Provide things honest in the sight of all men. If it be possible, as much as lieth in you, live peaceably with all men. Dearly beloved, avenge not yourselves, but rather give place unto wrath: for it is written, Vengeance is mine; I will repay, saith the Lord. Therefore if thine enemy hunger, feed him; if he thirst, give him drink: for in so doing thou shalt heap coals of fire on his head. Be not overcome of evil, but overcome evil with good. (Rom. 12:14–21)

33 Wherefore doth a living man complain, a man for the punishment of his sins? Let us search and try our ways, and turn again to the Lord. Let us lift up our heart with our hands unto God in the heavens. (Lam. 3:39–41)

And why beholdest thou the mote that is in thy brother's eye, but perceivest not the beam that is in thine own eye? Either how canst thou say to thy brother, Brother, let me pull out the mote that is in thine eye, when thou thyself beholdest not the beam that is in thine own eye? Thou hypocrite, cast out first the beam out of thine own eye, and then shalt thou see clearly to pull out the mote that is in thy brother's eye. (Luke 6:41–42)

But let a man examine himself, and so let him eat of that bread, and drink of that cup. (1 Cor. 11:28)

Examine yourselves, whether ye be in the faith; prove your own selves. (2 Cor. 13:5a)

34 They speak vanity every one with his neighbour: with flattering lips and with a double heart do they speak. (Ps. 12:2)

For as he thinketh in his heart, so is he: Eat and drink, saith he to thee; but his heart is not with thee. (Prov. 23:7)

35 Wherefore the Lord said, Forasmuch as this people draw near me with their mouth, and with their lips do honour me, but have removed their heart far from me, and their fear toward me is taught by the precept of men. (Isa. 29:13)

36 And thou, Solomon my son, know thou the God of thy father, and serve him with a perfect heart and with a willing mind: for the Lord searcheth all hearts, and understandeth all the imaginations of the thoughts: if thou seek him, he

will be found of thee; but if thou forsake him, he will cast thee off for ever. (1 Chron. 28:9)

I know also, my God, that thou triest the heart, and hast pleasure in uprightness. (1 Chron. 29:17a)

Therefore judge nothing before the time, until the Lord come, who both will bring to light the hidden things of darkness, and will make manifest the counsels of the hearts: and then shall every man have praise of God. (1 Cor. 4:5)

[37] And ye have forgotten the exhortation which speaketh unto you as unto children, My son, despise not thou the chastening of the Lord, nor faint when thou art rebuked of him: For whom the Lord loveth he chasteneth, and scourgeth every son whom he receiveth. (Heb. 12:5–6)

[38] For we know him that hath said, Vengeance belongeth unto me, I will recompense, saith the Lord. And again, The Lord shall judge his people. It is a fearful thing to fall into the hands of the living God. (Heb. 10:30–31)

[39] But the Lord shall endure for ever: he hath prepared his throne for judgment. And he shall judge the world in righteousness, he shall minister judgment to the people in uprightness. (Ps. 9:7–8)

Before the Lord: for he cometh, for he cometh to judge the earth: he shall judge the world with righteousness, and the people with his truth. (Ps. 96:13)

Before the Lord; for he cometh to judge the earth: with righteousness shall he judge the world, and the people with equity. (Ps. 98:90)

For God shall bring every work into judgment, with every secret thing, whether it be good, or whether it be evil. (Eccles. 12:14)

[40] And I saw a great white throne, and him that sat on it, from whose face the earth and the heaven fled away; and there was found no place for them. And I saw the dead, small and great, stand before God; and the books were opened: and another book was opened, which is the book of life: and the dead were judged out of those things which were written in the books, according to their works. And the sea gave up the dead which were in it; and death and hell delivered up the dead which were in them: and they were judged every man according to their works. And death and hell were cast into the lake of fire. This is the second death. And whosoever was not found written in the book of life was cast into the lake of fire. (Rev. 20:11–15)

How? Patient Endurance

Due to bad weather, my plane was late taking off. As the storm blew through Atlanta, I wondered if I could make my Miami connection to Brazil. In those days, I had to physically transfer my bags myself from the carousel of the first airline to the ticket counter of the connecting airline.

In Miami, I hired a skycap to help me. We threw my baggage on his cart and ran to the ticket counter. The counter agent was literally putting out the "closed" sign when I arrived. I explained my need to get on the flight while she was shaking her head no. My original seat had already been given away. Her boss was passing by, heard the conversation, and authorized me to receive the last seat available on my flight, which was leaving in just fifteen minutes.

With ticket in hand, I rushed through the security check, ran to the airplane, and stepped on board as they closed the door behind me. I fought to jam my carry-on into the small space left in the overhead compartment; squeezed into my seat; and pressed between two sprawled-out strangers, one drunk and the other sleeping. I prayed for grace to tolerate my cramped situation for this long flight.

After takeoff, the sleeping man awoke and pulled himself together, asking my forgiveness for his inconsideration. He was a representative to the Brazil National Congress from the area of our hospital ministry. For a long time I had wanted to meet him and tell him about our hospital ministry. We talked. At the end of the flight, he offered his services for any documentation we needed at the national level. He kept his word and was a tremendous help. My baggage even arrived with me at the next airport.

Not all difficulties work to our good in such an obvious way, but God is always working in all things.[1]

Patient Endurance: Accepting Where God Puts Us and What He Allows in Our Lives

God has the authority[2] to put us in *any* situation, in *any* place, and among *any* people as He desires.[3] He may put us in a town, neighborhood, school, or workplace next to many who are far from God.[4] Moreover, difficult problems will come.[5] But in all circumstances He is able[6] to keep us,[7] make us stand,[8] deliver us,[9] and help us when we are tempted.[10] He is able to give us all grace to abound in every good work.[11]

Cisterns

Can we live in the midst of a polluted world and not be a part of it? Contamination can seep into a cistern of water. This pool of water must be physically separate from any filth, the further the better. Still, contamination is always a danger. Legalists are like cisterns, afraid to be near the pollution of the world, afraid of contamination.[12] In Jesus's day these Pharisees avoided worldly people and criticized Jesus for going to sinners.[13]

Living Water

Unlike the stillness of cistern waters, in us is a well of overflowing living water[14] that cleanses us and ministers to those around us. This continual flow washes away any pollution.[15] Jesus is the very source of living water,[16] which water is the Word and ministry of the Spirit.[17]

Jesus's physical ministry often reflected His spiritual ministry, full of grace and blessing to those around Him. The legalists of Jesus's day would not touch an unclean leper because that person would make them ceremonially unclean.[18] By contrast, Jesus touched the lepers, healing and making them clean.[19] He went to sinners to minister grace and to be a testimony to them and called us to do the same.[20]

Circumstances of Life

We may be in a circumstance that we chose before God for the sake of testimony. For example, a man of God went to the evil king of Israel to testify before him while the king was worshipping at an idolatrous altar.[21] Or God may drop us in a new situation. Philip had a fruitful ministry in Samaria when God called him to go into a wilderness to witness to one man.[22]

God can put us next to the unsaved or those believers not walking right with Him, but we must not seek it so that we can enjoy the worldly influence.[23] We must be careful that our participation is for testimony and not a secret desire to fulfill the flesh.[24] We *are in* the world and a witness to it[25] but *are not* to be *of* the world.[26]

Question Our Choices in Our Circumstances and Friendships

A godly person should ask himself, "Am I here in this circumstance because God led me here, and I can be a witness, or am I here because I want to satisfy my fleshly lusts and enjoy the worldliness?" If we are there because God called us, then we should be a faithful witness.[27] If we are there because of our own desire, then we should flee.[28]

Persecution Response

As mentioned before, while witnessing to others, we may be persecuted.[29] Persecution is to be endured patiently,[30] returning good for evil when possible.[31] God will never abandon His children,[32] but instead will reward our faithfulness.[33] God knows, gives grace to His own,[34] and will judge our persecutors appropriately.[35]

We must be patient. We must be careful never to condemn God or become bitter with Him for what He has allowed.[36] Our response to Him must always be *trust* and *obedience*.[37]

With an attitude of patient endurance, we accept the circumstances God puts in our path, even when those circumstances bring us alongside those who do not follow the Word of God or bring us persecution. He intends us to be wells of His living water and to be ministering to those around us.

When I am in a circumstance with others who are not following God's Word, what do I focus on in their lives?

Notes

1   And we know that all things work together for good to them that love God, to them who are the called according to his purpose. (Rom. 8:28)

2   Thou art worthy, O Lord, to receive glory and honour and power: for thou hast created all things, and for thy pleasure they are and were created. (Rev. 4:11)

3   And God sent me [Joseph] before you [into Egypt] to preserve you a posterity in the earth, and to save your lives by a great deliverance. So now it was not you that sent me hither, but God: and he hath made me a father to Pharaoh, and lord of all his house, and a ruler throughout all the land of Egypt. (Gen. 45:7–8)

Come now therefore, and I will send thee [Moses] unto Pharaoh, that thou mayest bring forth my people the children of Israel out of Egypt. (Exod. 3:10)

Now the word of the Lord came unto Jonah the son of Amittai, saying, Arise, go to Nineveh, that great city, and cry against it; for their wickedness is come up before me. (Jonah 1:1–2)

But the Lord said unto him, Go thy way: for he [Paul] is a chosen vessel unto me, to bear my name before the Gentiles, and kings, and the children of Israel: For I will shew him how great things he must suffer for my name's sake. (Acts 9:15–16)

4   Behold, I send you forth as sheep in the midst of wolves: be ye therefore wise as serpents, and harmless as doves. (Matt. 10:16)

Therefore said he unto them, The harvest truly is great, but the labourers are few: pray ye therefore the Lord of the harvest, that he would send forth labourers into his harvest. Go your ways: behold, I send you forth as lambs among wolves. (Luke 10:2–3)

I wrote unto you in an epistle not to company with fornicators: Yet not altogether with the fornicators of this world, or with the covetous, or extortioners, or with idolaters; for then must ye needs go out of the world. (1 Cor. 5:9–10)

5   But in all things approving ourselves as the ministers of God, in much patience, in afflictions, in necessities, in distresses. (2 Cor. 6:4)

Knowing this, that the trying of your faith worketh patience. But let patience have her perfect work, that ye may be perfect and entire, wanting nothing. (James 1:3–4)

Take, my brethren, the prophets, who have spoken in the name of the Lord, for an example of suffering affliction, and of patience. Behold, we count them happy which endure. Ye have heard of the patience of Job, and have seen the end of the Lord; that the Lord is very pitiful, and of tender mercy. (James 5:10–11)

Wherein ye greatly rejoice, though now for a season, if need be, ye are in heaviness through manifold temptations: That the trial of your faith, being much more precious than of gold that perisheth, though it be tried with fire, might be found unto praise and honour and glory at the appearing of Jesus Christ. (1 Pet. 1:6–7)

Beloved, think it not strange concerning the fiery trial which is to try you, as though some strange thing happened unto you: But rejoice, inasmuch as ye are partakers of Christ's sufferings; that, when his glory shall be revealed, ye may be glad also with exceeding joy... Wherefore let them that suffer according to the will of God commit the keeping of their souls to him in well doing, as unto a faithful Creator. (1 Pet. 4:12–13, 19)

6 Now unto him that is able to do exceeding abundantly above all that we ask or think, according to the power that worketh in us. (Eph. 3:20)

7 [You] Who are kept by the power of God through faith unto salvation ready to be revealed in the last time. (1 Pet. 1:5)

8 Who art thou that judgest another man's servant? to his own master he standeth or falleth. Yea, he shall be holden up: for God is able to make him stand. (Rom. 14:4)

9 And lead us not into temptation, but deliver us from evil. (Matt. 6:13a)

Who delivered us from so great a death, and doth deliver: in whom we trust that he will yet deliver us. (2 Cor. 1:10)

Who gave himself for our sins, that he might deliver us from this present evil world, according to the will of God and our Father. (Gal. 1:4)

Persecutions, afflictions, which came unto me at Antioch, at Iconium, at Lystra; what persecutions I endured: but out of them all the Lord delivered me. (2 Tim. 3:11)

And the Lord shall deliver me from every evil work, and will preserve me unto his heavenly kingdom: to whom be glory for ever and ever. Amen. (2 Tim. 4:18)

The Lord knoweth how to deliver the godly out of temptations, and to reserve the unjust unto the Day of Judgment to be punished. (1 Pet. 2:9)

10 There hath no temptation taken you but such as is common to man: but God is faithful, who will not suffer you to be tempted above that ye are able; but will with the temptation also make a way to escape, that ye may be able to bear it. (1 Cor. 10:13)

For in that he himself hath suffered being tempted, he is able to succour them that are tempted. (Heb. 2:18)

11 And God is able to make all grace abound toward you; that ye, always having all sufficiency in all things, may abound to every good work. (2 Cor. 9:8)

12 Now when the Pharisee which had bidden him saw it, he spake within himself, saying, This man, if he were a prophet, would have known who and what manner of woman this is that toucheth him: for she is a sinner. (Luke 7:39)

Then led they Jesus from Caiaphas unto the hall of judgment: and it was early; and they themselves went not into the judgment hall, lest they should be defiled; but that they might eat the passover. (John 18:28)

¹³ And it came to pass, as Jesus sat at meat in the house, behold, many publicans and sinners came and sat down with him and his disciples. And when the Pharisees saw it, they said unto his disciples, Why eateth your Master with publicans and sinners? (Matt. 9:10–11)

And it came to pass, that, as Jesus sat at meat in his house, many publicans and sinners sat also together with Jesus and his disciples: for there were many, and they followed him. And when the scribes and Pharisees saw him eat with publicans and sinners, they said unto his disciples, How is it that he eateth and drinketh with publicans and sinners? (Mark 2:15–16)

And Levi made him a great feast in his own house: and there was a great company of publicans and of others that sat down with them. But their scribes and Pharisees murmured against his disciples, saying, Why do ye eat and drink with publicans and sinners? (Luke 5:29–30)

Then drew near unto him all the publicans and sinners for to hear him. And the Pharisees and scribes murmured, saying, This man receiveth sinners, and eateth with them. (Luke 15:1–2)

¹⁴ And the Lord shall guide thee continually, and satisfy thy soul in drough, and make fat thy bones: and thou shalt be like a watered garden, and like a spring of water, whose waters fail not. (Isa. 58:11)

Jesus answered and said unto her, Whosoever drinketh of this water shall thirst again: But whosoever drinketh of the water that I shall give him shall never thirst; but the water that I shall give him shall be in him a well of water springing up into everlasting life. (John 4:13–14)

He that believeth on me, as the scripture hath said, out of his belly shall flow rivers of living water. (John 7:38)

That he might sanctify and clease it with the wahing of water by the word. (Eph. 5:26)

Contrast: For my people have committed two evils; they have forsaken me the fountain of living waters, and hewed them out cisterns, broken cisterns, that can hold no water. (Jer. 2:13)

¹⁵ Let us draw near with a true heart in full assurance of faith, having our hearts sprinkled from an evil conscience, and our bodies washed with pure water. (Heb. 10:22)

¹⁶ Jesus answered and said unto her, Whosoever drinketh of this water shall thirst again: But whosoever drinketh of the water that I shall give him shall never thirst; but the water that I shall give him shall be in him a well of water springing up into everlasting life. (John 4:13–14)

He that believeth on me, as the scripture hath said, out of his belly shall flow rivers of living water. (John 7:38)

¹⁷ Jesus answered and said unto her, If thou knewest the gift of God, and who it is that saith to thee, Give me to drink; thou wouldest have asked of him, and he would have given thee living water... But whosoever drinketh of the water that

I shall give him shall never thirst; but the water that I shall give him shall be in him a well of water springing up into everlasting life. (John 4:10, 14)

In the last day, that great day of the feast, Jesus stood and cried, saying, If any man thirst, let him come unto me, and drink. He that believeth on me, as the scripture hath said, out of his belly shall flow rivers of living water. (But this spake he of the Spirit, which they that believe on him should receive: for the Holy Ghost was not yet given; because that Jesus was not yet glorified.) (John 7:37–39)

Husbands love your wives, even as Christ also loved the church, and gave himself for it; That he might sanctify and cleanse it with the washing of water by the word, That he might present it to himself a glorious church, not having spot, or wrinkle, or any such thing; but that it should be holy and without blemish. (Eph. 5:25–27)

[18] And whatsoever the unclean person toucheth shall be unclean; and the soul that toucheth it shall be unclean until even. (Num. 19:22)

And the leper in whom the plague is, his clothes shall be rent, and his head bare, and he shall put a covering upon his upper lip, and shall cry, Unclean, unclean. (Lev. 13:45)

[19] And, behold, there came a leper and worshipped him, saying, Lord, if thou wilt, thou canst make me clean. And Jesus put forth his hand, and touched him, saying, I will; be thou clean. And immediately his leprosy was cleansed. (Matt. 8:2–3)

The blind receive their sight, and the lame walk, the lepers are cleansed, and the deaf hear, the dead are raised up, and the poor have the gospel preached to them. (Matt. 11:5)

[20] These twelve Jesus sent forth, and commanded them... And as ye go, preach, saying, The kingdom of heaven is at hand. Heal the sick, cleanse the lepers, raise the dead, cast out devils: freely ye have received, freely give. (Matt. 10:5a, 7–8)

When Jesus heard it, he saith unto them, They that are whole have no need of the physician, but they that are sick: I came not to call the righteous, but sinners to repentance. (Mark 2:17)

And he said unto them, Go ye into all the world, and preach the gospel to every creature. (Mark 16:15)

Then he called his twelve disciples together... And he sent them to preach the kingdom of God, and to heal the sick. (Luke 9:1a, 2)

After these things the Lord appointed other seventy also, and sent them two and two before his face into every city and place, whither he himself would come. Therefore said he unto them, The harvest truly is great, but the labourers are few: pray ye therefore the Lord of the harvest, that he would send forth labourers into his harvest... And heal the sick that are therein, and say unto them, The kingdom of God is come nigh unto you. (Luke 10:1–2, 9)

Then said Jesus to them again, Peace be unto you: as my Father hath sent me, even so send I you. (John 20:21)

21 And, behold, there came a man of God out of Judah by the word of the Lord unto Bethel: and Jeroboam stood by the altar to burn incense. And he cried against the altar in the word of the Lord, and said, O altar, altar, thus saith the Lord; Behold, a child shall be born unto the house of David, Josiah by name; and upon thee shall he offer the priests of the high places that burn incense upon thee, and men's bones shall be burnt upon thee. (1 Kings 13:1–2)

22 Then Philip went down to the city of Samaria, and preached Christ unto them. And the people with one accord gave heed unto those things which Philip spake, hearing and seeing the miracles which he did… And the angel of the Lord spake unto Philip, saying, Arise, and go toward the south unto the way that goeth down from Jerusalem unto Gaza, which is desert. And he arose and went: and, behold, a man of Ethiopia, an eunuch of great authority under Candace queen of the Ethiopians, who had the charge of all her treasure, and had come to Jerusalem for to worship, Was returning, and sitting in his chariot read Esaias the prophet. Then the Spirit said unto Philip, Go near, and join thyself to this chariot. (Acts 8:5–6, 26–28)

23 Blessed is the man that walketh not in the counsel of the ungodly, nor standeth in the way of sinners, nor sitteth in the seat of the scornful. But his delight is in the law of the Lord; and in his law doth he meditate day and night. (Ps. 1:1–2)

Love not the world, neither the things that are in the world. If any man love the world, the love of the Father is not in him. (1 John 2:15)

24 Therefore, brethren, we are debtors, not to the flesh, to live after the flesh. For if ye live after the flesh, ye shall die: but if ye through the Spirit do mortify the deeds of the body, ye shall live. (Rom. 8:12–13)

But put ye on the Lord Jesus Christ, and make not provision for the flesh, to fulfill the lusts thereof. (Rom. 13:14)

Whether therefore ye eat, or drink, or whatsoever ye do, do all to the glory of God. (1 Cor. 10:31)

For, brethren, ye have been called unto liberty; only use not liberty for an occasion to the flesh, but by love serve one another… This I say then, Walk in the Spirit, and ye shall not fulfil the lust of the flesh. (Gal. 5:13, 16)

Dearly beloved, I beseech you as strangers and pilgrims, abstain from fleshly lusts, which war against the soul. (1 Pet. 2:11)

25 That ye may be blameless and harmless, the sons of God, without rebuke, in the midst of a crooked and perverse nation, among whom ye shine as lights in the world. (Phil. 2:15)

26 If ye were of the world, the world would love his own: but because ye are not of the world, but I have chosen you out of the world, therefore the world hateth you. (John 15:19)

I have given them thy word; and the world hath hated them, because they are not of the world, even as I am not of the world. I pray not that thou shouldest take them out of the world, but that thou shouldest keep them from the evil. They are not of the world, even as I am not of the world. (John 17:14–16)

[27] Moreover it is required in stewards, that a man be found faithful. (1 Cor. 4:2)

[28] Flee also youthful lusts: but follow righteousness, faith, charity, peace, with them that call on the Lord out of a pure heart. (2 Tim. 2:22)

But thou, O Man of God, flee these things; and follow after righteousness, godliness, faith, love, patience, meekness. (1 Tim. 6:11)

[29] Yea, and all that will live godly in Christ Jesus shall suffer persecution. (2 Tim. 3:12)

So that we ourselves glory in you in the churches of God for your patience and faith in all your persecutions and tribulations that ye endure. (2 Thess. 1:4)

[30] Rejoicing in hope; patient in tribulation; continuing instant in prayer. (Rom. 12:12)

My brethren, count it all joy when ye fall into divers temptations; Knowing this, that the trying of your faith worketh patience. But let patience have her perfect work, that ye may be perfect and entire, wanting nothing. (James 1:2–4)

[31] But I say unto you, Love your enemies, bless them that curse you, do good to them that hate you, and pray for them which despitefully use you, and persecute you. (Matt. 5:44)

Bless them which persecute you: bless and curse not... Recompense to no man evil for evil. Provide things honest in the sight of all men... Therefore if thine enemy hunger, feed him; if he thirst, give him drink: for in so doing thou shalt heap coals of fire on his head. Be not overcome of evil, but overcome evil with good. (Rom. 12:14, 17, 20–210)

See that none render evil for evil unto any man; but ever follow that which is good, both among yourselves, and to all men. (1 Thess. 5:15)

Having your conversation honest among the Gentiles: that, whereas they speak against you as evildoers, they may by your good works, which they shall behold, glorify God in the day of visitation. (1 Pet. 2:12)

Not rendering evil for evil, or railing for railing: but contrariwise blessing; knowing that ye are thereunto called, that ye should inherit a blessing... Having a good conscience; that, whereas they speak evil of you, as of evildoers, they may be ashamed that falsely accuse your good conversation in Christ. For it is better, if the will of God be so, that ye suffer for well doing, than for evil doing. (1 Pet. 3:9, 16–17)

[32] Let your conversation be without covetousness; and be content with such things as ye have: for he hath said, I will never leave thee, nor forsake thee. (Heb. 13:5)

[33] Blessed are ye, when men shall revile you, and persecute you, and shall say all manner of evil against you falsely, for my sake. Rejoice, and be exceeding glad: for great is your reward in heaven: for so persecuted they the prophets which were before you. (Matt. 5:11–12)

And Jesus answered and said, Verily I say unto you, There is no man that hath left house, or brethren, or sisters, or father, or mother, or wife, or children, or lands, for my sake, and the gospel's, But he shall receive an hundredfold now in this time, houses, and brethren, and sisters, and mothers, and children, and lands, with persecutions; and in the world to come eternal life. (Mark 10:29–30)

Blessed are ye, when men shall hate you, and when they shall separate you from their company, and shall reproach you, and cast out your name as evil, for the Son of man's sake. Rejoice ye in that day, and leap for joy: for, behold, your reward is great in heaven: for in the like manner did their fathers unto the prophets… But love ye your enemies, and do good, and lend, hoping for nothing again: and your reward shall be great, and ye shall be the children of the Highest: for he is kind unto the unthankful and to the evil. (Luke 6:22–23, 35)

For which cause we faint not; but though our outward man perish, yet the inward man is renewed day by day. For our light affliction, which is but for a moment, worketh for us a far more exceeding and eternal weight of glory. (2 Cor. 4:16–17)

Knowing that of the Lord ye shall receive the reward of the inheritance: for ye serve the Lord Christ. (Col. 3:24)

34 And he said unto me, My grace is sufficient for thee: for my strength is made perfect in weakness. Most gladly therefore will I rather glory in infirmities, that the power of Christ may rest upon me. Therefore I take pleasure in infirmities, in reproaches, in necessities, in persecutions, in distresses for Christ's sake: for when I am weak, then am I strong. (2 Cor. 12:9–10)

35 Dearly beloved, avenge not yourselves, but rather give place unto wrath: for it is written, Vengeance is mine; I will repay, saith the Lord. (Rom. 12:19)

He that leadeth into captivity shall go into captivity: he that killeth with the sword must be killed with the sword. Here is the patience and the faith of the saints. (Rev. 13:10)

36 Note Joseph's testimony: And Joseph said unto his brethren, Come near to me, I pray you. And they came near. And he said, I am Joseph your brother, whom ye sold into Egypt. Now therefore be not grieved, nor angry with yourselves, that ye sold me hither: for God did send me before you to preserve life… So now it was not you that sent me hither, but God. (Gen. 45:4–5, 8a)

He is the Rock, his work is perfect: for all his ways are judgment: a God of truth and without iniquity, just and right is he. (Deut. 32:4)

The Lord is righteous in all his ways, and holy in all his works. (Ps. 145:17)

Therefore hath the Lord watched upon the evil, and brought it upon us: for the Lord our God is righteous in all his works which he doeth. (Dan. 9:14a)

And they sing the song of Moses the servant of God, and the song of the Lamb, saying, Great and marvellous are thy works, Lord God Almighty; just and true are thy ways, thou King of saints. (Rev. 15:3)

And I heard another out of the altar say, Even so, Lord God Almighty, true and righteous are thy judgments. (Rev. 16:7)

37 Trust in the Lord with all thine heart; and lean not unto thine own understanding. In all thy ways acknowledge him, and he shall direct thy paths. (Prov. 3:5–6)

Knowing this, that the trying of your faith worketh patience. But let patience have her perfect work, that ye may be perfect and entire, wanting nothing… Blessed is the man that endureth temptation: for when he is tried, he shall receive the crown of life, which the Lord hath promised to them that love him. (James 1:3–4, 12)

How? Godliness

Seeking our help, a young mother brought her seizing infant to our simple jungle clinic in Brazil. Severe infection was driving a high fever that was causing the convulsions. We gave an injection and used a few grains from a crushed pill to stop the seizures.

By God's grace, the treatment worked. The infection started to respond, the fever diminished, and the seizures became mild and infrequent so the baby could nurse. Not having in-patient hospital care available at the time, we instructed the mother on a schedule of returning for treatment.

The mother never came back to me. She heard every word but decided not to follow our advice. Instead, she walked back to the witch doctor who had sent her to me in the first place. He had directed the baby to me, thinking it was about to die and knowing I would examine it. A common superstition in our town was that the last one to touch a dying person was responsible for the death. He wanted to make me responsible in everyone's eyes for the infant's demise.

With the baby improving under our care, he told the mother to bring the child back to him. She pointed her toes to him, listened to him, and followed his advice. We sent multiple messages for her to please return to our care. She ignored us. The baby died.

We could not help those who turned away and disregarded us. We could only help those who sincerely listened and responded.

Godliness: Following God's Example of Response to Listeners and Nonlisteners

God has called believers to *godliness*.[1] This is usually understood in the sense of following His commands and leaving sin for a virtuous life. Another application of godliness, or "God-likeness," can be observing to see if people will listen and act on God's Word[2] and then giving a scriptural response to both listeners and nonlisteners.

God has honored His Word,[3] giving testimony to the world by it.[4] Moreover, the importance of listening to His Word is a recurrent scriptural subject. In all senses, the word *hear* is used 386 times; the phrase *word of the Lord*, 242 times; and *thus saith the Lord*, 413 times.

Listen and Obey

We all have the responsibility to point our toes to Him,[5] to listen to His Word,[6] and to trust Him to guide us.[7] Obeying what God commands is the evidence that our toes are pointed to Him and His Word[8] and that we are sincerely seeking Him.[9] Among those that hear, some obey and some do not.[10] However, the choice to hear and to obey is a core issue of life for each of us.[11] And the way our toes are pointed is the main definer of our life path.[12]

Different Paths but Same Considerations

Regardless of our different live paths, how God works with us is based on the same two considerations:

- Where our toes are pointed—that is, what is our attitude to His Word.[13]
- Where our feet are located—that is, where are we spiritually on our life path.[14]

The believer's relationship to others is guided by the same two considerations: have they, do they, or will they listen to His Word and what life path are they on. We can understand the spiritual life of

145

others by their words[15] and the fruit of their lives.[16] By contrast, the self-righteous and legalists only look at the location of other people's feet—that is, they judge others by their current life situation and do not consider people's attitude toward the Lord's Word.[17]

Intersecting Paths

Though each of us is on a different life path, God occasionally directs us to come alongside others. We know this because the second great command is to love our neighbor.[18] In this world of physical, emotional, and spiritual needs, love means showing mercy,[19] being forgiving,[20] being kind,[21] and serving.[22] We show such compassion[23] because we are filled with God's love[24] and because we are followers of Jesus the Compassionate One.[25]

We can serve others in very simple ways.[26] However, we can be of *additional* help to those around us *if they* are listening[27] and *if we* have more spiritual understanding.[28] To help and teach others *more effectively*, we need to be grounded in the Word ourselves and continually growing in it.[29] Moreover, to be more useful, we must walk faithfully, without blame, and unspotted by the world.[30]

Our Approach to Those Who Will Listen

Turning away from all thoughts of personal condemnation and revenge, our own attitude toward others should be humble.[31] We must treat others with respect as we would our own father, mother, brother, and sister, particularly treating those of the opposite sex with all purity.[32] Elders of the church are to be treated with even more respect and with submissive hearts on our part.[33]

Our spiritual help to others is with the Word and by the Spirit. Both are the source of truth and conviction.[34] The scriptural role, especially of those in leadership, is to constantly preach and teach the Word[35] without partiality,[36] directly confronting those with wrong doctrine or conduct.[37] If the person in leadership is sinning, be careful that there is clear evidence with at least two or three witnesses, then the rebuke of him or her needs to be public.[38]

Our activities should not be centered on debates of someone's ideas,[39] but instead on praying for others[40] and serving others.[41] We must encourage others to remember what is right and caution them to do the right.[42] When people are walking contrary to scripture,[43] causing arguments and stirring up divisions,[44] then they need to be confronted with scripture.[45] If they will not repent, then they need to be disciplined by the church.[46] Part of the discipline is to consider them as both unsaved and nonmembers of the church, so they cannot even participate in the fellowship of the Lord's table.[47] In more severe, hard-hearted cases, we might even pray that they receive some of the consequences of their sin to help bring them back to Christ.[48]

Our Approach to Those Who Absolutely Will Not Repent and Who Clearly Turn Their Backs on the Faith

People who will not listen are proud and can cause strife in the church.[49] Sometimes those who turn their backs on God and His Word will just leave us.[50] If proud troublemakers will not leave us, then we must reject and withdraw from them.[51] Over time, these problems will get worse as the end nears.[52]

God is patient, kind[53], long-suffering, and not rushing to judgment.[54] However, if people will not listen to Him, He may not listen to them in the day of their need.[55] Even more, He may give them up to receive the full consequences of their sin and may condemn their words and actions with terrible penalties.[56] The Lord has reserved to Himself what the ultimate judgment should be.[57]

Fellowshipping as Believers

We separate coals of a fire to make it go out and push them together to make it burn better and brighter. God wants us to gather with believers to encourage and strengthen one another and to help our testimony burn brighter.[58] So within the body of Christ, we have fellowship with like-minded believers[59] and have close communion as in the local church.[60] However, we cannot have *spiritual* fellowship with unbelievers.[61]

Our fellowshipping will be closer with those whose path is closer to ours.[62] But whatever their path, we can still minister to the individual in the name of Christ, without accepting the differences.[63] Christ came to seek and to save the lost.[64] He ministered to us while we were lost in sin and enemies of God.[65] Can we do less to those who are born again, to those of the household of faith, even when we feel they are on a wrong path?[66]

Ministering Together

When two horses draw a cart along a road, their hooves are on the same trail. They are pointed the same direction. They are helping one another and are depending on one another. We may find ourselves on the same or similar path with others and with our toes pointed the same direction. Walking in the same doctrinal and moral truth, we may find we have the same goals and approach to ministry. Scripture gives multiple examples of believers working together.[67] For this working together, God has given each of us different abilities[68] and different functions in the Body of Christ, which we must recognize, accept, and respect. Moreover, our differences work to make us more effective in our ministry together.[69] These common paths of ministry may be physically next to ours, as in our own local church, or distant, as in missionary ministry.[70]

So our understanding and approach to people is partly based on the degree that they listen to and obey God's Word.

What about believers in my fellowship or ministry who sincerely follow God but prefer things in their lives that I do not allow? What are the limits to our preferences and our "Christian liberty"?

Notes

[1] But thou, O man of God, flee these things; and follow after righteousness, godliness, faith, love, patience, meekness. (1 Tim. 6:11)

Teaching us that, denying ungodliness and worldly lusts, we should live soberly, righteously, and godly, in this present world. (Titus 2:12)

Seeing then that all these things shall be dissolved, what manner of persons ought ye to be in all holy conversation and godliness. (2 Pet. 3:11)

[2] And thou shalt speak my words unto them, whether they will hear, or whether they will forbear. (2 Ezek. 2:7a)

And if any man hear my words, and believe not, I judge him not: for I came not to judge the world, but to save the world. He that rejecteth me, and receiveth not my words, hath one that judgeth him: the word that I have spoken, the same shall judge him in the last day. For I have not spoken of myself; but the Father which sent me, he gave me a commandment, what I should say, and what I should speak. And I know that his commandment is life everlasting: whatsoever I speak therefore, even as the Father said unto me, so I speak. (John 12:47–50)

[3] I will worship toward thy holy temple, and praise thy name for thy lovingkindness and for thy truth: for thou hast magnified thy word above all thy name. (Ps. 138:2)

[4] O earth, earth, earth, hear the word of the Lord. (Jer. 22:29)

And he said unto them, He that hath ears to hear, let him hear. (Mark 4:9)

For this cause also thank we God without ceasing, because, when ye received the word of God which ye heard of us, ye received it not as the word of men, but as it is in truth, the word of God, which effectually worketh also in you that believe. (1 Thess. 2:13)

[5] But if from thence thou shalt seek the LORD thy God, thou shalt find him, if thou seek him with all thy heart and with all thy soul. (Deut. 4:29)

Shew me thy ways, O LORD; teach me thy paths… What man is he that feareth the LORD? him shall he teach in the way that he shall choose. (Ps. 25:4, 12)

When thou saidst, Seek ye my face; my heart said unto thee, Thy face, LORD, will I seek… Teach me thy way, O LORD, and lead me in a plain path, because of mine enemies. (Ps. 27:8, 11)

O God, thou art my God; early will I seek thee: my soul thirsteth for thee, my flesh longeth for thee in a dry and thirsty land, where no water is. (Ps. 63:1)

Teach me thy way, O LORD; I will walk in thy truth: unite my heart to fear thy name. (Ps. 86:11)

Blessed art thou, O Lord: teach me thy statutes... I have chosen the way of truth: thy judgments have I laid before me... My hands also will I lift up unto thy commandments, which I have loved; and I will meditate in thy statutes... I thought on my ways, and turned my feet unto thy testimonies... I have refrained my feet from every evil way, that I might keep thy word... Thy word is a lamp unto my feet, and a light unto my path. (Ps. 119:12, 30, 48, 59, 101, 105)

And ye shall seek me, and find me, when ye shall search for me with all your heart. (Jer. 29:13)

In contrast: O Lord, I know the way of man is not in himself; it is not in man who walks to direct his own steps. (Jer. 10:23)

6 Observe and hear all these words which I command thee, that it may go well with thee, and with thy children after thee for ever, when thou doest that which is good and right in the sight of the Lord thy God. (Deut. 12:28)

A wise man will hear, and will increase learning; and a man of understanding shall attain unto wise counsels. (Prov. 1:5)

Hear instruction, and be wise, and refuse it not. (Prov. 8:33)

Hear counsel, and receive instruction, that thou mayest be wise in thy latter end. (Prov. 19:20)

But this thing commanded I them, saying, Obey my voice, and I will be your God, and ye shall be my people: and walk ye in all the ways that I have commanded you, that it may be well unto you. (Jer. 7:23)

If any man have ears to hear, let him hear. (Mark 7:16)

7 The steps of a good man are ordered by the Lord: and he delighteth in his way. (Ps. 37:23)

Cause me to hear thy lovingkindness in the morning; for in thee do I trust: cause me to know the way wherein I should walk; for I lift up my soul unto thee... Teach me to do thy will; for thou art my God: thy spirit is good; lead me into the land of uprightness. (Ps. 143:8, 10)

Trust in the Lord with all thine heart; and lean not unto thine own understanding. In all thy ways acknowledge him, and he shall direct thy paths. (Prov. 3:5–6)

And thine ears shall hear a word behind thee, saying, This is the way, walk ye in it, when ye turn to the right hand, and when ye turn to the left. (Isa. 30:21)

And seek not ye what ye shall eat, or what ye shall drink, neither be ye of doubtful mind. For all these things do the nations of the world seek after: and your Father knoweth that ye have need of these things. But rather seek ye the kingdom of God; and all these things shall be added unto you. (Luke 12:29–31)

In whom ye also trusted, after that ye heard the word of truth, the gospel of your salvation: in whom also after that ye believed, ye were sealed with that holy Spirit of promise. (Eph. 1:13)

8 Observe and hear all these words which I command thee, that it may go well with thee, and with thy children after thee for ever, when thou doest that which is good and right in the sight of the Lord thy God. (Deut. 12:28)

Thou shalt therefore obey the voice of the Lord thy God, and do his commandments and his statutes, which I command thee this day. (Deut. 27:10)

And Samuel said, Hath the Lord as great delight in burnt offerings and sacrifices, as in obeying the voice of the Lord? Behold, to obey is better than sacrifice, and to hearken than the fat of rams. (1 Sam. 15:22)

Know ye not, that to whom ye yield yourselves servants to obey, his servants ye are to whom ye obey; whether of sin unto death, or of obedience unto righteousness? But God be thanked, that ye were the servants of sin, but ye have obeyed from the heart that form of doctrine which was delivered you. (Rom. 6:16–17)

But be ye doers of the word, and not hearers only, deceiving your own selves. (James 1:22)

9 Blessed are the undefiled in the way, who walk in the law of the Lord. Blessed are they that keep his testimonies, and that seek him with the whole heart. They also do no iniquity: they walk in his ways... With my whole heart have I sought thee: O let me not wander from thy commandments... Teach me, O Lord, the way of thy statutes; and I shall keep it unto the end... Give me understanding, and I shall keep thy law; yea, I shall observe it with my whole heart... So shall I keep thy law continually for ever and ever... I have remembered thy name, O Lord, in the night, and have kept thy law... I have inclined mine heart to perform thy statutes alway, even unto the end... I am thy servant; give me understanding, that I may know thy testimonies... I have kept thy precepts and thy testimonies: for all my ways are before thee. (Ps. 119:1–3, 10, 33–34, 44, 55, 112, 125, 168)

My sheep hear my voice, and I know them, and they follow me. (John 10:27)

10 And afterward Moses and Aaron went in, and told Pharaoh, Thus saith the Lord God of Israel, Let my people go, that they may hold a feast unto me in the wilderness. And Pharaoh said, Who is the Lord, that I should obey his voice to let Israel go? I know not the Lord, neither will I let Israel go. (Exod. 5:1–2)

Hear now this, O foolish people, and without understanding; which have eyes, and see not; which have ears, and hear not. (Jer. 5:21)

To whom shall I speak, and give warning, that they may hear? behold, their ear is uncircumcised, and they cannot hearken: behold, the word of the Lord is unto them a reproach; they have no delight in it... Thus saith the Lord, Stand ye in the ways, and see, and ask for the old paths, where is the good way, and walk therein, and ye shall find rest for your souls. But they said, We will not walk therein. (Jer. 6:10, 16)

And now, because ye have done all these works, saith the Lord, and I spake unto you, rising up early and speaking, but ye heard not; and I called you, but ye answered not. (Jer. 7:13)

And the Lord hath sent unto you all his servants the prophets, rising early and sending them; but ye have not hearkened, nor inclined your ear to hear. (Jer. 25:4)

Howbeit I sent unto you all my servants the prophets, rising early and sending them, saying, Oh, do not this abominable thing that I hate. But they hearkened not, nor inclined their ear to turn from their wickedness, to burn no incense unto other gods... As for the word that thou hast spoken unto us in the name of the LORD, we will not hearken unto thee. (Jer. 44:4–5, 16)

And thou shalt speak my words unto them, whether they will hear, or whether they will forbear: for they are most rebellious. (Ezek. 2:7)

Moreover he said unto me, Son of man, all my words that I shall speak unto thee receive in thine heart, and hear with thine ears. And go, get thee to them of the captivity, unto the children of thy people, and speak unto them, and tell them, Thus saith the Lord God; whether they will hear, or whether they will forbear... Son of man, I have made thee a watchman unto the house of Israel: therefore hear the word at my mouth, and give them warning from me... But when I speak with thee, I will open thy mouth, and thou shalt say unto them, Thus saith the Lord God; He that heareth, let him hear; and he that forbeareth, let him forbear: for they are a rebellious house. (Ezek. 3:10–11, 17, 27)

Be ye not as your fathers, unto whom the former prophets have cried, saying, Thus saith the Lord of hosts; Turn ye now from your evil ways, and from your evil doings: but they did not hear, nor hearken unto me, saith the Lord. (Zech. 1:4)

And when Felix heard these things, having more perfect knowledge of that way, he deferred them, and said, When Lysias the chief captain shall come down, I will know the uttermost of your matter... And after certain days, when Felix came with his wife Drusilla, which was a Jewess, he sent for Paul, and heard him concerning the faith in Christ. And as he reasoned of righteousness, temperance, and judgment to come, Felix trembled, and answered, Go thy way for this time; when I have a convenient season, I will call for thee. (Acts 24:22, 24–25)

Then they that gladly received his word were baptized: and the same day there were added unto them about three thousand souls. (Acts 2:41)

How be it many of them which heard the word believed; and the number of the men was about five thousand. (Acts 4:4)

Which was with the deputy of the country, Sergius Paulus, a prudent man; who called for Barnabas and Saul, and desired to hear the word of God... Then the deputy...believed, being astonished at the doctrine of the Lord. And the next sabbath day came almost the whole city together to hear the word of God. (Acts 13:7, 12, 44)

[11] Hear ye, and give ear; be not proud: for the Lord hath spoken. (Jer. 13:15)

But he answered and said, It is written, Man shall not live by bread alone, but by every word that proceedeth out of the mouth of God. (Matt. 4:4)

Therefore whosoever heareth these sayings of mine, and doeth them, I will liken him unto a wise man, which built his house upon a rock: And the rain descended, and the floods came, and the winds blew, and beat upon that house; and it fell not: for it was founded upon a rock. And every one that heareth these sayings of mine, and doeth them not, shall be likened unto a foolish man, which built his house upon the sand: And the rain descended, and the floods came, and the winds blew, and beat upon that house; and it fell: and great was the fall of it. And the rain descended, and the floods came, and the winds blew, and beat upon that house; and it fell: and great was the fall of it. (Matt. 7:24–27)

But he said, Yea rather, blessed are they that hear the word of God, and keep it. (Luke 11:28)

He that hath my commandments, and keepeth them, he it is that loveth me: and he that loveth me shall be loved of my Father, and I will love him, and will manifest myself to him. Judas saith unto him, not Iscariot, Lord, how is it that thou wilt manifest thyself unto us, and not unto the world? Jesus answered and said unto him, If a man love me, he will keep my words: and my Father will love him, and we will come unto him, and make our abode with him. He that loveth me not keepeth not my sayings: and the word which ye hear is not mine, but the Father's which sent me. (John 14:21–24)

As the Father hath loved me, so have I loved you: continue ye in my love. If ye keep my commandments, ye shall abide in my love; even as I have kept my Father's commandments, and abide in his love. These things have I spoken unto you, that my joy might remain in you, and that your joy might be full. This is my commandment, That ye love one another, as I have loved you. Greater love hath no man than this, that a man lay down his life for his friends. Ye are my friends, if ye do whatsoever I command you. (John 15:9–14)

12 Teach me, O LORD, the way of thy statutes; and I shall keep it unto the end. Give me understanding, and I shall keep thy law; yea, I shall observe it with my whole heart. Make me to go in the path of thy commandments; for therein do I delight… I thought on my ways, and turned my feet unto thy testimonies. I made haste, and delayed not to keep thy commandments… Unless thy law had been my delights, I should then have perished in mine affliction. I will never forget thy precepts: for with them thou hast quickened me. I am thine, save me; for I have sought thy precepts… I have refrained my feet from every evil way, that I might keep thy word… Thy word is a lamp unto my feet, and a light unto my path… I have inclined mine heart to perform thy statutes alway, even unto the end… Thy testimonies are wonderful: therefore doth my soul keep them… Order my steps in thy word: and let not any iniquity have dominion over me… The righteousness of thy testimonies is everlasting: give me understanding, and I shall live… I have kept thy precepts and thy testimonies: for all my ways are before thee. (Ps. 119:33–35, 59–60, 92–94, 101, 105, 112, 129, 133, 144, 168)

And the two disciples heard him speak, and they followed Jesus. (John 1:37)

Since we heard of your faith in Christ Jesus, and of the love which ye have to all the saints, For the hope which is laid up for you in heaven, whereof ye heard before in the word of the truth of the gospel; Which is come unto you, as it is in all the world; and bringeth forth fruit, as it doth also in you, since the day ye heard of it, and knew the grace of God in truth. (Col. 1:4–6)

13 And now, Israel, what doth the LORD thy God require of thee, but to fear the LORD thy God, to walk in all his ways, and to love him, and to serve the LORD thy God with all thy heart and with all thy soul, To keep the commandments of the LORD, and his statutes, which I command thee this day for thy good? (Deut. 10:12–13)

Only be thou strong and very courageous, that thou mayest observe to do according to all the law, which Moses my servant commanded thee: turn not from it to the right hand or to the left, that thou mayest prosper withersoever thou goest. This book of the law shall not depart out of thy mouth; but thou shalt meditate therein day and night, that thou mayest observe to do according to all that is written therein: for then thou shalt make thy way prosperous, and then thou shalt have good success. (Josh. 1:7–8)

And keep the charge of the LORD thy God, to walk in his ways, to keep his statutes, and his commandments, and his judgments, and his testimonies, as it is written in the law of Moses, that thou mayest prosper in all that thou doest, and whithersoever thou turnest thyself. (1 Kings 2:3)

He that hath my commandments, and keepeth them, he it is that loveth me: and he that loveth me shall be loved of my Father, and I will love him, and will manifest myself to him. Judas saith unto him, not Iscariot, Lord, how is it that thou wilt manifest thyself unto us, and not unto the world? Jesus answered and said unto him, If a man love me, he will keep my words: and my Father will love him, and we will come unto him, and make our abode with him. He that loveth me not keepeth not my sayings: and the word which ye hear is not mine, but the Father's which sent me. (John 14:21–24)

14 The LORD rewarded me according to my righteousness: according to the cleanness of my hands hath he recompensed me. For I have kept the ways of the LORD, and have not wickedly departed from my God. For all his judgments were before me: and as for his statutes, I did not depart from them. I was also upright before him, and have kept myself from mine iniquity. Therefore the LORD hath recompensed me according to my righteousness; according to my cleanness in his eye sight. (2 Sam. 22:21–25)

If my people, which are called by my name, shall humble themselves, and pray, and seek my face, and turn from their wicked ways; then will I hear from heaven, and will forgive their sin, and will heal their land. (2 Chron. 7:14)

Shall not God search this out? for he knoweth the secrets of the heart. (Ps. 44:21)

O God, thou knowest my foolishness; and my sins are not hid from thee. (Ps. 69:5)

O lord, thou hast searched me, and known me. Thou knowest my downsitting and mine uprising, thou understandest my thought afar off. Thou compassest my path and my lying down, and art acquainted with all my ways. For there is not a word in my tongue, but, lo, O LORD, thou knowest it altogether... Search me, O God, and know my heart: try me, and know my thoughts. (Ps. 139:1–4, 23)

For the ways of man are before the eyes of the LORD, and he pondereth all his goings. (Prov. 5:21)

For mine eyes are upon all their ways: they are not hid from my face, neither is their iniquity hid from mine eyes. (Jer. 16:17)

I the LORD search the heart, I try the reins, even to give every man according to his ways, and according to the fruit of his doings. (Jer. 17:10)

Great in counsel, and mighty in work: for thine eyes are open upon all the ways of the sons of men: to give every one according to his ways, and according to the fruit of his doings. (Jer. 32:19)

Who is wise, and he shall understand these things? prudent, and he shall know them? for the ways of the LORD are right, and the just shall walk in them: but the transgressors shall fall therein. (Hos. 14:9)

Now therefore thus saith the LORD of hosts; Consider your ways... Thus saith the LORD of hosts; Consider your ways. (Hag. 1:5, 7)

But my words and my statutes, which I commanded my servants the prophets, did they not take hold of your fathers? and they returned and said, Like as the LORD of hosts thought to do unto us, according to our ways, and according to our doings, so hath he dealt with us. (Zech. 1:6)

He that believeth on the Son hath everlasting life: and he that believeth not the Son shall not see life; but the wrath of God abideth on him. (John 3:36)

Verily, verily, I say unto you, He that heareth my word, and believeth on him that sent me, hath everlasting life, and shall not come into condemnation; but is passed from death unto life. (John 5:24)

15 And he called the multitude, and said unto them, Hear, and understand: Not that which goeth into the mouth defileth a man; but that which cometh out of the mouth, this defileth a man... Do not ye yet understand, that whatsoever entereth in at the mouth goeth into the belly, and is cast out into the draught? But those things which proceed out of the mouth come forth from the heart; and they defile the man. (Matt. 15:10–11, 17–18)

A good man out of the good treasure of his heart bringeth forth that which is good; and an evil man out of the evil treasure of his heart bringeth forth that which is evil: for of the abundance of the hear this mouth speaketh. (Luke 6:15)

That if thou shalt confess with thy mouth the Lord Jesus, and shalt believe in thine heart that God hath raised him from the dead, thou shalt be saved. For with the heart man believeth unto righteousness; and with the mouth confession is made unto salvation. (Rom. 10:9–10)

16 Ye shall know them by their fruits. Do men gather grapes of thorns, or figs of thistles? Even so every good tree bringeth forth good fruit; but a corrupt tree bringeth forth evil fruit. A good tree cannot bring forth evil fruit, neither can a corrupt tree bring forth good fruit. Every tree that bringeth not forth good fruit is hewn down, and cast into the fire. Wherefore by their fruits ye shall know them. (Matt. 7:16–20)

Either make the tree good, and his fruit good; or else make the tree corrupt, and his fruit corrupt: for the tree is known by his fruit. (Matt. 12:33)

For a good tree bringeth not forth corrupt fruit; neither doth a corrupt tree bring forth good fruit. For every tree is known by his own fruit. For of thorns men do not gather figs, nor of a bramble bush gather they grapes. (Luke 6:43–44)

17 *Note*: In the scriptures we see the Pharisees constantly condemning the publicans and sinners. However, we can see how the toes of those same publicans and sinners were pointed in these verses:

Whether of them twain did the will of his father? They say unto him, The first. Jesus saith unto them, Verily I say unto you, That the publicans and the harlots go into the kingdom of God before you. For John came unto you in the way of righteousness, and ye believed him not: but the publicans and the harlots believed him: and ye, when ye had seen it, repented not afterward, that ye might believe him. (Matt. 21:31–32)

And all the people that heard him, and the publicans, justified God, being baptized with the baptism of John. (Luke 7:29)

Then drew near unto him all the publicans and sinners for to hear him. (Luke 15:1)

18 And thou shalt love the Lord thy God with all thy heart, and with all thy soul, and with all thy mind, and with all thy strength: this is the first commandment. And the second is like, namely this, Thou shalt love thy neighbour as thy self. There is none other commandment greater than these. (Mark 12:31–32)

19 He hath shewed thee, O man, what is good; and what doth the LORD require of thee, but to do justly, and to love mercy, and to walk humbly with thy God? (Mic. 6:8)

We then that are strong ought to bear the infirmities of the weak, and not to please ourselves. (Rom. 15:1)

But the wisdom that is from above is first pure, then peaceable, gentle, and easy to be intreated, full of mercy and good fruits, without partiality, and without hypocrisy. (James 3:17)

20 Then came Peter to him, and said, Lord, how oft shall my brother sin against me, and I forgive him? till seven times? Jesus saith unto him, I say not unto thee, Until seven times: but, Until seventy times seven… So likewise shall my heavenly Father do also unto you, if ye from your hearts forgive not every one his brother their trespasses. (Matt. 18:21–22, 35)

And when ye stand praying, forgive, if ye have ought against any: that your Father also which is in heaven may forgive you your trespasses. But if ye do not forgive, neither will your Father which is in heaven forgive your trespasses. (Mark 11:25–26)

And be ye kind one to another, tenderhearted, forgiving one another, even as God for Christ's sake hath forgiven you. (Eph. 4:32)

21 Be kindly affectioned one to another with brotherly love; in honour preferring one another. (Rom. 12:10)

Charity [love] suffereth long, and is kind; charity envieth not; charity vaunteth not itself, is not puffed up. (1 Cor. 13:4)

22 But he that is greatest among you shall be your servant. (Matt. 23:11)

But ye shall not be so: but he that is greatest among you, let him be as the younger; and he that is chief, as he that doth serve. (Luke 22:26)

For, brethren, ye have been called unto liberty; only use not liberty for an occasion to the flesh, but by love serve one another. (Gal. 5:13)

23 Unto the upright there ariseth light in the darkness: he is gracious, and full of compassion, and righteous. (Ps. 112:4)

Finally, be ye all of one mind, having compassion one of another, love as brethren, be pitiful, be courteous. (1 Pet. 3:8)

But whoso hath this world's good, and seeth his brother have need, and shutteth up his bowels of compassion from him, how dwelleth the love of God in him? (1 John 3:17)

24 And I have declared unto them thy name, and will declare it: that the love wherewith thou hast loved me may be in them, and I in them. (John 17:26)

And hope maketh not ashamed; because the love of God is shed abroad in our hearts by the Holy Ghost which is given unto us. For when we were yet without strength, in due time Christ died for the ungodly. For scarcely for a righteous man will one die: yet peradventure for a good man some would even dare to die. But God commendeth his love toward us, in that, while we were yet sinners, Christ died for us. (Rom. 5:5–8)

Nay, in all these things we are more than conquerors through him that loved us. For I am persuaded, that neither death, nor life, nor angels, nor principalities, nor powers, nor things present, nor things to come, Nor height, nor depth, nor any other creature, shall be able to separate us from the love of God, which is in Christ Jesus our Lord. (Rom. 8:37–39)

I am crucified with Christ: nevertheless I live; yet not I, but Christ liveth in me: and the life which I now live in the flesh I live by the faith of the Son of God, who loved me, and gave himself for me. (Gal. 2:20)

And to know the love of Christ, which passeth knowledge, that ye might be filled with all the fulness of God. (Eph. 3:19)

And walk in love, as Christ also hath loved us, and hath given himself for us an offering and a sacrifice to God for a sweet smelling savour. (Eph. 5:2)

But whoso hath this world's good, and seeth his brother have need, and shutteth up his bowels of compassion from him, how dwelleth the love of God in him? (1 John 3:17)

Beloved, let us love one another: for love is of God; and every one that loveth is born of God, and knoweth God. He that loveth not knoweth not God; for God is love... And we have known and believed the love that God hath to us. God is love; and he that dwelleth in love dwelleth in God, and God in him... We love him, because he first loved us. (1 John 4:7–8, 16, 19)

25 But when he saw the multitudes, he was moved with compassion on them, because they fainted, and were scattered abroad, as sheep having no shepherd. (Matt. 9:36)

And Jesus went forth, and saw a great multitude, and was moved with compassion toward them, and he healed their sick. (Matt. 14:14)

So Jesus had compassion on them, and touched their eyes: and immediately their eyes received sight, and they followed him. (Matt. 20:34)

And Jesus, when he came out, saw much people, and was moved with compassion toward them, because they were as sheep not having a shepherd: and he began to teach them many things. (Mark 6:34)

And when the Lord saw her, he had compassion on her, and said unto her, Weep not. And he came and touched the bier: and they that bare him stood still. And he said, Young man, I say unto thee, Arise. And he that was dead sat up, and began to speak. And he delivered him to his mother. (Luke 7:13–15)

26 And if thou draw out thy soul to the hungry, and satisfy the afflicted soul; then shall thy light rise in obscurity, and thy darkness be as the noon day. (Isa. 58:10)

And whosoever shall give to drink unto one of these little ones a cup of cold water only in the name of a disciple, verily I say unto you, he shall in no wise lose his reward. (Matt. 10:42)

For whosoever shall give you a cup of water to drink in my name, because ye belong to Christ, verily I say unto you, he shall not lose his reward. (Mark 9:41)

Then shall the King say unto them on his right hand, Come, ye blessed of my Father, inherit the kingdom prepared for you from the foundation of the world: For I was an hungred, and ye gave me meat: I was thirsty, and ye gave me drink: I was a stranger, and ye took me in: Naked, and ye clothed me: I was sick, and ye visited me: I was in prison, and ye came unto me. (Matt. 25:34–36)

But whoso hath this world's good, and seeth his brother have need, and shutteth up his bowels of compassion from him, how dwelleth the love of God in him? 18 My little children, let us not love in word, neither in tongue; but in deed and in truth. (1 John 3:17–18)

27 Blessed is the man that heareth me, watching daily at my gates, waiting at the posts of my doors. (Prov. 8:34)

He that refuseth instruction despiseth his own soul: but he that heareth reproof getteth understanding. (Prov. 15:32)

He that getteth wisdom loveth his own soul: he that keepeth understanding shall find good. (Prov. 19:8)

Therefore whosoever heareth these sayings of mine, and doeth them, I will liken him unto a wiseman, which built his house upon a rock: And the rain descended, and the floods came, and the winds blew, and beat upon that house; and it fell not :for it was founded upon a rock. And every one that heareth these sayings of mine, and doeth them not, shall be likened unto a foolish man, which built his house upon the sand: And the rain descended, and the floods came, and the winds blew, and beat upon that house; and it fell: and great was the fall of it. (Matt. 7:24–27)

But he that received seed into the good ground is he that heareth the word, and understandeth it; which also beareth fruit, and bringeth forth, some an hundredfold, some sixty, some thirty. (Matt. 13:23)

And with many such parables spake he the word unto them, as they were able to hear it. (Mark 4:33)

[28] I am thy servant; give me understanding, that I may know thy testimonies... The entrance of thy words giveth light; it giveth understanding unto the simple. (Ps. 119:125, 130)

The Lord God hath given me the tongue of the learned, that I should know how to speak a word in season to him that is weary: he wakeneth morning by morning, he wakeneth mine ear to hear as the learned. (Isa. 50:4)

For I say, through the grace given unto me, to every man that is among you, not to think of himself more highly than he ought to think ; but to think soberly, according as God hath dealt to every man the measure of faith. (Rom. 12:3)

And I myself also am persuaded of you, my brethren, that ye also are full of goodness, filled with all knowledge, able also to admonish one another. (Rom. 15:14)

But in all things approving ourselves as the ministers of God, in much patience, in afflictions, in necessities, in distresses... By pureness, by knowledge, by long suffering, by kindness, by the Holy Ghost, by love unfeigned. (2 Cor. 6:4, 6)

Brethren, if a man be overtaken in a fault, ye which are spiritual, restore such an one in the spirit of meekness; considering thyself, lest thou also be tempted. (Gal. 6:1)

Wherefore be ye not unwise, but understanding what the will of the Lord is. (Eph. 5:17)

And this I pray, that your love may abound yet more and more in knowledge and in all judgment. (Phil. 1:9)

For this cause we also, since the day we heard it, do not cease to pray for you, and to desire that ye might be filled with the knowledge of his will in all wisdom and spiritual understanding; That ye might walk worthy of the Lord unto all pleasing, being fruitful in every good work, and increasing in the knowledge of God. (Col. 1:9–10)

29 This book of the law shall not depart out of thy mouth; but thou shalt meditate therein day and night, that thou mayest observe to do according to all that is written therein: for then thou shalt make thy way prosperous, and then thou shalt have good success. (Josh. 1:8)

But his delight is in the law of the LORD; and in his law doth he meditate day and night. And he shall be like a tree planted by the rivers of water, that bringeth forth his fruit in his season; his leaf also shall not wither; and whatsoever he doeth shall prosper. (Ps. 1:2–3)

And I myself also am persuaded of you, my brethren, that ye also are full of goodness, filled with all knowledge, able also to admonish one another. (Rom. 15:14)

Meditate upon these things; give thyself wholly to them; that thy profiting may appear to all. Take heed unto thyself, and unto the doctrine; continue in them: for in doing this thou shalt both save thyself, and them that hear thee. (1 Tim. 4:15–16)

But thou, O man of God, flee these things; and follow after righteousness, godliness, faith, love, patience, meekness. Fight the good fight of faith, lay hold on eternal life, where unto thou art also called, and hast professed a good profession before many witnesses… That thou keep this commandment without spot, unrebukeable, until the appearing of our Lord Jesus Christ:… O Timothy, keep that which is committed to thy trust, avoiding profane and vain babblings, and oppositions of science falsely so called. (1 Tim. 6:11–12, 14, 20)

Wherefore I put thee in remembrance that thou stir up the gift of God, which is in thee by the putting on of my hands. For God hath not given us the spirit of fear; but of power, and of love, and of a sound mind. Be not thou therefore ashamed of the testimony of our Lord, nor of me his prisoner: but be thou partaker of the afflictions of the gospel according to the power of God;… Hold fast the form of sound words, which thou hast heard of me, in faith and love which is in Christ Jesus. That good thing which was committed unto thee keep by the Holy Ghost which dwelleth in us. (2 Tim. 1:6–8, 13–14)

Thou therefore, my son, be strong in the grace that is in Christ Jesus. And the things that thou hast heard of me among many witnesses, the same commit thou to faithful men, who shall be able to teach others also… Study to shew thyself approved unto God, a workman that needeth not to be ashamed, rightly dividing the word of truth. (2 Tim. 2:1–2, 15)

But continue thou in the things which thou hast learned and hast been assured of, knowing of whom thou hast learned them; And that from a child thou hast known the holy scriptures, which are able to make thee wise unto salvation through faith which is in Christ Jesus. (2 Tim. 3:14–15)

30 Therefore we ought to give the more earnest heed to the things which we have heard, lest at any time we should let them slip. (Heb. 2:1)

This charge I commit unto thee, son Timothy, according to the prophecies which went before on thee, that thou by them migh test war a good warfare; Holding faith, and a good conscience; which some having put away concerning faith have made shipwreck. (1 Tim. 1:18–19)

But refuse profane and old wives' fables, and exercise thyself rather unto godliness. For bodily exercise profiteth little: but godliness is profitable unto all things, having promise of the life that now is, and of that which is to come... Let no man despise thy youth; but be thou an example of the believers, in word, in conversation, in charity, in spirit, in faith, in purity. (1 Tim. 4:7–8, 12)

Lay hands suddenly on no man, neither be partaker of other men's sins: keep thyself pure. (1 Tim. 5:22)

But thou, O man of God, flee these things; and follow after righteousness, godliness, faith, love, patience, meekness. Fight the good fight of faith, lay hold on eternal life, where unto thou art also called, and hast professed a good profession before many witnesses... That thou keep this commandment without spot, unrebukeable, until the appearing of our Lord Jesus Christ:... O Timothy, keep that which is committed to thy trust, avoiding profane and vain babblings, and oppositions of science falsely so called. (1 Tim. 6:11–12, 14, 20)

Wherefore I put thee in remembrance that thou stir up the gift of God, which is in thee by the putting on of my hands. For God hath not given us the spirit of fear; but of power, and of love, and of a sound mind. Be not thou therefore ashamed of the testimony of our Lord, nor of me his prisoner: but be thou partaker of the afflictions of the gospel according to the power of God;... Hold fast the form of sound words, which thou hast heard of me, in faith and love which is in Christ Jesus. That good thing which was committed unto thee keep by the Holy Ghost which dwelleth in us. (2 Tim. 1:6–8, 13–14)

Thou therefore endure hardness, as a good soldier of Jesus Christ. No man that warreth entangleth himself with the affairs of this life; that he may please him who hath chosen him to be a soldier. And if a man also strive for masteries, yet is he not crowned, except he strive lawfully... If a man therefore purge himself from these, he shall be a vessel unto honour, sanctified, and meet for the master's use, and prepared unto every good work. Flee also youthful lusts: but follow righteousness, faith, charity, peace, with them that call on the Lord out of a pure heart. (2 Tim. 2:3–5, 21–22)

31 Put on therefore, as the elect of God, holy and beloved, bowels of mercies, kindness, humbleness of mind, meekness, longsuffering. (Col. 3:12)

But foolish and unlearned questions avoid, knowing that they do gender strifes. And the servant of the Lord must not strive; but be gentle unto all men, apt to teach, patient, In meekness instructing those that oppose themselves; if God peradventure will give them repentance to the acknowledging of the truth; And that they may recover themselves out of the snare of the devil, who are taken captive by him at his will. (2 Tim. 2:23–26)

Yea, all of you…be clothed with humility: for God resisteth the proud, and giveth grace to the humble. (1 Pet. 5:5)

32 Rebuke not an elder, but intreat him as a father; and the younger men as brethren; The elder women as mothers; the younger as sisters, with all purity. (1 Tim. 5:1–2)

33 Rebuke not an elder, but intreat him as a father; and the younger men as brethren;… Let the elders that rule well be counted worthy of double honour, especially they who labour in the word and doctrine. (1 Tim. 5:1, 17)

Likewise, ye younger, submit yourselves unto the elder. Yea, all of you be subject one to another, and be clothed with humility: for God resisteth the proud, and giveth grace to the humble. (1 Pet. 5:5)

34 And I will pray the Father, and he shall give you another Comforter, that he may abide with you for ever; Even the Spirit of truth; whom the world cannot receive, because it seeth him not, neither knoweth him: but ye know him; for he dwelleth with you, and shall be in you… But the Comforter, which is the Holy Ghost, whom the Father will send in my name, he shall teach you all things, and bring all things to your remembrance, whatsoever I have said unto you. (John 14:16–17, 26)

But when the Comforter is come, whom I will send unto you from the Father, even the Spirit of truth, which proceedeth from the Father, he shall testify of me. (John 15:26)

Nevertheless I tell you the truth; It is expedient for you that I go away: for if I go not away, the Comforter will not come unto you; but if I depart, I will send him unto you. And when he is come, he will reprove the world of sin, and of righteousness, and of judgment: Of sin, because they believe not on me; Of righteousness, because I go to my Father, and ye see me no more; Of judgment, because the prince of this world is judged… Howbeit when he, the Spirit of truth, is come, he will guide you into all truth: for he shall not speak of himself; but whatsoever he shall hear, that shall he speak: and he will shew you things to come. He shall glorify me: for he shall receive of mine, and shall shew it unto you. (John 16:7–11, 13–14)

All scripture is given by inspiration of God, and is profitable for doctrine, for reproof, for correction, for instruction in righteousness: That the man of God may be perfect, throughly furnished unto all good works. (2 Tim. 3:16–17)

I charge thee therefore before God, and the Lord Jesus Christ, who shall judge the quick and the dead at his appearing and his kingdom; Preach the word; be instant in season, out of season; reprove, rebuke, exhort with all longsuffering and doctrine. (2 Tim. 4:1–2)

For the word of God is quick, and powerful, and sharper than any two edged sword, piercing even to the dividing asunder of soul and spirit, and of the joints and marrow, and is a discerner of the thoughts and intents of the heart. (Heb. 4:12)

35 And straightway many were gathered together, insomuch that there was no room to receive them, no, not so much as about the door: and he preached the word unto them. (Mark 2:2)

And he ordained twelve, that they should be with him, and that he might send them forth to preach. (Mark 3:14)

And he said unto them, Go ye into all the world, and preach the gospel to every creature. (Mark 16:15)

Therefore they that were scattered abroad went every where preaching the word. (Acts 8:4)

Whom we preach, warning every man, and teaching every man in all wisdom; that we may present every man perfect in Christ Jesus. (Col. 1:28)

These things command and teach. Let no man despise thy youth; but be thou an example of the believers, in word, in conversation, in charity, in spirit, in faith, in purity. Till I come, give attendance to reading, to exhortation, to doctrine. (1 Tim. 4:11–13)

Hold fast the form of sound words, which thou hast heard of me, in faith and love which is in Christ Jesus. (2 Tim. 1:13)

Preach the word; be instant in season, out of season; reprove, rebuke, exhort with all long suffering and doctrine. (2 Tim. 4:2)

But speak thou the things which become sound doctrine:... Sound speech, that cannot be condemned; that he that is of the contrary part may be ashamed, having no evil thing to say of you. (Titus 2:1, 8)

36 I charge thee before God, and the Lord Jesus Christ, and the elect angels, that thou observe these things without preferring one before another, doing nothing by partiality. (1 Tim. 5:21)

My brethren, have not the faith of our Lord Jesus Christ, the Lord of glory, with respect of persons... Are ye not then partial in yourselves, and are become judges of evil thoughts?... But if ye have respect to persons, ye commit sin, and are convinced of the law as transgressors. (James 2:1, 4, 9)

But the wisdom that is from above is first pure, then peaceable, gentle, and easy to be intreated, full of mercy and good fruits, without partiality, and without hypocrisy. (James 3:17)

37 Open rebuke is better than secret love. Faithful are the wounds of a friend; but the kisses of an enemy are deceitful. (Prov. 27:5–6)

It is better to hear the rebuke of the wise, than for a man to hear the song of fools. (Eccles. 7:5)

But when Peter was come to Antioch, I withstood him to the face, because he was to be blamed. For before that certain came from James, he did eat with the Gentiles: but when they were come, he withdrew and separated himself, fearing them which were of the circumcision. And the other Jews dissembled likewise with him; insomuch that Barnabas also was carried away with their dissimulation. But when I saw that they walked not uprightly according to the truth of the gospel, I said unto Peter before them all, If thou, being a Jew, livest after the manner of Gentiles, and not as do the Jews, why compellest thou the Gentiles to live as do the Jews? (Gal. 2:11–14)

As I besought thee to abide still at Ephesus, when I went into Macedonia, that thou mightest charge some that they teach no other doctrine. (1 Tim. 1:3)

38 But when I saw that they walked not uprightly according to the truth of the gospel, I said unto Peter before them all, If thou, being a Jew, livest after the manner of Gentiles, and not as do the Jews, why compellest thou the Gentiles to live as do the Jews? (Gal. 2:14)

Against an elder receive not an accusation, but before two or three witnesses. Them that sin rebuke before all, that others also may fear. (1 Tim. 5:19–20)

39 Son of man, prophesy against the prophets of Israel that prophesy, and say thou unto them that prophesy out of their own hearts, Hear ye the word of the Lord;… And will ye pollute me among my people for handfuls of barley and for pieces of bread, to slay the souls that should not die, and to save the souls alive that should not live, by your lying to my people that hear your lies? (Ezek. 13:2, 19)

As I besought thee to abide still at Ephesus, when I went into Macedonia, that thou mightest charge some that they teach no other doctrine, Neither give heed to fables and endless genealogies, which minister questions, rather than godly edifying which is in faith: so do. (1 Tim. 1:3–4)

But shun profane and vain babblings: for they will increase unto more ungodliness. And their word will eat as doth a canker: of whom is Hymenaeus and Philetus; Who concerning the truth have erred, saying that the resurrection is past already; and overthrow the faith of some… But foolish and unlearned questions avoid, knowing that they do gender strifes. (2 Tim. 2:16–18, 23)

40 I exhort therefore, that, first of all, supplications, prayers, intercessions, and giving of thanks, be made for all men; For kings, and for all that are in authority; that we may lead a quiet and peaceable life in all godliness and honesty. For this is good and acceptable in the sight of God our Saviour; Who will have all men to be saved, and to come unto the knowledge of the truth… I will therefore that men pray every where, lifting up holy hands, without wrath and doubting. (1 Tim. 2:1–4, 8)

41 For, brethren, ye have been called unto liberty; only use not liberty for an occasion to the flesh, but by love serve one another. (Gal. 5:13)

As every man hath received the gift, even so minister the same one to another, as good stewards of the manifold grace of God. (1 Pet. 4:10)

42 Now we exhort you, brethren, warn them that are unruly, comfort the feebleminded, support the weak, be patient toward all men. (1 Thess. 5:14)

Now the end of the commandment is charity out of a pure heart, and of a good conscience, and of faith unfeigned. (1 Tim. 1:5)

If thou put the brethren in remembrance of these things, thou shalt be a good minister of Jesus Christ, nourished up in the words of faith and of good doctrine, whereunto thou hast attained. (1 Tim. 4:6)

Charge them that are rich in this world, that they be not highminded, nor trust in uncertain riches, but in the living God, who giveth us richly all things to enjoy; That they do good, that they be rich in good works, ready to distribute, willing to communicate. (1 Tim. 6:17–18)

Of these things put them in remembrance, charging them before the Lord that they strive not about words to no profit, but to the subverting of the hearers. (2 Tim. 2:14)

But speak thou the things which become sound doctrine: That the aged men be sober, grave, temperate, sound in faith, in charity, in patience. The aged women likewise, that they be in behaviour as becometh holiness, not false accusers, not given to much wine, teachers of good things; That they may teach the young women to be sober, to love their husbands, to love their children, To be discreet, chaste, keepers at home, good, obedient to their own husbands, that the word of God be not blasphemed. Young men likewise exhort to be sober minded. In all things shewing thyself a pattern of good works: in doctrine shewing uncorruptness, gravity, sincerity, Sound speech, that cannot be condemned; that he that is of the contrary part may be ashamed, having no evil thing to say of you... For the grace of God that bringeth salvation hath appeared to all men, Teaching us that, denying ungodliness and worldly lusts, we should live soberly, righteously, and godly, in this present world; Looking for that blessed hope, and the glorious appearing of the great God and our Saviour Jesus Christ; Who gave himself for us, that he might redeem us from all iniquity, and purify unto himself a peculiar people, zealous of good works. These things speak, and exhort, and rebuke with all authority. Let no man despise thee. (Titus 2:1–8, 11–15)

Put them in mind to be subject to principalities and powers, to obey magistrates, to be ready to every good work, to speak evil of no man, to be no brawlers, but gentle, shewing all meekness unto all men... This is a faithful saying, and these things I will that thou affirm constantly, that they which have believed in God might be careful to maintain good works. These things are good and profitable unto men... And let ours also learn to maintain good works for necessary uses, that they be not unfruitful. (Titus 3:1–2, 8, 14)

43 From which some having swerved have turned aside unto vain jangling; Desiring to be teachers of the law; understanding neither what they say, nor whereof they affirm. (1 Tim. 1:6–7)

44 Where no wood is, there the fire goeth out: so where there is no talebearer, the strife ceaseth. As coals are to burning coals, and wood to fire; so is a contentious man to kindle strife. (Prov. 26:20–21)

An angry man stirreth up strife, and a furious man aboundeth in transgression. (Prov. 29:22)

Now I beseech you, brethren, by the name of our Lord Jesus Christ, that ye all speak the same thing, and that there be no divisions among you; but that ye be perfectly joined together in the same mind and in the same judgment.

For it hath been declared unto me of you, my brethren, by them which are of the house of Chloe, that there are contentions among you. Now this I say, that every one of you saith, I am of Paul; and I of Apollos; and I of Cephas; and I of Christ. (1 Cor. 1:10–12)

For ye are yet carnal: for whereas there is among you envying, and strife, and divisions, are ye not carnal, and walk as men? For while one saith, I am of Paul; and another, I am of Apollos; are ye not carnal? Who then is Paul, and who is Apollos, but ministers by whom ye believed, even as the Lord gave to every man? (1 Cor. 3:3–5)

But if any man seem to be contentious, we have no such custom, neither the churches of God... For first of all, when ye come together in the church, I hear that there be divisions among you; and I partly believe it. For there must be also heresies among you, that they which are approved may be made manifest among you. (1 Cor. 11:16, 18–19)

But avoid foolish questions, and genealogies, and contentions, and strivings about the law; for they are unprofitable and vain. (Titus 3:9)

45 And have no fellowship with the unfruitful works of darkness, but rather reprove them. (Eph. 5:11)

Whom [Christ] we preach, warning every man, and teaching every man in all wisdom; that we may present every man perfect in Christ Jesus. (Col. 1:28)

Preach the word; be instant in season, out of season; reprove, rebuke, exhort with all longsuffering and doctrine. (2 Tim. 4:2)

For there are many unruly and vain talkers and deceivers, specially they of the circumcision: Whose mouths must be stopped, who subvert whole houses, teaching things which they ought not, for filthy lucre's sake... This witness is true. Wherefore rebuke them sharply, that they may be sound in the faith; Not giving heed to Jewish fables, and commandments of men, that turn from the truth. Unto the pure all things are pure: but unto them that are defiled and unbelieving is nothing pure; but even their mind and conscience is defiled. They profess that they know God; but in works they deny him, being abominable, and disobedient, and unto every good work reprobate. (Titus 1:10–11, 13–16)

46 It is actually reported that there is sexual immorality among you, and such sexual immorality as is not even named among the Gentiles—that a man has his father's wife! And ye are puffed up, and have not rather mourned, that he that hath done this deed might be taken away from among you. For I verily, as absent in body, but present in spirit, have judged already, as though I were present, concerning him that hath so done this deed, In the name of our Lord Jesus Christ, when ye are gathered together, and my spirit, with the power of our Lord Jesus Christ, To deliver such an one unto Satan for the destruction of the flesh, that the spirit may be saved in the day of the Lord Jesus. (1 Cor. 5:1–5)

47 I wrote unto you in an epistle not to company with fornicators: Yet not altogether with the fornicators of this world, or with the covetous, or extortioners, or

with idolaters; for then must ye needs go out of the world. But now I have written unto you not to keep company, if any man that is called a brother be a fornicator, or covetous, or an idolater, or a railer, or a drunkard, or an extortioner; with such an one no not to eat. For what have I to do to judge them also that are without? do not ye judge them that are within? But them that are without God judgeth. Therefore put away from among yourselves that wicked person. (1 Cor. 5:9–13)

48 In the name of our Lord Jesus Christ, when ye are gathered together, and my spirit, with the power of our Lord Jesus Christ, To deliver such an one unto Satan for the destruction of the flesh, that the spirit may be saved in the day of the Lord Jesus. (1 Cor. 5:4–5)

Holding faith, and a good conscience; which some having put away concerning faith have made shipwreck: Of whom is Hymenaeus and Alexander; whom I have delivered unto Satan, that they may learn not to blaspheme. (1 Tim. 1:19–20)

Alexander the coppersmith did me much evil: the Lord reward him according to his works: Of whom be thou ware also; for he hath greatly withstood our words. (2 Tim. 4:14–15)

49 Hatred stirreth up strifes: but love covereth all sins. (Prov. 10:12)

A wise son heareth his father's instruction: but a scorner heareth not rebuke. (Prov. 13:1)

A scorner loveth not one that reproveth him: neither will he go unto the wise... A wrathful man stirreth up strife: but he that is slow to anger appeaseth strife. (Prov. 15:12, 18)

He loveth transgression that loveth strife: and he that exalteth his gate seeketh destruction. (Prov. 17:19)

He that is of a proud heart stirreth up strife: but he that putteth his trust in the LORD shall be made fat. (Prov. 28:25)

If any man teach otherwise, and consent not to wholesome words, even the words of our Lord Jesus Christ, and to the doctrine which is according to godliness; He is proud, knowing nothing, but doting about questions and strifes of words, whereof cometh envy, strife, railings, evil surmisings, Perverse disputings of men of corrupt minds, and destitute of the truth, supposing that gain is godliness: from such withdraw thyself. (1 Tim. 6:3–5)

But foolish and unlearned questions avoid, knowing that they do gender strifes. (2 Tim. 2:23)

50 This thou knowest, that all they which are in Asia be turned away from me; of whom are Phygellus and Hermogenes. (2 Tim. 1:15)

For of this sort are they which creep into houses, and lead captive silly women laden with sins, led away with divers lusts, Ever learning, and never able to come to the knowledge of the truth. Now as Jannes and Jambres withstood Moses, so do these also resist the truth: men of corrupt minds, reprobate concerning the faith. But they shall proceed no further: for their folly shall be manifest unto all men, as theirs also was. (2 Tim. 3:6–9)

These be they who separate themselves, sensual, having not the Spirit. (Jude 1:19)

51 Let the lying lips be put to silence; which speak grievous things proudly and contemptuously against the righteous. (Ps. 31:18)

Blessed is that man that maketh the LORD his trust, and respecteth not the proud, nor such as turn aside to lies. (Ps. 40:4)

Whoso privily slandereth his neighbour, him will I cut off: him that hath an high look and a proud heart will not I suffer. (Ps. 101:5)

Thou hast rebuked the proud that are cursed, which do err from thy commandments. (Ps. 119:21)

Cast out the scorner, and contention shall go out; yea, strife and reproach shall cease. (Prov. 22:10)

Now I beseech you, brethren, mark them which cause divisions and offences contrary to the doctrine which ye have learned; and avoid them. For they that are such serve not our Lord Jesus Christ, but their own belly; and by good words and fair speeches deceive the hearts of the simple. For your obedience is come abroad unto all men. I am glad therefore on your behalf: but yet I would have you wise unto that which is good, and simple concerning evil. (Rom. 16:17–19)

But now I have written unto you not to keep company, if any man that is called a brother be a fornicator, or covetous, or an idolater, or a railer, or a drunkard, or an extortioner; with such an one no not to eat. For what have I to do to judge them also that are without? do not ye judge them that are within? But them that are without God judgeth. Therefore put away from among yourselves that wicked person. (1 Cor. 5:11–13)

But though we, or an angel from heaven, preach any other gospel unto you than that which we have preached unto you, let him be accursed. As we said before, so say I now again, If any man preach any other gospel unto you than that ye have received, let him be accursed. (Gal. 1:8–9)

Proving what is acceptable unto the Lord. 11 And have no fellowship with the unfruitful works of darkness, but rather reprove them. For it is a shame even to speak of those things which are done of them in secret. (Eph. 5:10–12)

Now we command you, brethren, in the name of our Lord Jesus Christ, that ye withdraw yourselves from every brother that walketh disorderly, and not after the tradition which he received of us. For yourselves know how ye ought to follow us: for we behaved not ourselves disorderly among you; Neither did we eat any man's bread for nought; but wrought with labour and travail night and day, that we might not be chargeable to any of you: Not because we have not power, but to make ourselves an ensample unto you to follow us. For even when we were with you, this we commanded you, that if any would not work, neither should he eat. For we hear that there are some which walk among you disorderly, working not at all, but are busybodies. Now them that are such we command and exhort by our Lord Jesus Christ, that with quietness they work, and eat their own bread. But ye, brethren, be not weary in well doing. And if any man obey not our word by this epistle, note that man, and have no company with him, that he may be ashamed. Yet count him not as an enemy, but admonish him as a brother. (Thess. 3:6–15)

If any man teach otherwise, and consent not to wholesome words, even the words of our Lord Jesus Christ, and to the doctrine which is according to godliness; He is proud, knowing nothing, but doting about questions and strifes of words, whereof cometh envy, strife, railings, evil surmisings, Perverse disputings of men of corrupt minds, and destitute of the truth, supposing that gain is godliness: from such withdraw thyself. (1 Tim. 6:3–5)

This know also, that in the last days perilous times shall come. For men shall be lovers of their own selves, covetous, boasters, proud, blasphemers, disobedient to parents, unthankful, unholy, Without natural affection, trucebreakers, false accusers, incontinent, fierce, despisers of those that are good, Traitors, heady, highminded, lovers of pleasures more than lovers of God; Having a form of godliness, but denying the power thereof: from such turn away. (2 Tim. 3:1–5)

A man that is an heretick after the first and second admonition reject; Knowing that he that is such is subverted, and sinneth, being condemned of himself. (Titus 3:10–11)

Wherefore, beloved, seeing that ye look for such things, be diligent that ye may be found of him in peace, without spot, and blameless... Ye therefore, beloved, seeing ye know these things before, beware lest ye also, being led away with the error of the wicked, fall from your own stedfastness. But grow in grace, and in the knowledge of our Lord and Saviour Jesus Christ. To him be glory both now and for ever. Amen. (2 Pet. 3:14, 17–18)

If there come any unto you, and bring not this doctrine, receive him not into your house, neither bid him God speed: For he that biddeth him God speed is partaker of his evil deeds. (2 John 1:10–11)

[52] Now the Spirit speaketh expressly, that in the latter times some shall depart from the faith, giving heed to seducing spirits, and doctrines of devils; Speaking lies in hypocrisy; having their conscience seared with a hot iron; Forbidding to marry, and commanding to abstain from meats, which God hath created to be received with thanksgiving of them which believe and know the truth. (1 Tim. 4:1–3)

But evil men and seducers shall wax worse and worse, deceiving, and being deceived. (2 Tim. 3:13)

For the time will come when they will not endure sound doctrine; but after their own lusts shall they heap to themselves teachers, having itching ears; 4 And they shall turn away their ears from the truth, and shall be turned unto fables. (2 Tim. 4:3–4)

This second epistle, beloved, I now write unto you; in both which I stir up your pure minds by way of remembrance: That ye may be mindful of the words which were spoken before by the holy prophets, and of the commandment of us the apostles of the Lord and Saviour: Knowing this first, that there shall come in the last days scoffers, walking after their own lusts, And saying, Where is the promise of his coming? for since the fathers fell asleep, all things continue as they were from the beginning of the creation. (2 Pet. 3:1–4)

53 And the Lord passed by before him, and proclaimed, The Lord, The Lord God, merciful and gracious, longsuffering, and abundant in goodness and truth. (Exod. 34:6)

The Lord is longsuffering, and of great mercy, forgiving iniquity and transgression, and by no means clearing the guilty, visiting the iniquity of the fathers upon the children unto the third and fourth generation. (Num. 14:18)

But thou, O Lord, art a God full of compassion, and gracious, longsuffering, and plenteous in mercy and truth. (Ps. 86:15)

The LORD is merciful and gracious, slow to anger, and plenteous in mercy. (Ps. 103:8)

But love ye your enemies, and do good, and lend, hoping for nothing again; and your reward shall be great, and ye shall be the children of the Highest: for he is kind unto the unthankful and to the evil. (Luke 6:35)

What if God, willing to shew his wrath, and to make his power known, endured with much longsuffering the vessels of wrath fitted to destruction. (Rom. 9:22)

Or despisest thou the riches of his goodness and forbearance and longsuffering; not knowing that the goodness of God leadeth thee to repentance? (Rom. 2:4)

The Lord is not slack concerning his promise, as some men count slackness; but is longsuffering to us-ward, not willing that any should perish, but that all should come to repentance. (2 Pet. 3:9)

54 If I regard iniquity in my heart, the Lord will not hear me. (Ps. 66:18)

And when ye spread forth your hands, I will hide mine eyes from you: yea, when ye make many prayers, I will not hear: your hands are full of blood. (Isa. 1:15)

But your iniquities have separated between you and your God, and your sins have hid his face from you, that he will not hear. (Isa. 59:2)

Therefore will I also deal in fury: mine eye shall not spare, neither will I have pity: and though they cry in mine ears with a loud voice, yet will I not hear them. (Ezek. 8:18)

But they refused to hearken, and pulled away the shoulder, and stopped their ears, that they should not hear. Therefore it is come to pass, that as he cried, and they would not hear; so they cried, and I would not hear, saith the Lord of hosts. (Zech. 7:11, 13)

55 Even as I have seen, they that plow iniquity, and sow wickedness, reap the same. (Job 4:8)

He [the wicked] made a pit, and digged it, and is fallen into the ditch which he made. His mischief shall return upon his own head, and his violent dealing shall come down upon his own pate. (Ps. 7:15–16)

The heart is deceitful above all things, and desperately wicked: who can know it? I the LORD search the heart, I try the reins, even to give every man according to his ways, and according to the fruit of his doings. (Jer. 17:9–10)

But I will punish you according to the fruit of your doings, saith the LORD: and I will kindle a fire in the forest thereof, and it shall devour all things round about it. (Jer. 21:14)

But as for them whose heart walketh after the heart of their detestable things and their abominations, I will recompense their way upon their own heads, saith the Lord GOD. (Ezek. 11:21)

For the wrath of God is revealed from heaven against all ungodliness and unrighteousness of men, who hold the truth in unrighteousness; Because that which may be known of God is manifest in them; for God hath shewed it unto them... Because that, when they knew God, they glorified him not as God, neither were thankful; but became vain in their imaginations, and their foolish heart was darkened. Professing themselves to be wise, they became fools... Wherefore God also gave them up to uncleanness through the lusts of their own hearts, to dishonour their own bodies between themselves... For this cause God gave them up unto vile affections: for even their women did change the natural use into that which is against nature... And even as they did not like to retain God in their knowledge, God gave them over to a reprobate mind, to do those things which are not convenient. (Rom. 1:18–19, 21–22, 24, 26, 28)

Be not deceived; God is not mocked: for whatsoever a man soweth, that shall he also reap. (Gal. 6:7)

56 The Lord shall send upon thee cursing, vexation, and rebuke, in all that thou settest thine hand unto for to do, until thou be destroyed, and until thou perish quickly; because of the wickedness of thy doings, whereby thou hast forsaken me. (Gal. 6:7)

You answered them, O Lord our God; You were to them God-Who-Forgives, though You took vengeance on their deeds. (Ps. 99:8)

Then shall they call upon me, but I will not answer; they shall seek me early, but they shall not find me: For that they hated knowledge, and did not choose the fear of the LORD: They would none of my counsel: they despised all my reproof. Therefore shall they eat of the fruit of their own way, and be filled with their own devices. (Prov. 1:28–31)

Therefore will I number you to the sword, and ye shall all bow down to the slaughter: because when I called, ye did not answer; when I spake, ye did not hear; but did evil before mine eyes, and did choose that wherein I delighted not. (Isa. 65:12)

I also will choose their delusions, and will bring their fears upon them; because when I called, none did answer; when I spake, they did not hear: but they did evil before mine eyes, and chose that in which I delighted not. (Isa. 66:4)

Thus saith the Lord of hosts, the God of Israel; Behold, I will bring upon this city and upon all her towns all the evil that I have pronounced against it, because they have hardened their necks, that they might not hear my words. (Jer. 19:15)

And they came in, and possessed it; but they obeyed not thy voice, neither walked in thy law; they have done nothing of all that thou commandedst them to do: therefore thou hast caused all this evil to come upon them... And they have turned unto me the back, and not the face: though I taught them, rising up early and teaching them, yet they have not hearkened to receive instruction. (Jer. 32:23, 33)

If ye will not hear, and if ye will not lay it to heart, to give glory unto my name, saith the Lord of hosts, I will even send a curse upon you, and I will curse your blessings: yea, I have cursed them already, because ye do not lay it to heart. (Mal. 2:2)

57 He is the Rock, his work is perfect: for all his ways are judgment: a God of truth and without iniquity, just and right is he... To me belongeth vengeance and recompence... (Deut. 32:4, 35a)

But the Lord shall endure for ever: he hath prepared his throne for judgment. And he shall judge the world in righteousness, he shall minister judgment to the people in uprightness... The LORD is known by the judgment which he executeth: the wicked is snared in the work of his own hands. (Ps. 9:7–8, 16)

O Lord God, to whom vengeance belongeth; O God, to whom vengeance belongeth, shew thyself. (Ps. 94:1)

For God shall bring every work into judgment, with every secret thing, whether it be good, or whether it be evil. (Eccles. 12:14)

Dearly beloved, avenge not yourselves, but rather give place unto wrath: for it is written, Vengeance is mine; I will repay, saith the Lord. (Rom. 12:19)

For we know him that hath said, Vengeance belongeth unto me, I will recompense, saith the Lord. And again, The Lord shall judge his people. (Heb. 10:30)

And I saw the dead, small and great, stand before God; and the books were opened: and another book was opened, which is the book of life: and the dead were judged out of those things which were written in the books, according to their works. And the sea gave up the dead which were in it; and death and hell delivered up the dead which were in them: and they were judged every man according to their works. (Rev. 20:12–13)

58 And they continued stedfastly in the apostles' doctrine and fellowship, and in breaking of bread, and in prayers. (Acts 2:42)

Praying us with much intreaty that we would receive the gift, and take upon us the fellowship of the ministering to the saints. (2 Cor. 8:4)

Not forsaking the assembling of ourselves together, as the manner of some is; but exhorting one another: and so much the more, as ye see the day approaching. (Heb. 10:25)

59 That which we have seen and heard declare we unto you, that ye also may have fellowship with us: and truly our fellowship is with the Father, and with his Son Jesus Christ... If we say that we have fellowship with him, and walk in darkness, we lie, and do not the truth: But if we walk in the light, as he is in the light, we have fellowship one with another, and the blood of Jesus Christ his Son cleanseth us from all sin. (1 John 1:3, 6–7)

And when she was baptized, and her household, she besought us, saying, If ye have judged me to be faithful to the Lord, come into my house, and abide there. And she constrained us. (Acts 16:15)

60 Paul wrote to the church in Rome, in Philippi, in Colossi, and in Thessalonica, commenting on their love, fellowship, and service to one another.

For I long to see you, that I may impart unto you some spiritual gift, to the end ye may be established; That is, that I may be comforted together with you by the mutual faith both of you and me. (Rom. 1:11–12)

I thank my God upon every remembrance of you, Always in every prayer of mine for you all making request with joy, For your fellowship in the gospel from the first day until now. (Phil. 1:3–5)

We give thanks to God and the Father of our Lord Jesus Christ, praying always for you, Since we heard of your faith in Christ Jesus, and of the love which ye have to all the saints. (Col. 1:3–4)

We are bound to thank God always for you, brethren, as it is meet, because that your faith groweth exceedingly, and the charity of every one of you all toward each other aboundeth. (2 Thess. 1:3)

61 And have no fellowship with the unfruitful works of darkness, but rather reprove them. (Eph. 5:11)

Be ye not unequally yoked together with unbelievers: for what fellowship hath righteousness with unrighteousness? and what communion hath light with darkness? And what concord hath Christ with Belial? or what part hath he that believeth with an infidel? And what agreement hath the temple of God with idols? for ye are the temple of the living God; as God hath said, I will dwell in them, and walk in them; and I will be their God, and they shall be my people. Wherefore come out from among them, and be ye separate saith the Lord, and touch not the unclean thing; and I will receive you, And will be a Father unto you, and ye shall be my sons and daughters, saith the Lord Almighty. (2 Cor. 6:14–18)

62 Can two walk together, except they be agreed? (Amos 3:3)

63 Brethren, if a man be overtaken in a fault, ye which are spiritual, restore such an one in the spirit of meekness; considering thyself, lest thou also be tempted. (Gal. 6:1)

Save others by snatching them from the fire; to others show mercy, mixed with fear—hating even the clothing stained by corrupted flesh. (Jude 1:23)

64 For the Son of man is come to save that which was lost. (Matt. 18:11)

For the Son of man is come to seek and to save that which was lost. (Luke 19:10)

65 For if, when we were enemies, we were reconciled to God by the death of his Son, much more, being reconciled, we shall be saved by his life. (Rom. 5:10)

And you, that were sometime alienated and enemies in your mind by wicked works, yet now hath he reconciled. (Col. 1:21)

66 And all things are of God, who hath reconciled us to himself by Jesus Christ, and hath given to us the ministry of reconciliation; to wit, that God was in Christ, reconciling the world unto himself, not imputing their trespasses unto them; and hath committed unto us the word of reconciliation. (2 Cor. 5:18–19)

Praying us with much intreaty that we would receive the gift, and take upon us the fellowship of the ministering to the saints. (2 Cor. 8:4)

As we have therefore opportunity, let us do good unto all men, especially unto them who are of the household of faith. (Gal. 6:10)

Now therefore ye are no more strangers and foreigners, but fellow citizens with the saints, and of the household of God. (Eph. 2:19)

67 I have planted, Apollos watered; but God gave the increase. For we are labourers together with God: ye are God's husbandry, ye are God's buildin. (1 Cor. 3:6, 9)

Whether any do enquire of Titus, he is my partner and fellow helper concerning you: or our brethren be enquired of, they are the messengers of the churches, and the glory of Christ. (2 Cor. 8:23)

For as touching the ministering to the saints, it is superfluous for me to write to you: For I know the forwardness of your mind, for which I boast of you to them of Macedonia, that Achaia was ready a year ago; and your zeal hath provoked very many. Yet have I sent the brethren, lest our boasting of you should be in vain in this behalf; that, as I said, ye may be ready: Lest haply if they of Macedonia come with me, and find you unprepared, we (that we say not, ye) should be ashamed in this same confident boasting. Therefore I thought it necessary to exhort the brethren, that they would go before unto you, and make up beforehand your bounty, whereof ye had notice before, that the same might be ready, as a matter of bounty, and not as of covetousness. But this I say, He which soweth sparingly shall reap also sparingly; and he which soweth bountifully shall reap also bountifully. (2 Cor. 9:1–6)

Yet I supposed it necessary to send to you Epaphroditus, my brother, and companion in labour, and fellow soldier, but your messenger, and he that ministered to my wants. (Phil. 2:25)

As ye also learned of Epaphras our dear fellowservant, who is for you a faithful minister of Christ. (Col. 1:7)

And sent Timotheus, our brother, and minister of God, and our fellow labourer in the gospel of Christ, to establish you, and to comfort you concerning your faith. (1 Thess. 3:2)

Beloved, thou doest faithfully whatsoever thou doest to the brethren, and to strangers; Which have borne witness of thy charity before the church: whom if thou bring forward on their journey after a godly sort, thou shalt do well: Because that for his name's sake they went forth, taking nothing of the Gentiles. We therefore ought to receive such, that we might be fellow helpers to the truth. (3 John 1:5–8)

68 Now ye are the body of Christ, and members in particular. And God hath set some in the church, first apostles, secondarily prophets, thirdly teachers, after that miracles, then gifts of healings, helps, governments, diversity of tongues. (1 Cor. 12:27–28)

And he gave some, apostles; and some, prophets; and some, evangelists; and some, pastors and teachers; for the perfecting of the saints, for the work of the ministry, for the edifying of the body of Christ: Till we all come in the unity of the faith, and of the knowledge of the Son of god, unto a perfect man, unto the measure of the stature of the fullness of Christ:... From whom the whole body fitly joined together and compacted by that which every joint supplieth, according to the effectual working in the measure of every part, maketh increase of the body unto the edifying of itself in love. (Eph. 4:11–13, 16)

69 For as we have many members in one body, and all members have not the same office: So we, being many, are one body in Christ, and every one members one of another. Having then gifts differing according to the grace that is given to us, whether prophecy, let us prophesy according to the proportion of faith; Or ministry, let us wait on our ministering: or he that teacheth, on teaching; Or he that exhorteth, on exhortation: he that giveth, let him do it with simplicity; he that ruleth, with diligence; he that sheweth mercy, with cheerfulness. (Rom. 12:4–8)

That we henceforth be no more children, tossed to and fro, and carried about with every wind of doctrine, by the sleight of men, and cunning craftiness, whereby they lie in wait to deceive; But speaking the truth in love, may grow up into him in all things, which is the head, even Christ: From whom the whole body fitly joined together and compacted by that which every joint supplieth, according to the effectual working in the measure of every part, maketh increase of the body unto the edifying of itself in love. (Eph. 4:14–16)

For as the body is one, and hath many members, and all the members of that one body, being many, are one body: so also is Christ. For by one Spirit are we all baptized into one body, whether we be Jews or Gentiles, whether we be bond or free; and have been all made to drink into one Spirit. For the body is not one member, but many. If the foot shall say, Because I am not the hand, I am not of the body; is it therefore not of the body? And if the ear shall say, Because I am not the eye, I am not of the body; is it therefore not of the body? If the whole body were an eye, where were the hearing? If the whole were hearing, where were the smelling? But now hath God set the members every one of them in the body, as it hath pleased him. And if they were all one member, where were the body? But now are they many members, yet but one body. And the eye cannot say unto the hand, I have no need of thee: nor again the head to the feet, I have no need of you. Nay, much more those members of the body, which seem to be more feeble, are necessary: And those members of the body, which we think to be less honourable, upon these we bestow more abundant honour; and our uncomely parts have more abundant comeliness. For our comely parts have no need: but God hath tempered the body together, having given more abundant honour to that part which lacked. That there should be no schism in the body; but that the members should have the same care one for another. And whether one member suffer, all the members suffer with it; or one member be honoured, all the members rejoice with it. Now ye are the body of Christ, and members in particular. (1 Cor. 12:12–27)

70 As ye also learned of Epaphras our dear fellowservant, who is for you a faithful minister of Christ. (Col. 1:7)

And sent Timotheus, our brother, and minister of God, and our fellow labourer in the gospel of Christ, to establish you, and to comfort you concerning your faith. (1 Thess. 3:2)

The Lord grant unto him that he may find mercy of the Lord in that day: and in how many things he ministered unto me at Ephesus, thou knowest very well. (2 Tim. 1:18)

For God is not unrighteous to forget your work and labour of love, which ye have shewed toward his name, in that ye have ministered to the saints, and do minister. (Heb. 6:10)

As every man hath received the gift, even so minister the same one to another, as good stewards of the manifold grace of God. If any man speak, let him speak as the oracles of God; if any man minister, let him do it as of the ability which God giveth: that God in all things may be glorified through Jesus Christ, to whom be praise and dominion for ever and ever. Amen. (1 Pet. 4:10–11)

How? Brotherly Kindness and the Law of Liberty

John and Jason sat down to eat at Jason's house and prayed over the meal. Seeing the perfectly cooked food in the serving bowl, John asked, "Where did you buy the meat?" As Jason cut off a large slice for himself, he explained at which market he had bought it.

John sat back in his chair with an expression of disgust. "This meat is from the pagan temple sacrifices. You call yourself a Christian and a true follower of Jesus, but you eat meat that was sacrificed to idols!"

Jason swallowed his first bite and protested, "I did not participate in the sacrifice to the idol at the temple. This is just the extra meat that was sold in the market. This is the best and freshest meat in the city. We know an idol is nothing. All the food in the world is owned by the Lord. What we eat does not make us unclean.[1] Further, we have thanked God for it and asked His sanctifying blessing.[2] So eat and enjoy."[3]

John stared at Jason and pronounced his condemnation: "Eating meat sacrificed to an idol of the devil means you are joining in the sacrifice itself, honoring that false god. You have participated in idol worship and have severely dirtied your Christian testimony. If I eat even one bite, my whole testimony as a believer will be called into question by my family and relatives."

The two men in this hypothetical conversation were members of the first-century church. Saved out of a very conservative Jewish background, John had been taught that eating some of a sacrifice was equal to taking part in the sacrifice.[4] Further, the Old Testament strictly forbade participating in idol worship.[5] As a believer in Christ, he continued to have a deep respect for his Jewish heritage.

Jason had been a Gentile idol worshiper who became a Christian.[6] As a believer, he understood that idols were just so much stone, metal, and wood that men have fashioned. Now he counted his former idolatry as worthless and the idols as nothing.[7]

Most of the earliest believers in the Lord Jesus Christ were out of the Jewish religion. Then believers from among the Gentiles began pouring into the churches. Each group brought in their preferences as to how the Christian faith should be lived. A major disagreement between the Jewish and pagan background believers centered on eating meat that had been offered to idols. These groups struggled to understand and accept one another's liberty in Christ.

Brotherly Kindness: Understanding Our Liberty in Christ and Its Limits under the Law of Liberty

The Meaning of the Word *Liberty*

One Greek noun, translated in the New Testament as *liberty*, is *eleutheros*, which has the basic meaning of freedom.[8] Another Greek noun translated *liberty* is *exousia*, which has several shades of meaning: permission, authority, right, liberty, or power to do something.[9]

Consider the illustration of a very rich man who bought a huge house for his large family. As each member of his family came into the dwelling for the first time, he presented them with a key to the house. The door going in was always unlocked for more to enter, but the key signified their father-granted authority to be in that house. They each had the right, the freedom, and the liberty to live as his family in that house.

The Breadth of Our Liberty in Christ

As God's children in His house, we have a glorious liberty.[10] To comprehend the greatness of that liberty, we must understand the completeness of our salvation. Before we were born again, we walked in this world condemned by the law under *God the Righteous Judge.*[11] When we accepted Jesus and His sacrifice for our sin,[12] God identified us with Jesus in His death, burial, and resurrection.[13] In Scripture, death signifies complete separation.[14] So through Jesus's sacrificial death, we were separated from the Law,[15] the power of sin,[16] and the second death.[17]

Walking through life, and eventually into eternity, we have the Everlasting Key to the household of God, which is the Seal of the Spirit of God.[18] In the illustration of the rich man's house, no one goes out, turning in their key, losing their status as family. Scripture says we are born into God's kingdom.[19] Once born, we cannot be "unborn." Moreover, the seal of the Spirit remains a part of us until our final redemption in eternal glory.[20]

We live by grace[21] as new creations in God's family.[22] We no longer live as slaves of sin but servants and children of *God our loving Father.*[23] Thankfully, we are no longer under *condemnation* by *God the Judge.*[24] In Christ, we have that glorious freedom[25] and should not seek to go back into living as if we are under the Law.[26]

We are eternally separated from condemnation under the law in the courtroom of *God the Judge.* However, that separation does not mean that we have freedom to sin.[27] When we do disobey, our sin is against our loving *Father.*[28] We must repent but still may receive His *discipline.*[29]

What Areas of Our Christian Life Have Liberty?

While we believers already have received a gracious entry into God's family,[30] we also should seek entry into a local fellowship of believers.[31] In that fellowship, we may have differing *preferences* of what foods we can eat, what is appropriate to wear, what activities are permissible, what special days to observe and how to observe them, what should be included in the church service or not included, what to watch on TV, what music to listen to, and more. Many *personal preferences* in our *Christian conduct* are due to our own personal background and culture. Christian liberty applies to these conduct areas.

In contrast to preferences, biblical doctrine is true in all cultures all the time. Such truth as salvation only through Jesus[32] and salvation by grace through faith[33] never changes. Further, basic moral principles—such as do not lie, do not steal, and do not commit adultery—always apply to our lives.[34] Problems arise when we see some *conduct as a simple personal preference* while others rightly or wrongly view it as a moral or even a doctrinal issue.

What Are the Limits of Our Preferences within Our Father's Family?

The Word of God, especially in the teachings of Paul, uses the issue of eating meat offered to idols to explain the limits to our Christian liberty. Understanding and carefully obeying these limits will bring blessing to our ministry.[35]

Do Not Let Preferences Be Driven by Pride

Pride is always a problem.[36] It causes strife,[37] bringing disaster to us and others.[38] Imagine one member of a large household who thinks he or she is always right, who always pushes his or her own ideas, and who never listens respectfully to others.

The fact is that none of us have all the answers.[39] Instead, we need to be humbly grateful for the tremendous mercy and grace of God that saved wretched sinners like us.[40] We should be thankful our names are written in the Lamb's Book of Life.[41] A further antidote to pride is focusing on loving the Lord and others with a servant heart.[42]

We Should Limit Our Preferences If They Have a Bad Effect on Others

What we consider a permissible preference in our Christian liberty, others may see as sinful.[43] Moreover, if a fellow believer sees us do something that he considers wrong, he might follow our example, sinning against his own conscience before God. Thus, his Christian life will be hindered.[44] When we harm another believer in this manner, we are sinning both against him and against Christ.[45]

When we allow a preference in our lives, a personal struggle is in our hearts while living and fellowshipping with those who do not allow it. In our hearts, we are free, but we may be judged by others.[46] What should we do? We must walk through life being sensitive to those around us[47] because whatever we do impacts the lives of others.[48] Paul tells us to walk in love toward others,[49] not offending them,[50] and to continue seeking what is good for them.[51] When no one is offended, we can continue in what we allow in our lives. But when fellow believers are troubled by what we allow, we should stop and deny ourselves[52] so as not to offend or weaken them.[53]

Be Patient, Seeking Unity and Not Judging

Imagine someone in a large family mentally and emotionally beating down another with constant criticism and coldly pushing them to the fringes of the family fellowship. By contrast, faithful believers are patient, not arguing with the person who struggles with his or her liberty.[54] We should not judge them, leaving instead all judgment to God.[55] Let us not be self-righteous Pharisees in our treatment of others.[56] Instead, we must judge ourselves[57] so that we are careful not to harm another believer.[58]

Conflicts will arise and must be addressed.[59] When we have a conflict with others, we should go to them personally, whether they have a problem with us[60] or we with them.[61] We should strive to follow God's example of mercy and forgiveness[62] so that we do not become divided.[63] If we cannot resolve it just between us, then we need to bring in others who can help mediate a solution. If we cannot resolve it as a group, then we bring it to the church to decide.[64]

We have all seen disaster in families whose conflicts never have been properly addressed. In a church fellowship, moral and doctrinal problems should be dealt with directly.[65] And liberty issues also may become problems church wide and need attention.[66] Unity and being of one mind should be our goal in the church.[67]

We Should Limit Our Preferences If They Hinder Our Service to God

Within a well-run large family, each person has responsibilities. Picture one person being so involved in his or her own personal activity, no longer considering important responsibilities to the group. That activity may not be wrong and may be perfectly acceptable. However, it still interferes with a task they were given.

For example, Paul certainly had the liberty to be married.[68] However, for him, in his ministry, marriage would have been a hindrance.[69] Also, he had the scriptural authority to be supported by the churches that he was starting.[70] Yet he worked to sustain himself and did not live by funds from the new churches. He was an example of self-denial to them.[71] Instead of pleasing himself, he aimed to be of service wherever he went, humbly working to be of spiritual benefit to others so that he could reach more people.[72] A basic goal of believers is not our own pleasure or advancement but the salvation and spiritual growth of others.[73]

We Should Limit Our Preferences If They Are Not Helpful to Us Personally

Envisage someone in a large family trying to perform his responsibilities while performing some useless activity. The activity itself may not be wrong, so it does not offend anyone. But it does not help us grow in Christ. Of all the liberty choices we have, some are just not beneficial to us in our Christian walk.[74]

We Should Limit Our Preferences If They Encourage Sin in Our Lives

In our walk with Christ, we may secretly want to keep an activity of the old life or some sinful association. We may wrongly use our liberty in Christ as a covering of the activity or association, hiding our wrong desires[75] and creating an idol in our heart.[76] However, we must be careful to judge our own lives, or we can fall into sin.[77] The goal of our lives is to glorify God,[78] not to satisfy our own lusts and desires.[79]

Certainly, we should never seek wicked activities and harden our hearts against the convicting work of the Lord and His Word.[80] The example of the nation of Israel teaches us about the consequences of turning back into sin.[81] They were called out of Egypt to be a nation that follows God, and they received multiple blessings.[82] However, some still wanted to pursue things that they had back in Egypt instead of following God.[83] Their lust of the flesh was a form of idolatry, which led to immorality. Consequently, God severely judged them.[84]

Believers should not fool themselves that they have "arrived," but walk circumspectly,[85] guarding against displeasing the Lord.[86] Thankfully, our gracious Father God is ready and able to help us escape sinful temptations.[87]

Each of us needs to be fully persuaded in our own mind what is a permissible preference in our liberty.[88]

Throwing aside any harmful or sinful use of liberty, our desire is to serve God and others in love.[89]

What is the special character of that love?

Notes

1 And he saith unto them, Are ye so without understanding also? Do ye not perceive, that whatsoever thing from without entereth into the man, it cannot defile him; Because it entereth not into his heart, but into the belly, and goeth out into the draught, purging all meats? And he said, That which cometh out of the man, that defileth the man. For from within, out of the heart of men, proceed evil thoughts, adulteries, fornications, murders, Thefts, covetousness, wickedness, deceit, lasciviousness, an evil eye, blasphemy, pride, foolishness: All these evil things come from within, and defile the man. (Mark 7:18–23)

2 For every creature of God is good, and nothing to be refused, if it be received with thanksgiving: for it is sanctified by the word of God and prayer. (1 Tim. 4:4–5)

3 Whatsoever is sold in the shambles, that eat, asking no question for conscience sake. (1 Cor. 10:25)

4 Behold Israel after the flesh: are not they which eat of the sacrifices partakers of the altar. (1 Cor. 10:18)

5 For thou shalt worship no other god: for the Lord, whose name is Jealous, is a jealous God: Lest thou make a covenant with the inhabitants of the land, and they go a whoring after their gods, and do sacrifice unto their gods, and one call thee, and thou eat of his sacrifice. (Exod. 34:14–15)

And they shall no more offer their sacrifices unto devils, after whom they have gone a whoring. This shall be a statute for ever unto them throughout their generations. (Lev. 17:7)

6 For they themselves shew of us what manner of entering in we had unto you, and how ye turned to God from idols to serve the living and true God. (1 Thess. 1:9)

For the time past of our life may suffice us to have wrought the will of the Gentiles, when we walked in lasciviousness, lusts, excess of wine, revelings, banquetings, and abominable idolatries. (1 Pet. 4:3)

7 Their idols are silver and gold, the work of men's hands. They have mouths, but they speak not: eyes have they, but they see not: They have ears, but they hear not: noses have they, but they smell not: They have hands, but they handle not: feet have they, but they walk not: neither speak they through their throat. They that make them are like unto them; so is ever one that trusteth in them. (Ps. 115:4–8) (See also Psalm 135:15–18.)

As concerning therefore the eating of those things that are offered in sacrifice unto idols, we know that an idol is nothing in the world, and that there is none other God but One. For though there be that are called gods, whether in heaven or in earth, (as there be gods many, and lords many,) But to us there is but one

God, the Father, of whom are all things, and we in him; and one Lord Jesus Christ, by whom are all things, and we by him. (1 Cor. 8:4–6)

8 Spiros Zodhiates, *The Complete Word Study Dictionary, New Testament* (Iowa Falls: World Bible Publishers, 1992), 566.

9 Zodhiates, 606.

10 Because the creature itself also shall be delivered from the bondage of corruption into the glorious liberty [*eleutheros*: freedom] of the children of God. (Rom. 8:21)

11 But the Lord shall endure for ever: he hath prepared his throne for judgment. And he shall judge the world in righteousness, he shall minister judgment to the people in uprightness. (Ps. 9:7–8)

And the heavens shall declare his righteousness: for God is judge himself... (Ps. 50:6)

But after thy hardness and impenitent heart treasurest up unto thyself wrath against the day of wrath and revelation of the righteous judgment of God; Who will render to every man according to his deeds:... For there is no respect of persons with God. (Rom. 2:5–6, 11)

12 For even Christ our Passover is sacrificed for us. (1 Cor. 5:7b)

And walk in love, as Christ also hath loved us, and hath given himself for us an offering and a sacrifice to God for a sweet-smelling savour. (Eph. 5:2)

But now once in the end of the world hath he appeared to put away sin by the sacrifice of himself. (Heb. 9:26b)

But this man, after he had offered one sacrifice for sins for ever, sat down on the right hand of God. (Heb. 10:12)

13 Know ye not, that so many of us as were baptized into Jesus Christ were baptized into his death? Therefore we are buried with him by baptism into death: that like as Christ was raised up from the dead by the glory of the Father, even so we also should walk in newness of life... Knowing this, that our old man is crucified with him, that the body of sin might be destroyed, that henceforth we should not serve sin. For he that is dead is freed from sin. Now if we be dead with Christ, we believe that we shall also live with him... For in that he died, he died unto sin once: but in that he liveth, he liveth unto God. Likewise reckon ye also yourselves to be dead indeed unto sin, but alive unto God through Jesus Christ our Lord. (Rom. 6:3–4, 6-8, 10–11)

In whom also ye are circumcised with the circumcision made without hands, in putting off the body of the sins of the flesh by the circumcision of Christ: Buried with him in baptism, wherein also ye are risen with him through the faith of the operation of God, who hath raised him from the dead. And you, being dead in your sins and the uncircumcision of your flesh, hath he quickened together with him, having forgiven you all trespasses; Blotting out the handwriting of ordinances that was against us, which was contrary to us, and took it out of the way, nailing it to his cross. (Col. 2:11–14)

¹⁴ The wife is bound by the law as long as her husband liveth; but if her husband be dead, she is at liberty [*eleatheros*: freedom] to be married to whom she will; only in the Lord. (1 Cor. 7:39)

¹⁵ Know ye not, brethren, (for I speak to them that know the law,) how that the law hath dominion over a man as long as he liveth? For the woman which hath an husband is bound by the law to her husband so long as he liveth; but if the husband be dead, she is loosed from the law of her husband. So then if, while her husband liveth, she be married to another man, she shall be called an adulteress: but if her husband be dead, she is free from that law; so that she is no adulteress, though she be married to another man. Wherefore, my brethren, ye also are become dead to the law by the body of Christ; that ye should be married to another, even to him who is raised from the dead, that we should bring forth fruit unto God. For when we were in the flesh, the motions of sins, which were by the law, did work in our members to bring forth fruit unto death. But now we are delivered from the law, that being dead wherein we were held; that we should serve in newness of spirit, and not in the oldness of the letter. (Rom. 7:1–6)

For Christ is the end of the law for righteousness to everyone that believeth. (Rom. 10:4)

Christ hath redeemed us from the curse of the law, being made a curse for us: for it is written, Cursed is every one that hangeth on a tree. (Gal. 3:13)

Having abolished in his flesh the enmity, even the law of commandments contained in ordinances; for to make in himself of twain one new man, so making peace. (Eph. 2:15)

¹⁶ As far as the east is from the west, so far hath he removed our transgressions from us. (Ps. 103:12)

For he that is dead is freed from sin… For sin shall not have dominion over you: for ye are not under the law, but under grace. (Rom. 6:7, 14)

But God forbid that I should glory, save in the cross of our Lord Jesus Christ, by whom the world is crucified unto me, and I unto the world. (Gal. 6:14)

Who hath delivered us from the power of darkness, and hath translated us into the kingdom of his dear Son. (Col. 1:13)

For by one offering he hath perfected forever them that are sanctified… And their sins and iniquities will I remember no more. (Heb. 10:14, 17)

¹⁷ For the law of the Spirit of life in Christ Jesus hath made me free from the law of sin and death. For what the law could not do, in that it was weak through the flesh, God sending his own Son in the likeness of sinful flesh, and for sin, condemned sin in the flesh: That the righteousness of the law might be fulfilled in us, who walk not after the flesh, but after the Spirit. (Rom. 8:2–4)

[God] Who delivered us from so great a death, and doth deliver: in whom we trust that he will yet deliver us. (2 Cor. 2:10)

But we see Jesus, who was made a little lower than the angels for the suffering of death, crowned with glory and honor; that he by the grace of God should taste death for every man… Forasmuch then as the children are partakers of flesh and blood, he also himself likewise took part of the same; that through death he might destroy him that had the power of death, that is, the devil; And deliver them who through fear of death were all their lifetime subject to bondage. (Heb. 2:9, 14–15)

Verily, verily, I say unto you, He that heareth my word, and believeth on him that sent me, hath everlasting life, and shall not come into condemnation; but is passed from death unto life. (John 5:24)

18 For all the promises of God in him are yea, and in him Amen, unto the glory of God by us. Now he which stablisheth us with you in Christ, and hath anointed us, is God; Who hath also sealed us, and given the earnest of the Spirit in our hearts. (2 Cor. 1:20–22)

In whom [Christ] also we have obtained an inheritance, being predestinated according to the purpose of him who worketh all things after the counsel of his own will: That we should be to the praise of his glory, who first trusted in Christ. In whom ye also trusted, after that ye heard the word of truth, the gospel of your salvation: in whom also after that ye believed, ye were sealed with that holy Spirit of promise, Which is the earnest of our inheritance until the redemption of the purchased possession, unto the praise of his glory. (Eph. 1:11–14)

19 But as many as received him, to them gave he power to become the sons of God, even to them that believe on his name: Which were born, not of blood, nor of the will of the flesh, nor of the will of man, but of God. (John 1:12–13)

Jesus answered and said unto him, Verily, verily, I say unto thee, Except a man be born again, he cannot see the kingdom of God. Nicodemus saith unto him, How can a man be born when he is old? can he enter the second time into his mother's womb, and be born? Jesus answered, Verily, verily, I say unto thee, Except a man be born of water and of the Spirit, he cannot enter into the kingdom of God. That which is born of the flesh is flesh; and that which is born of the Spirit is spirit. Marvel not that I said unto thee, Ye must be born again. The wind bloweth where it listeth, and thou hearest the sound thereof, but canst not tell whence it cometh, and whither it goeth: so is every one that is born of the Spirit. (John 3:3–8)

Blessed be the God and Father of our Lord Jesus Christ, which according to his abundant mercy hath begotten us again unto a lively hope by the resurrection of Jesus Christ from the dead, To an inheritance incorruptible, and undefiled, and that fadeth not away, reserved in heaven for you, Who are kept by the power of God through faith unto salvation ready to be revealed in the last time… Being born again, not of corruptible seed, but of incorruptible, by the word of God, which liveth and abidethfor ever. (1 Pet. 1:3–5, 23)

Whosoever believeth that Jesus is the Christ is born of God: and every one that loveth him that begat loveth him also that is begotten of him. (1 John 5:1)

²⁰ In whom ye also trusted, after that ye heard the word of truth, the gospel of your salvation: in whom also after that ye believed, ye were sealed with that holy Spirit of promise, Which is the earnest of our inheritance until the redemption of the purchased possession, unto the praise of his glory. (Eph. 1:13–14)

And grieve not the holy Spirit of God, whereby ye are sealed unto the day of redemption. (Eph. 4:30)

Nevertheless the foundation of God standeth sure, having this seal, The Lord knoweth them that are his. And, let every one that nameth the name of Christ depart from iniquity. (2 Tim. 2:19)

And when the chief Shepherd shall appear, ye shall receive a crown of glory that fadeth not away... But the God of all grace, who hath called us unto his eternal glory by Christ Jesus, after that ye have suffered a while, make you perfect, stablish, strengthen, settle you. (1 Pet. 5:4, 10)

Now unto him that is able to keep you from falling, and to present you faultless before the presence of his glory with exceeding joy. (Jude 1:24)

²¹ By whom also we have access by faith into this grace wherein we stand, and rejoice in hope of the glory of God. (Rom. 5:2)

For sin shall not have dominion over you: for ye are not under the law, but under grace. (Rom. 6:14)

For the law was given by Moses, but grace and truth came by Jesus Christ. (John 1:17)

Being justified freely by His grace through the redemption that is in Christ Jesus. (Rom. 3:24)

To the praise of the glory of his grace, wherein he hath made us accepted in the beloved. In whom we have redemption through his blood, the forgiveness of sins, according to the riches of his grace. (Eph. 1:6–7)

²² Who hath delivered us from the power of darkness, and hath translated us into the kingdom of his dear Son. (Col. 1:13)

But after that the kindness and love of God our Savior toward man appeared,... Which he shed on us abundantly through Jesus Christ our Savior; That being justified by grace, we should be made heirs according to the hope of eternal life. (Titus 3:4, 6–7)

For ye have not received the spirit of bondage again to fear; but ye have received the Spirit of adoption, whereby we cry, Abba, Father... And if children, then heirs; heirs of God, and join-heirs with Christ. (Rom. 8:15, 17a)

And because ye are sons, God hath sent forth the Spirit of his son into your hearts, crying, Abba, Father. (Gal. 4:6)

²³ For the Father himself loveth you, because ye have loved me, and have believed that I came out from God. (John 16:27)

But God be thanked, that ye were the servants of sin, but ye have obeyed from the heart that form of doctrine which was delivered you. Being then made free from sin, ye became the servants of righteousness... For when ye were the servants of sin, ye were free from righteousness... But now being made free from sin, and become servants to God, ye have your fruit unto holiness, and the end everlasting life. (Rom. 6:17–18, 20, 22)

But when the fullness of the time was come, God sent forth his Son, made of a woman, made under the law, To redeem them that were under the law, that we might receive the adoption of sons. And because ye are sons, God hath sent forth the Spirit of his Son into your hearts, crying, Abba, Father. (Gal. 4:4–6)

Peace be to the brethren, and love with faith, from God the Father and the Lord Jesus Christ. (Eph. 6:23)

And the Lord make you to increase and abound in love one toward another, and toward all men, even as we do toward you: To the end he may stablish your hearts unblameable in holiness before God, even our Father, at the coming of our Lord Jesus Christ with all his saints. (1 Thess. 3:12–13)

Behold, what manner of love the Father hath bestowed upon us, that we should be called the sons of God: therefore the world knoweth us not, because it knew him not. (1 John 3:1)

24 Verily, verily, I say unto you, He that heareth my word, and believeth on him that sent me, hath everlasting life, and shall not come into condemnation; but is passed from death unto life. (John 5:24)

There is therefore now no condemnation to them which are in Christ Jesus. (Rom. 8:1a)

25 And ye shall know the truth, and the truth shall make you free… If the Son therefore shall make you free, ye shall be free indeed. (John 8:32, 36)

Because the creature itself also shall be delivered from the bondage of corruption into the glorious liberty [eleutheros: freedom] of the children of God. (Rom. 8:21)

Now the Lord is that Spirit: and where the Spirit of the Lord is, there is liberty [*eleutheros*: freedom]. (2 Cor. 3:17)

26 But when the fulness of the time was come, God sent forth his Son, made of a woman, made under the law, To redeem them that were under the law, that we might receive the adoption of sons… But now, after that ye have known God, or rather are known of God, how turn ye again to the weak and beggarly elements, whereunto ye desire again to be in bondage? Ye observe days, and months, and times, and years… Stand fast therefore in the liberty [*eleutheros*: freedom] wherewith Christ hath made us free, and be not entangled again with the yoke of bondage. (Gal. 4:4–5, 9–10, 5:1)

27 What shall we say then? Shall we continue in sin, that grace may abound? God forbid. How shall we, that are dead to sin, live any longer therein? (Rom. 6:1–2)

28 But if ye do not forgive, neither will your Father which is in heaven forgive your trespasses. (Mark 11:26)

But if we walk in the light, as he is in the light, we have fellowship one with another, and the blood of Jesus Christ his Son cleanseth us from all sin. If we say that we have no sin, we deceive ourselves, and the truth is not in us. If we confess our sins, he is faithful and just to forgive us our sins, and to cleanse us from all unrighteousness. If we say that we have not sinned, we make him a liar, and his word is not in us... My little children, these things write I unto you, that ye sin not. And if any man sin, we have an advocate with the Father, Jesus Christ the righteous. (1 John 1:7–2:1)

29 And ye have forgotten the exhortation which speaketh unto you as unto children, My Son, despise not thou the chastening of the Lord, nor faint when thou art rebuked of him: For whom the Lord loveth He chasteneth, and sourgeth every son whom he receiveth. If ye endure chastening, God dealeth with you as with sons; for what son is he whom the father chasteneth not? But if ye be without chastisement, whereof all are partakers, then are ye bastards, and not sons. Furthermore we have had fathers of our flesh which corrected us, and we gave them reverence: shall we not much rather be in subjection unto the Father of spirits, and live? For they verily for a few days chastened us after their own pleasure; but he for our profit, that we might be partakers of his holiness. Now no chastening for the present seemeth to be joyous, but grievous: nevertheless afterward it yieldeth the peaceable fruit of righteousness unto them which are exercised thereby. (Heb. 12:5–11)

30 Now therefore ye are not more strangers and foreigners, but fellow citizens with the saints, and of the household of God. (Eph. 2:19)

For this cause I bow my knees unto the Father of our Lord Jesus Christ, Of whom the whole family in heaven and earth is named. (Eph. 3:14–15)

As we have therefore opportunity, let us do good unto all men, especially unto them who are of the household of faith. (Gal. 6:10)

31 Not forsaking the assembling of ourselves together, as the manner of some is; but exhorting one another: and so much the more, as ye see the day approaching. (Heb. 10:25)

32 Jesus saith unto him, I am the way, the truth, and the life: no man cometh unto the Father, but by me. (John 14:6)

Neither is there salvation in any other: for there is none other name under heaven given among men, whereby we must be saved. (Acts 4:12)

33 By whom also we have access by faith into this grace wherein we stand, and rejoice in hope of the glory of God. (Rom. 5:2)

Even when we were dead in sins, hath quickened us together with Christ, (by grace ye are saved;) And hath raised us up together, and made us sit together in heavenly places in Christ Jesus: That in the ages to come he might shew the exceeding riches of his grace in his kindness toward us through Christ Jesus. For by grace are ye saved through faith; and that not of yourselves: it is the gift of God: Not of works, lest any man should boast. (Eph. 2:5–8)

34 For this, Thou shalt not commit adultery, Thou shalt not kill, Thou shalt not steal, Thou shalt not bear false witness, Thou shalt not covet; and if there be any other commandment, it is briefly comprehended in this saying, namely, Thou shalt love thy neighbour as thyself. Love worketh no ill to his neighbour: therefore love is the fulfilling of the law. (Rom. 13:9–10)

35 But whoso looketh into the perfect law of liberty[*eleutheros*: freedom], and continueth therein, he being not a forgetful hearer, but a doer of the work, this man shall be blessed in his deed. (James 1:25)

36 The fear of the LORD is to hate evil: pride, and arrogancy, and the evil way, and the froward mouth, do I hate. (Prov. 8:13)

He is in the way of life that keepeth instruction: but he that refuseth reproof erreth. (Prov. 10:17)

And these things, brethren, I have in a figure transferred to myself and to Apollos for your sakes; that ye might learn in us not to think of men above that which is written, that no one of you be puffed up for one against another. For who maketh thee to differ from another? and what hast thou that thou didst not receive? now if thou didst receive it, why dost thou glory, as if thou hadst not received it? (1 Cor. 4:6–7)

Now as touching things offered unto idols, we know that we all have knowledge. Knowledge puffeth up, but charity edifieth. (1 Cor. 8:1)

For all that is in the world, the lust of the flesh, and the lust of the eyes, and the pride of life, is not of the Father, but is of the world. (1 John 2:16)

37 Only by pride cometh contention: but with the well advised is wisdom. (Prov. 13:10)

He that is of a proud heart stirreth up strife: but he that putteth his trust in the Lord shall be made fat. (Prov. 28:25)

38 Wherefore let him that thinketh he standeth take heed lest he fall. (1 Cor. 10:12)

When pride cometh, then cometh shame: but with the lowly is wisdom. (Prov. 11:2)

Pride goeth before destruction, and an haughty spirit before a fall. (Prov. 16:18)

A man's pride shall bring him low: but honour shall uphold the humble in spirit. (Prov. 29:23)

39 And if any man think that he knoweth any thing, he knoweth nothing yet as he ought to know. (1 Cor. 8:2)

40 There is no soundness in my flesh because of thine anger; neither is there any rest in my bones because of my sin. For mine iniquities are gone over mine head: as an heavy burden they are too heavy for me. My wounds stink and are corrupt because of my foolishness. I am troubled; I am bowed down greatly; I go mourning all the day long... I am feeble and sore broken: I have roared by reason of the disquietness of my heart... My heart panteth, my strength faileth me: as for the light of mine eyes, it also is gone from me... For I am ready to halt, and my sorrow is continually before me. For I will declare mine iniquity; I will be sorry for my sin... Make haste to help me, O Lord my salvation. (Ps. 38:3–6, 8, 10, 17–18, 220)

And the publican, standing afar off, would not lift up so much as his eyes unto heaven, but smote upon his breast, saying, God be merciful to me a sinner. (Luke 18:13)

O wretched man that I am! Who shall deliver me from the body of this death? (Rom. 7:24)

But God commendeth his love toward us, in that, while we were yet sinners, Christ died for us. (Rom. 5:8)

And you hath he quickened, who were dead in trespasses and sins; Wherein in time past ye walked according to the course of this world, according to the prince of the power of the air, the spirit that now worketh in the children of disobedience: Among whom also we all had our conversation in times past in the lusts of our flesh, fulfilling the desires of the flesh and of the mind; and were by nature the children of wrath, even as others. But God, who is rich in mercy, for his great love wherewith he loved us, Even when we were dead in sins, hath quickened us together with Christ, (by grace ye are saved;) And hath raised us up together, and made us sit together in heavenly places in Christ Jesus: That in the ages to come he might shew the exceeding riches of his grace in his kindness toward us through Christ Jesus. (Eph. 2:1–7)

41 Notwithstanding in this rejoice not, that the spirits are subject unto you; but rather rejoice, because your names are written in heaven. (Luke 10:20)

But if any man love God, the same is known of him. (1 Cor. 8:3)

And I intreat thee also, true yokefellow, help those women which laboured with me in the gospel, with Clement also, and with other my fellowlabourers, whose names are in the book of life. (Phil. 4:3)

He that overcometh, the same shall be clothed in white raiment; and I will not blot out his name out of the book of life, but I will confess his name before my Father, and before his angels. (Rev. 3:5)

And I saw the dead, small and great, stand before God; and the books were opened: and another book was opened, which is the book of life: and the dead were judged out of those things which were written in the books, according to their works... And whosoever was not found written in the book of life was cast into the lake of fire. (Rev. 20:12, 15)

And there shall in no wise enter into it any thing that defileth, neither whatsoever worketh abomination, or maketh a lie: but they which are written in the Lamb's book of life. (Rev. 21:27)

42 And thou shalt love the Lord thy God with all thy heart, and with all thy soul, and with all thy mind, and with all thy strength: this is the first commandment. And the second is like, namely this, Thou shalt love thy neighbour as thyself. There is none other commandment greater than these. (Mark 12:30–31)

But ye shall not be so: but he that is greatest among you, let him be as the younger; and he that is chief, as he that doth serve. (Luke 22:26)

If any man serve me, let him follow me; and where I am, there shall also my servant be: if any man serve me, him will my Father honour. (John 12:26)

For he that in these things serveth Christ is acceptable to God, and approved of men. (Rom. 14:18)

For though I be free from all men, yet have I made myself servant unto all, that I might gain the more. And unto the Jews I became as a Jew, that I might gain the Jews; to them that are under the law, as under the law, that I might gain them that are under the law; To them that are without law, as without law, (being not without law to God, but under the law to Christ,) that I might gain them that are without law. To the weak became I as weak, that I might gain the weak: I am made all things to all men, that I might by all means save some. And this I do for the gospel's sake, that I might be partaker thereof with you. (1 Cor. 9:19–23)

Wherefore we receiving a kingdom which cannot be moved, let us have grace, whereby we may serve God acceptably with reverence and godly fear. (Heb. 12:28)

43 As concerning therefore the eating of those things that are offered in sacrifice unto idols, we know that an idol is nothing in the world, and that there is none other God but one… Howbeit there is not in every man that knowledge: for some with conscience of the idol unto this hour eat it as a thing offered unto an idol; and their conscience being weak is defiled. (1 Cor. 8:4, 7)

44 But take heed lest by any means this liberty [*exousia*: liberty] of yours become a stumbling block to them that are weak. For if any man see thee which hast knowledge sit at meat in the idol's temple, shall not the conscience of him which is weak be emboldened to eat those things which are offered to idols; And through thy knowledge shall the weak brother perish, for whom Christ died? (1 Cor. 8:9–11)

For meat destroy not the work of God. All things indeed are pure; but it is evil for that man who eateth with offence. (Rom. 14:20)

45 But when ye sin so against the brethren, and wound their weak conscience, ye sin against Christ. (1 Cor. 8:12)

46 Conscience, I say, not thine own, but of the other: for why is my liberty judged of another man's conscience? For if I by grace be a partaker, why am I evil spoken of for that for which I give thanks? (1 Cor. 10:29–30)

47 But if thy brother be grieved with thy meat, now walkest thou not charitably. Destroy not him with thy meat, for whom Christ died. (Rom. 14:15)

For ye were sometimes darkness, but now are ye light in the Lord: walk as children of light… See then that ye walk circumspectly, not as fools, but as wise. (Eph. 5:8, 15)

Nevertheless, whereto we have already attained, let us walk by the same rule, let us mind the same thing. (Phil. 3:16)

48 For none of us liveth to himself, and no man dieth to himself. (Rom. 14:7)

49 And walk in love, as Christ also hath loved us, and hath given himself for us an offering and a sacrifice to God for a sweet smelling savour. (Eph. 5:2)

50 Give none offence, neither to the Jews, nor to the Gentiles, nor to the church of God. (1 Cor. 10:32)

51 Let no man seek his own, but every man another's wealth. (1 Cor. 10:24)

52 It is good neither to eat flesh, nor to drink wine, nor any thing whereby thy brother stumbleth, or is offended, or is made weak. Hast thou faith? have it to thyself before God. Happy is he that condemneth not himself in that thing which he alloweth. And he that doubteth is damned if he eat, because he eateth not of faith: for whatsoever is not of faith is sin. (Rom. 14:21–23)

Wherefore, if meat make my brother to offend, I will eat no flesh while the world standeth, lest I make my brother to offend. (1 Cor. 8:13)

53 It is good neither to eat flesh, nor to drink wine, nor any thing whereby thy brother stumbleth, or is offended, or is made weak. (Rom. 14:21)

54 We then that are strong ought to bear the infirmities of the weak, and not to please ourselves. Let every one of us please his neighbour for his good to edification. For even Christ pleased not himself. (Rom. 15:1–3a)

Him that is weak in the faith receive ye, but not to doubtful disputations. For one believeth that he may eat all things: another, who is weak, eateth herbs. Let not him that eateth despise him that eateth not; and let not him which eateth not judge him that eateth: for God hath received him. Who art thou that judgest another man's servant? to his own master he standeth or falleth. Yea, he shall be holden up: for God is able to make him stand. (Rom. 14:1–4)

55 Dearly beloved, avenge not yourselves, but rather give place unto wrath: for it is written, Vengeance is mine; I will repay, saith the Lord. (Rom. 12:19)

Who art thou that judgest another man's servant? to his own master he standeth or falleth. Yea, he shall be holden up: for God is able to make him stand... But why dost thou judge thy brother? or why dost thou set at nought thy brother? for we shall all stand before the judgment seat of Christ. For it is written, As I live, saith the Lord, every knee shall bow to me, and every tongue shall confess to God. So then every one of us shall give account of himself to God. Let us not therefore judge one another any more: but judge this rather, that no man put a stumbling block or an occasion to fall in his brother's way. (Rom. 14:4, 10–13)

Grudge not one against another, brethren, lest ye be condemned: behold, the judge standeth before the door. (James 5:9)

56 And as he said these things unto them, the scribes and the Pharisees began to urge him vehemently, and to provoke him to speak of many things. (Luke 11:53)

And when Peter was come up to Jerusalem, they that were of the circumcision contended with him. (Acts 11:2)

57 But let a man examine himself... For if we would judge ourselves, we should not be judged. (1 Cor. 11:28a, 31)

Having therefore these promises, dearly beloved, let us cleanse ourselves from all filthiness of the flesh and spirit, perfecting holiness in the fear of God. (2 Cor. 7:1)

Examine yourselves, whether ye be in the faith. (2 Cor. 13:5a)

58 Let us not therefore judge one another any more: but judge this rather, that no man put a stumbling block or an occasion to fall in his brother's way… It is good neither to eat flesh, nor to drink wine, nor any thing whereby thy brother stumbleth, or is offended, or is made weak. (Rom. 14:13, 21)

59 Now I beseech you, brethren, by the name of our Lord Jesus Christ, that ye all speak the same thing, and that there be no divisions among you; but that ye be perfectly joined together in the same mind and in the same judgment. For it hath been declared unto me of you, my brethren, by them which are of the house of Chloe, that there are contentions among you. (1 Cor. 1:10–11)

For ye are yet carnal: for whereas there is among you envying, and strife, and divisions, are ye not carnal, and walk as men? (1 Cor. 3:3)

For first of all, when ye come together in the church, I hear that there be divisions among you; and I partly believe it. (1 Cor. 11:18)

I beseech Euodias, and beseech Syntyche, that they be of the same mind in the Lord. And I intreat thee also, true yokefellow, help those women which laboured with me in the gospel, with Clement also, and with other my fellow labourers, whose names are in the book of life. (Phil. 4:2–3)

60 Therefore if thou bring thy gift to the altar, and there rememberest that thy brother hath ought against thee; Leave there thy gift before the altar, and go thy way; first be reconciled to thy brother, and then come and offer thy gift. (Matt. 5:23–24)

Confess your faults one to another, and pray one for another, that ye may be healed. The effectual fervent prayer of a righteous man availeth much. (James 5:16)

61 Take heed to yourselves: If thy brother trespass against thee, rebuke him; and if he repent, forgive him. (Luke 17:3)

Moreover if thy brother shall trespass against thee, go and tell him his fault between thee and him alone: if he shall hear thee, thou hast gained thy brother… Then came Peter to him, and said, Lord, how oft shall my brother sin against me, and I forgive him? till seven times? Jesus saith unto him, I say not unto thee, Until seven times: but, Until seventy times seven. (Matt. 18:15, 21–22)

62 Be ye therefore merciful, as your Father also is merciful. Judge not, and ye shall not be judged: condemn not, and ye shall not be condemned: forgive, and ye shall be forgiven: Give, and it shall be given unto you; good measure, pressed down, and shaken together, and running over, shall men give into your bosom. For with the same measure that ye mete withal it shall be measured to you again. (Luke 6:36–38)

And forgive us our sins; for we also forgive every one that is indebted to us. And lead us not into temptation; but deliver us from evil. (Luke 11:4)

Take heed to yourselves: If thy brother trespass against thee, rebuke him; and if he repent, forgive him. And if he trespass against thee seven times in a day, and seven times in a day turn again to thee, saying, I repent; thou shalt forgive him. (Luke 17:3–4)

63 But he, knowing their thoughts, said unto them, Every kingdom divided against itself is brought to desolation; and a house divided against a house falleth. (Luke 11:17)

64 Moreover if thy brother shall trespass against thee, go and tell him his fault between thee and him alone: if he shall hear thee, thou hast gained thy brother. But if he will not hear thee, then take with thee one or two more, that in the mouth of two or three witnesses every word may be established. And if he shall neglect to hear them, tell it unto the church: but if he neglect to hear the church, let him be unto thee as an heathen man and a publican. (Matt. 18:15–17)

65 But now I have written unto you not to keep company, if any man that is called a brother be a fornicator, or covetous, or an idolator, or a railer, or a drunkard, or an extortioner; with such an one no not to eat. For what have I to do to judge them also that are without? do not ye judge them that are within? But them that are without God judgeth. Therefore put away from among yourselves that wicked person. (1 Cor. 5:11–13)

And that because of false brethren unawares brought in, who came in privily to spy out our liberty [*eleutheros*: freedom] which we have in Christ Jesus, that they might bring us into bondage: To whom we gave place by subjection, no, not for an hour; that the truth of the gospel might continue with you... But when Peter was come to Antioch, I withstood him to the face, because he was to be blamed. For before that certain came from James, he did eat with the Gentiles: but when they were come, he withdrew and separated himself, fearing them which were of the circumcision. And the other Jews dissembled likewise with him; insomuch that Barnabas also was carried away with their dissimulation. But when I saw that they walked not uprightly according to the truth of the gospel, I said unto Peter before them all, If thou, being a Jew, livest after the manner of Gentiles, and not as do the Jews, why compellest thou the Gentiles to live as do the Jews? (Gal. 2:4–5, 11–14)

66 And this I say, lest any man should beguile you with enticing words... Beware lest any man spoil you through philosophy and vain deceit, after the tradition of men, after the rudiments of the world, and not after Christ... Let no man therefore judge you in meat, or in drink, or in respect of an holyday, or of the new moon, or of the sabbath days:... Let no man beguile you of your reward in a voluntary humility and worshipping of angels, intruding into those things which he hath not seen, vainly puffed up by his fleshly mind,... Wherefore if ye be dead with Christ from the rudiments of the world, why, as though living in the world, are ye subject to ordinances (Touch not; taste not; handle not; which all are to perish with the using;) after the commandments and doctrines of men?

Which things have indeed a shew of wisdom in will worship, and humility, and neglecting of the body: not in any honour to the satisfying of the flesh. (Col. 2:4, 8, 16, 18, 20–23)

67 Now the God of patience and consolation grant you to be likeminded one toward another according to Christ Jesus: That ye may with one mind and one mouth glorify God, even the Father of our Lord Jesus Christ. Wherefore receive ye one another, as Christ also received us to the glory of God. (Rom. 15:5–7)

Now I beseech you, brethren, by the name of our Lord Jesus Christ, that ye all speak the same thing, and that there be no divisions among you; but that ye be perfectly joined together in the same mind and in the same judgment. (1 Cor. 1:10)

Fulfil ye my joy, that ye be likeminded, having the same love, being of one accord, of one mind. (Phil. 2:2)

68 Am I am not an apostle? am I not free? have I not seen Jesus Christ our Lord? are not ye my work in the Lord?... Have we not power [*exousia*: liberty] to lead about a sister, a wife, as well as other apostles, and as the brethren of the Lord, and Cephas? (1 Cor. 9:1, 5)

69 For I would that all men were even as I myself. But every man hath his proper gift of God, one after this manner, and another after that. I say therefore to the unmarried and widows, it is good for them if they abide even as I... But as God hath distributed to every man, as the Lord hath called every one, so let him walk. And so ordain I in all churches. (1 Cor. 7:7–8, 17)

70 Who goeth a warfare any time at his own charges? who planteth a vineyard, and eateth not of the fruit thereof? or who feedeth a flock, and eateth not of the milk of the flock? Say I these things as a man? or saith not the law the same also? For it is written in the Law of Moses, thou shalt not muzzle the mouth of the ox that treadeth out the corn. Doth God take care for oxen? Or saith he it altogether for our sakes? For our sakes, no doubt, this is written: that he that ploweth should plow in hope; and that he that thresheth in hope should be partaker of his hope. If we have sown unto you spiritual things, is it a great thing if we shall reap your carnal things?... Do ye not know that they which minister about holy things live of the things of the temple? And they which wait at the altar are partakers with the altar? Even so hath the Lord ordained that they which preach the gospel should live of the gospel. (1 Cor. 9:7–11, 13–14)

71 What is my reward then? Verily that, when I preach the gospel, I may make the gospel of Christ without charge, that I abuse not my power [*exousia*: liberty] in the gospel. (1 Cor. 9:18)

But as we were allowed of God to be put in trust with the gospel, even so we speak; not as pleasing men, but God, which trieth our hearts. For neither at any time used we flattering words, as ye know, nor a cloke of covetousness; God is witness: Nor of men sought we glory, neither of you, nor yet of others, when we might have been burdensome, as the apostles of Christ. (1 Thess. 2:4–6)

Neither did we eat any man's bread for nought; but wrought with labour and travail night and day, that we might not be chargeable to any of you: Not because we have not power [*exousia*: liberty], but to make ourselves an ensample unto you to follow us. (2 Thess. 3:8–9)

72 For the kingdom of God is not meat and drink; but righteousness, and peace, and joy in the Holy Ghost. For he that in these things serveth Christ is acceptable to God, and approved of men. Let us therefore follow after the things which make for peace, and things wherewith one may edify another. (Rom. 14:17–19)

For though I be free from all men, yet have I made myself servant unto all, that I might gain the more. And unto the Jews I became as a Jew, that I might gain the Jews; to them that are under the law, as under the law, that I might gain them that are under the law; To them that are without law, as without law, (being not without law to God, but under the law to Christ,) that I might gain them that are without law. To the weak became I as weak, that I might gain the weak: I am made all things to all men, that I might by all means save some. And this I do for the gospel's sake, that I might be partaker thereof with you. (1 Cor. 9:19–23)

73 Even as I please all men in all things, not seeking mine own profit, but the profit of many that they may be saved. (1 Cor. 10:33)

74 All things are lawful for me, but all things are not expedient: all things are lawful for me, but all things edify not. (1 Cor. 10:23)

75 As free, and not using your liberty [*eleutheros*: freedom] for a cloke of maliciousness, but as the servants of God. (1 Pet. 2:16)

For, brethren, ye have been called unto liberty [*eleutheros*: freedom]; only use not liberty [*eleutheros*: freedom] for an occasion to the flesh, but by love serve one another. (Gal. 5:13)

76 Son of man, these men have set up their idols in their heart, and put the stumbling block of their iniquity before their face: should I be enquired of at all by them? (Ezek. 14:3)

Wherefore, my dearly beloved, flee from idolatry. I speak as to wise men; judge ye what I say. (1 Cor. 10:14–15)

77 Wherefore let him that thinketh he standeth take heed lest he fall. (1 Cor. 10:12)

78 Whether therefore ye eat, or drink, or whatsoever ye do, do all to the glory of God. (1 Cor. 10:31)

And whatsoever ye do in word or deed, do all in the name of the Lord Jesus, giving thanks to God and the Father by him… And whatsoever ye do, do it heartily, as to the Lord, and not unto men. (Col. 3:17, 23)

79 All things are lawful unto me, but all things are not expedient: all things are lawful for me, but I will not be brought under the power of any. Meats for the belly, and the belly for meats: but God shall destroy both it and them. Now the body is not for fornication, but for the Lord; and the Lord for the body. (1 Cor. 6:12–13)

Know ye not that they which run in a race run all, but one receiveth the prize? So run, that ye may obtain. And every man that striveth for the mastery is temperate in all things. Now they do it to obtain a corruptible crown; but we an incorruptible. I therefore so run, not as uncertainly; so fight I, not as one that beateth the air: But I keep under my body, and bring it into subjection: lest that by any means, when I have preached to others, I myself should be a castaway. (1 Cor. 9:24–27)

80 But exhort one another daily, while it is called to day; lest any of you be hardened through the deceitfulness of sin... While it is said, To day if ye will hear his voice, harden not your hearts, as in the provocation. (Heb. 3:13, 15)

For the word of God is quick, and powerful, and sharper than any two edged sword, piercing even to the dividing asunder of soul and spirit, and of the joints and marrow, and is a discerner of the thoughts and intents of the heart. Neither is there any creature that is not manifest in his sight: but all things are naked and opened unto the eyes of him with whom we have to do. (Heb. 4:12–13)

And ye have forgotten the exhortation which speaketh unto you as unto children, My son, despise not thou the chastening of the Lord, nor faint when thou art rebuked of him: For whom the Lord loveth he chasteneth, and scourgeth every son whom he receiveth... And make straight paths for your feet, lest that which is lame be turned out of the way; but let it rather be healed. Follow peace with all men, and holiness, without which no man shall see the Lord: Looking diligently lest any man fail of the grace of God; lest any root of bitterness springing up trouble you, and thereby many be defiled;... See that ye refuse not him that speaketh. For if they escaped not who refused him that spake on earth, much more shall not we escape, if we turn away from him that speaketh from heaven:... Wherefore we receiving a kingdom which cannot be moved, let us have grace, whereby we may serve God acceptably with reverence and godly fear: For our God is a consuming fire. (Heb. 12:5–6, 13–15, 25, 28–29)

Turn away mine eyes from beholding vanity; and quicken thou me in thy way... I thought on my ways, and turned my feet unto thy testimonies. (Ps. 119:37, 59)

81 Now these things were our examples, to the intent we should not lust after evil things, as they [Israel] also lusted. Now all these things happened unto them for examples: and they are written for our admonition, upon whom the ends of the world are come. (1 Cor. 10:6, 11)

82 Moreover, brethren, I would not that ye should be ignorant, how that all our fathers were under the cloud, and all passed through the sea; And were all baptized unto Moses in the cloud and in the sea; And did all eat the same spiritual meat; And did all drink the same spiritual drink: for they drank of that spiritual Rock that followed them: and that Rock was Christ. (1 Cor. 10:1–4)

83 And they said unto Moses, Because there were no graves in Egypt, hast thou taken us away to die in the wilderness? wherefore hast thou dealt thus with us,

to carry us forth out of Egypt? Is not this the word that we did tell thee in Egypt, saying, Let us alone, that we may serve the Egyptians? For it had been better for us to serve the Egyptians, than that we should die in the wilderness. (Exod. 14:11–12)

And the children of Israel said unto them, Would to God we had died by the hand of the LORD in the land of Egypt, when we sat by the flesh pots, and when we did eat bread to the full; for ye have brought us forth into this wilderness, to kill this whole assembly with hunger. (Exod. 16:3)

We remember the fish, which we did eat in Egypt freely; the cucumbers, and the melons, and the leeks, and the onions, and the garlick. (Num. 11:5)

And all the children of Israel murmured against Moses and against Aaron: and the whole congregation said unto them, Would God that we had died in the land of Egypt! or would God we had died in this wilderness! (Num. 14:2)

We have sinned with our fathers, we have committed iniquity, we have done wickedly. Our fathers understood not thy wonders in Egypt; they remembered not the multitude of thy mercies; but provoked him at the sea, even at the Red sea... They soon forgat his works; they waited not for his counsel: But lusted exceedingly in the wilderness, and tempted God in the desert. And he gave them their request; but sent leanness into their soul... They made a calf in Horeb, and worshipped the molten image. Thus they changed their glory into the similitude of an ox that eateth grass. They forgat God their saviour, which had done great things in Egypt;... Yea, they despised the pleasant land, they believed not his word: But murmured in their tents, and hearkened not unto the voice of the LORD... They joined themselves also unto Baalpeor, and ate the sacrifices of the dead. Thus they provoked him to anger with their inventions: and the plague brake in upon them... Therefore was the wrath of the LORD kindled against his people, insomuch that he abhorred his own inheritance. And he gave them into the hand of the heathen; and they that hated them ruled over them. Their enemies also oppressed them, and they were brought into subjection under their hand. (Ps. 106:6–7, 13–15, 19–21, 24–25, 28–29, 40–42)

84 But with many of them God was not well pleased: for they were overthrown in the wilderness. Now these things were our examples, to the intent we should not lust after evil things, as they also lusted. Neither be ye idolaters, as were some of them; as it is written, The people sat down to eat and drink, and rose up to play. Neither let us commit fornication, as some of them committed, and fell in one day three and twenty thousand. Neither let us tempt Christ, as some of them also tempted, and were destroyed of serpents. Neither murmur ye, as some of them also murmured, and were destroyed of the destroyer. (1 Cor. 10:5–10)

Correction is grievous unto him that forsaketh the way: and he that hateth reproof shall die. (Prov. 15:10)

85 See then that ye walk circumspectly, not as fools, but as wise. (Eph. 5:15)

[86] Do we provoke the Lord to jealousy? Are we stronger than he? (1 Cor. 10:22)

[87] There hath no temptation taken you but such as is common to man: but God is faithful, who will not suffer you to be tempted above that ye are able; but will with the temptation also make a way to escape, that ye may be able to bear it. (1 Cor. 10:13)

[88] One man esteemeth one day above another: another esteemeth every day alike. Let every man be fully persuaded in his own mind. He that regardeth the day, regardeth it unto the Lord; and he that regardeth not the day, to the Lord he doth not regard it. He that eateth, eateth to the Lord, for he giveth God thanks; and he that eateth not, to the Lord he eateth not, and giveth God thanks... I know, and am persuaded by the Lord Jesus, that there is nothing unclean of itself: but to him that esteemeth any thing to be unclean, to him it is unclean... Hast thou faith? have it to thyself before God. Happy is he that condemneth not himself in that thing which he alloweth. And he that doubteth is damned if he eat, because he eateth not of faith: for whatsoever is not of faith is sin. (Rom. 14:5–6, 14, 22–23)

[89] For, brethren, ye have been called unto liberty [eleutheros: freedom]; only use not liberty [*eleutheros*: freedom] for an occasion to the flesh, but by love serve one another. For all the law is fulfilled in one word, even in this; Thou shalt love thy neighbour as thyself. (Gal. 5:13–14)

How? The Law of Love

When Sandy and I were married, we stood like so many couples before the pastor and congregation, saying our wedding vows to one another. I admit to a great mix of emotion that filled my heart. On the one hand, I felt love toward my bride and, on the other hand, apprehension over the breadth and seriousness of those promises before God. We knew the vows would bring joyous union but also would bring sacrifices down the road. Love brought us through the ceremony and over fifty years of marriage. Real love is willing to sacrifice.

The Law of Love: Serving God and Others with Sacrificial Love

God and the Height of Love

The degree of sacrifice is a measure of the greatness of love. God so loved the world that *He gave Himself* in the Person of His Son to die on a cross for our sin.[1] The Son so loved us that *He surrendered Himself* to bear the Father's wrath for sin and carry it to the grave.[2]

We have all used our two hands to demonstrate the size of something, spreading them apart to illustrate a larger object. Someone took this simple human gesture and made a breathtaking illustration of God's love. Asking Jesus how much He loved us, He stretched His hands as far as He could and allowed them to be nailed to the cross.[3] The height of God's sacrificial love for us is beyond our comprehension.[4] And by that love, He has made us everlasting heirs of all things in Jesus.[5] We will live forever with the Triune God, filled with the eternal love that exists between the Father and the Son.[6]

Our Response to God's Love

In this vertical relation we have with God, we must surrender ourselves completely to Him.[7] Loving God is the first and great commandment,[8] and we show our love by humble obedience.[9] This command to believers is *not* from a *Judge* Who condemns us for each of our failures. It is from our *loving Father* Who is teaching us the right focus for our life[10] and Who is helping us to grow in that focus.[11]

Avoiding sinful behavior because we fear punishment is good. Doing what is right out of love is better.[12] In love, we offer up to God the sacrifices of sincere repentance,[13] praise,[14] worship,[15] giving,[16] prayer,[17] and service.[18] Further, we endure temptation, hard times, and persecution out of love for the Lord.[19]

Pride Hinders Love

We all struggle with pride and have looked at this problem in earlier chapters. Doing something that we would normally consider "beneath" us does not come easy. As we surrender to the law of love, we give up our pride and sacrifice it to God.[20]

At the Last Supper, while the disciples were arguing over who among them would be greatest in the kingdom,[21] King Jesus knelt and washed their feet, giving us an example of humble service to follow.[22] Even more, He humbled Himself for us, enduring cruel torture, shame, and death on the cross.[23]

We must be willing to follow Christ's example of *going wherever* God leads us and *doing whatever* He commands.[24] Jesus came to earth. At the will of the Father, He left the absolutely glorious throne of glory to be born in a stable to a poor family, becoming a helpless, humble baby, totally cared for by a teenage girl. His life path was to walk among people who, at best, did not completely understand Him[25] and who, at worst, absolutely despised Him.[26] In the midst of such difficulties, He testified that He was here in this world to serve.[27] He challenges to us to serve in this world, just like the Father had sent Him.[28]

The Breadth of Our Love to Others

In the horizontal relationships with those around us, we are commanded to take the normal self-care, which we all have, and focus it on others,[29] even strangers[30] and enemies[31]—that is, anyone in need.[32] He gave us a further commandment to love one another *as He loves us*.[33] But how do we live out that love? Only occasionally do we make some grand sacrifice for others. More usual are day-to-day actions as summarized in verses that often include "one another."

We must seek peace, unity, and being of one mind in our ministry with one another[34] and in honor preferring one another.[35] As we assemble and fellowship together,[36] our conduct must be harmless,[37] comforting, encouraging, and edifying to one another.[38] Such an attitude includes understanding and respecting our differences in character and ministry[39] without partiality.[40]

We are challenged not to argue, criticize, or speak evil of one another.[41] We should think the better of folks unless they say or prove otherwise.[42] Be patient, willing to suffer wrong, and be kind to one another,[43] helping to recover the saints and to win the lost.[44] Be merciful and forgive one another without judging.[45] We are *not to be judges but servants* toward others.[46] Serving others is love in action.[47]

Love does not lead us to condemn others but to guide them to the Word of God.[48] And that love may include confronting them with the Word,[49] even as Christ Himself used the Word of God to confront others.[50] But we must speak the truth in love.[51]

In that wondrous passage on love in 1 Corinthians 13,[52] we understand that service without love is worthless. Whether we preach, or teach, or become experts in scripture knowledge, without love toward God and others, it is vain. Faith without sincere love leaves us empty. Sacrifices even unto death have no eternal value without love. Love is patient toward others, forgiving, kind, helpful, and does not assume evil motives in others. Love does not enjoy sin but rejoices in truth. Love abandons pride and does not envy others. Instead, love seeks the best outcome for a situation and for others.

Loving God through Our Love of Others

In our jungle mission work, we built some wood houses using multiple concrete pillars. Between each two pillars, we laid a cross beam upon which we built the rest of the structure. When we put one end of the beam on one pillar, we did not leave the other end on the ground. Each beam had to be supported at *both* ends.

Glorifying God is the beam upon which we build our conduct. Glorifying Him rests on the two great commandments, not just one.[53] We cannot say we love God if we hate others, because hatred of God and hatred of people go together.[54] Neither can we say we have Christian love of others while ignoring God's commands.[55] Loving God and loving others are intertwined, because we are serving God and growing in faith when we are loving and serving others.[56]

**Love of God and others is both the
motive and the attitude of a life
that is pleasing to the Lord. Do all in love.[57]**

**Can we bring together all these admonitions
into a few simple words?
Does Scripture Itself give us some summary verses?**

Notes

[1] For God so loved the world, that he gave his only begotten Son, that whosoever believeth in him should not perish, but have everlasting life. (John 3:16)

In this was manifested the love of God toward us, because that God sent his only begotten Son into the world, that we might live through him. Herein is love, not that we loved God, but that he loved us, and sent his Son to be the propitiation for our sins. (1 John 4:9–10)

[2] Therefore doth my Father love me, because I lay down my life, that I might take it again. No man taketh it from me, but I lay it down of myself. I have power to lay it down, and I have power to take it again. This commandment have I received of my Father. (John 10:17–18)

This is my commandment, That ye love one another, as I have loved you. Greater love hath no man than this, that a man lay down his life for his friends. (John 15:12–13)

For what the law could not do, in that it was weak through the flesh, God sending his own Son in the likeness of sinful flesh, and for sin, condemned sin in the flesh. (Rom. 8:3)

For he hath made him to be sin for us, who knew no sin; that we might be made the righteousness of God in him. (2 Cor. 5:21)

For ye know the grace of our Lord Jesus Christ, that, though he was rich, yet for your sakes he became poor, that ye through his poverty might be rich. (2 Cor. 8:9)

For then must he often have suffered since the foundation of the world: but now once in the end of the world hath he appeared to put away sin by the sacrifice of himself. (Heb. 9:26)

But this man, after he had offered one sacrifice for sins for ever, sat down on the right hand of God. (Heb. 10:12)

And from Jesus Christ, who is the faithful witness, and the first begotten of the dead, and the prince of the kings of the earth. Unto him that loved us, and washed us from our sins in his own blood, And hath made us kings and priests unto God and his Father; to him be glory and dominion for ever and ever. Amen. (Rev. 1:5–6)

[3] Therefore doth my Father love me, because I lay down my life, that I might take it again. No man taketh it from me, but I lay it down of myself. I have power to lay it down, and I have power to take it again. This commandment have I received of my Father. (John 10:17–18)

[4] God thundereth marvellously with his voice; great things doeth he, which we cannot comprehend. (Job 37:5)

Let the wicked forsake his way, and the unrighteous man his thoughts: and let him return unto the LORD, and he will have mercy upon him; and to our God, for he will abundantly pardon. For my thoughts are not your thoughts, neither are your ways my ways, saith the LORD. For as the heavens are higher than the earth, so are my ways higher than your ways, and my thoughts than your thoughts. (Isa. 55:7–9)

Blessed be the God and Father of our Lord Jesus Christ, who hath blessed us with all spiritual blessings in heavenly places in Christ: According as he hath chosen us in him before the foundation of the world, that we should be holy and without blame before him in love: Having predestinated us unto the adoption of children by Jesus Christ to himself, according to the good pleasure of his will, To the praise of the glory of his grace, wherein he hath made us accepted in the beloved... In whom also we have obtained an inheritance, being predestinated according to the purpose of him who worketh all things after the counsel of his own will. (Eph. 1:3–6, 11)

5 The Spirit itself beareth witness with our spirit, that we are the children of God: And if children, then heirs; heirs of God, and joint-heirs with Christ;... He that spared not his own Son, but delivered him up for us all, how shall he not with him also freely give us all things? (Rom. 8:16–17a, 32)

But as it is written, Eye hath not seen, nor ear heard, neither have entered into the heart of man, the things which God hath prepared for them that love him... Now we have received, not the spirit of the world, but the spirit which is of God; that we might know the things that are freely given to us of God. (1 Cor. 2:9, 12)

And if ye be Christ's, then are ye Abraham's seed, and heirs according to the promise. (Gal. 3:29)

Wherefore thou art no more a servant, but a son; and if a son, then an heir of God through Christ. (Gal. 4:7)

But God, who is rich in mercy, for his great love wherewith he loved us, Even when we were dead in sins, hath quickened us together with Christ, (by grace ye are saved;) And hath raised us up together, and made us sit together in heavenly places in Christ Jesus: That in the ages to come he might shew the exceeding riches of his grace in his kindness toward us through Christ Jesus. (Eph. 2:4–7)

Now our Lord Jesus Christ himself, and God, even our Father, which hath loved us, and hath given us everlasting consolation and good hope through grace. (2 Thess. 2:16)

According as his divine power hath given unto us all things that pertain unto life and godliness, through the knowledge of him that hath called us to glory and virtue: Whereby are given unto us exceeding great and precious promises: that by these ye might be partakers of the divine nature, having escaped the corruption that is in the world through lust. (2 Pet. 1:3–4)

Behold, what manner of love the Father hath bestowed upon us, that we should be called the sons of God: therefore the world knoweth us not, because it knew him not. Beloved, now are we the sons of God, and it doth not yet appear what we shall be: but we know that, when he shall appear, we shall be like him; for we shall see him as he is. (1 John 3:1–2)

And this is the record, that God hath given to us eternal life, and this life is in his Son. (1 John 5:11)

6 Father, I will that they also, whom thou hast given me, be with me where I am; that they may behold my glory, which thou hast given me: for thou lovedst me before the foundation of the world... And I have declared unto them thy name, and will declare it: that the love wherewith thou hast loved me may be in them, and I in them. (John 17:24, 26)

According as he hath chosen us in him before the foundation of the world, that we should be holy and without blame before him in love. (Eph. 1:4)

7 Neither yield ye your members as instruments of unrighteousness unto sin: but yield yourselves unto God, as those that are alive from the dead, and your members as instruments of righteousness unto God. (Rom. 6:13)

I beseech you therefore, brethren, by the mercies of God, that ye present your bodies a living sacrifice, holy, acceptable unto God, which is your reasonable service. And be not conformed to this world: but be ye transformed by the renewing of your mind, that ye may prove what is that good, and acceptable, and perfect, will of God. (Rom. 12:1–2)

And that he died for all, that they which live should not henceforth live unto themselves, but unto him which died for them, and rose again. (2 Cor. 5:15)

Ye also, as lively stones, are built up a spiritual house, an holy priesthood, to offer up spiritual sacrifices, acceptable to God by Jesus Christ. (1 Pet. 2:5)

And they overcame him by the blood of the Lamb, and by the word of their testimony; and they loved not their lives unto the death. (Rev. 12:11)

8 And thou shalt love the LORD thy God with all thine heart, and with all thy soul, and with all thy might. (Deut. 6:5)

And now, Israel, what doth the LORD thy God require of thee, but to fear the LORD thy God, to walk in all his ways, and to love him, and to serve the LORD thy God with all thy heart and with all thy soul. (Deut. 10:12)

Take good heed therefore unto yourselves, that ye love the LORD your God. (Josh. 23:11)

Jesus said unto him, Thou shalt love the Lord thy God with all thy heart, and with all thy soul, and with all thy mind. (Matt. 22:37)

Jesus said unto him, Thou shalt love the Lord thy God with all thy heart, and with all thy soul, and with all thy mind. (Matt. 22:37)

And thou shalt love the Lord thy God with all thy heart, and with all thy soul, and with all thy mind, and with all thy strength: this is the first commandment. (Mark 12:30)

And he answering said, Thou shalt love the Lord thy God with all thy heart, and with all thy soul, and with all thy strength, and with all thy mind; and thy neighbor as thyself. (Luke 10:27)

[9] Know therefore that the LORD thy God, he is God, the faithful God, which keepeth covenant and mercy with them that love him and keep his commandments to a thousand generations. (Deut. 7:9)

And now, Israel, what doth the LORD thy God require of thee, but to fear the LORD thy God, to walk in all his ways, and to love him, and to serve the LORD thy God with all thy heart and with all thy soul, To keep the commandments of the LORD, and his statutes, which I command thee this day for thy good? (Deut. 10:12–13)

If ye love me, keep my commandments... He that hath my commandments, and keepeth them, he it is that loveth me: and he that loveth me shall be loved of my Father, and I will love him, and will manifest myself to him... Jesus answered and said unto him, If a man love me, he will keep my words: and my Father will love him, and we will come unto him, and make our abode with him... But that the world may know that I love the Father; and as the Father gave me commandment, even so I do. Arise, let us go hence. (John 14:15, 21, 23, 31)

Therefore doth my Father love me, because I lay down my life, that I might take it again. (John 10:17)

[10] And now, Israel, what doth the LORD thy God require of thee, but to fear the LORD thy God, to walk in all his ways, and to love him, and to serve the LORD thy God with all thy heart and with all thy soul. (Deut. 10:12)

And walk in love, as Christ also hath loved us, and hath given himself for us an offering and a sacrifice to God for a sweet smelling savour. (Eph. 5:2)

And the Lord direct your hearts into the love of God, and into the patient waiting for Christ. (2 Thess. 3:5)

And we have known and believed the love that God hath to us. God is love; and he that dwelleth in love dwelleth in God, and God in him. (1 John 4:16)

For this is the love of God, that we keep his commandments: and his commandments are not grievous. For whatsoever is born of God overcometh the world: and this is the victory that overcometh the world, even our faith. Who is he that overcometh the world, but he that believeth that Jesus is the Son of God? (1 John 5:3–5)

[11] For whom the LORD loveth he correcteth; even as a father the son in whom he delighteth. (Prov. 3:12)

I am crucified with Christ: nevertheless I live; yet not I, but Christ liveth in me: and the life which I now live in the flesh I live by the faith of the Son of God, who loved me, and gave himself for me. (Gal. 2:20)

That he would grant you, according to the riches of his glory, to be strengthened with might by his Spirit in the inner man; that Christ may dwell in your hearts by faith; that ye, being rooted and grounded in love, may be able to comprehend with all saints what is the breadth, and length, and depth, and height; And to know the love of Christ, which passeth knowledge, that ye might be filled with all the fulness of God. (Eph. 3:16–19)

And the Lord make you to increase and abound in love one toward another, and toward all men, even as we do toward you. (1 Thess. 3:12)

And the Lord direct your hearts into the love of God, and into the patient waiting for Christ. (2 Thess. 3:5)

12 For the love of Christ constraineth us; because we thus judge, that if one died for all, then were all dead: And that he died for all, that they which live should not henceforth live unto themselves, but unto him which died for them, and rose again. (2 Cor. 5:14–15)

For to their power, I bear record, yea, and beyond their power they were willing of themselves; Praying us with much intreaty that we would receive the gift, and take upon us the fellowship of the ministering to the saints. And this they did, not as we hoped, but first gave their own selves to the Lord, and unto us by the will of God. (2 Cor. 8:3–5)

13 For thou desirest not sacrifice; else would I give it: thou delightest not in burnt offering. The sacrifices of God are a broken spirit: a broken and a contrite heart, O God, thou wilt not despise. (Ps. 51:16–17)

14 Therefore I will give thanks unto thee, O Lord, among the heathen, and I will sing praises unto thy name. (2 Sam. 22:50)

I will praise the Lord according to his righteousness: and will sing praise to the name of the Lord most high. (Ps. 7:17)

I will praise thee, O Lord, with my whole heart; I will shew forth all thy marvellous works. I will be glad and rejoice in thee: I will sing praise to thy name, O thou most High. (Ps. 9:1–2)

I will declare thy name unto my brethren: in the midst of the congregation will I praise thee. (Ps. 22:22)

The Lord is my strength and my shield; my heart trusted in him, and I am helped: therefore my heart greatly rejoiceth; and with my song will I praise him. (Ps. 28:7)

Rejoice in the Lord, O ye righteous: for praise is comely for the upright. (Ps. 33:1)

Then will I go unto the altar of God, unto God my exceeding joy: yea, upon the harp will I praise thee, O God my God. (Ps. 43:4)

According to thy name, O God, so is thy praise unto the ends of the earth: thy right hand is full of righteousness. (Ps. 48:10)

I will freely sacrifice unto thee: I will praise thy name, O Lord; for it is good. (Ps. 54:6)

I will praise thee, O Lord my God, with all my heart: and I will glorify thy name for evermore. (Ps. 86:12)

Enter into his gates with thanksgiving, and into his courts with praise: be thankful unto him, and bless his name. (Ps. 100:4)

And let them sacrifice the sacrifices of thanksgiving, and declare his works with rejoicing… Oh that men would praise the Lord for his goodness, and for his wonderful works to the children of men! Let them exalt him also in the congregation of the people, and praise him in the assembly of the elders. (Ps. 107:22, 31–32)

Praise ye the LORD. I will praise the LORD with my whole heart, in the assembly of the upright, and in the congregation. (Ps. 111:1)

I will offer to thee the sacrifice of thanksgiving, and will call upon the name of the LORD. (Ps. 116:17)

I will praise thee: for thou hast heard me, and art become my salvation... Thou art my God, and I will praise thee: thou art my God, I will exalt thee. (Ps. 118:21, 28)

Praise the LORD of hosts: for the LORD is good; for his mercy endureth for ever: and of them that shall bring the sacrifice of praise into the house of the LORD. (Jer. 33:11b)

And again, Praise the Lord, all ye Gentiles; and laud him, all ye people. (Rom. 15:11)

By him therefore let us offer the sacrifice of praise to God continually, that is, the fruit of our lips giving thanks to his name. (Heb. 13:15)

15 Give unto the LORD the glory due unto his name; worship the LORD in the beauty of holiness. (Ps. 29:2)

All the ends of the world shall remember and turn unto the LORD: and all the kindreds of the nations shall worship before thee. (Ps. 22:27)

O come, let us worship and bow down: let us kneel before the LORD our maker. (Ps. 95:6)

Exalt ye the LORD our God, and worship at his footstool; for he is holy. (Ps. 99:5)

But the hour cometh, and now is, when the true worshippers shall worship the Father in spirit and in truth: for the Father seeketh such to worship him. God is a Spirit: and they that worship him must worship him in spirit and in truth. (John 4:23–24)

Speaking to yourselves in psalms and hymns and spiritual songs, singing and making melody in your heart to the Lord; Giving thanks always for all things unto God and the Father in the name of our Lord Jesus Christ. (Eph. 5:19–20)

The four and twenty elders fall down before him that sat on the throne, and worship him that liveth for ever and ever, and cast their crowns before the throne, saying, Thou art worthy, O Lord, to receive glory and honour and power: for thou hast created all things, and for thy pleasure they are and were created. (Rev. 4:10–11)

16 The righteous giveth and spareth not. (Prov. 21:26b)

Moreover, brethren, we do you to wit of the grace of God bestowed on the churches of Macedonia; How that in a great trial of affliction the abundance of their joy and their deep poverty abounded unto the riches of their liberality. For to their power, I bear record, yea, and beyond their power they were willing of themselves; Praying us with much intreaty that we would receive the gift, and take upon us the fellowship of the ministering to the saints. And this they did, not as we hoped, but first gave their own selves to the Lord, and unto us by the will of God. (2 Cor. 8:1–5)

Every man according as he purposeth in his heart, so let him give; not grudgingly, or of necessity: for God loveth a cheerful giver. And God is able to make all grace abound toward you; that ye, always having all sufficiency in all things, may abound to every good work. (2 Cor. 9:7–8)

17 Yet the LORD will command his lovingkindness in the day time, and in the night his song shall be with me, and my prayer unto the God of my life. (Ps. 42:8)

Let my prayer be set forth before thee as incense; and the lifting up of my hands as the evening sacrifice. (Ps. 141:2)

After this manner therefore pray ye: Our Father which art in heaven, Hallowed be thy name. (Matt. 6:9)

18 Only fear the LORD, and serve him in truth with all your heart: for consider how great things he hath done for you. (1 Sam. 12:24)

Serve the LORD with fear, and rejoice with trembling. (Ps. 2:11)

For, brethren, ye have been called unto liberty; only use not liberty for an occasion to the flesh, but by love serve one another. (Gal. 5:13)

And whatsoever ye do, do it heartily, as to the Lord, and not unto men; Knowing that of the Lord ye shall receive the reward of the inheritance: for ye serve the Lord Christ. (Col. 3:23–24)

For they themselves shew of us what manner of entering in we had unto you, and how ye turned to God from idols to serve the living and true God. (1 Thess. 1:9)

How much more shall the blood of Christ, who through the eternal Spirit offered himself without spot to God, purge your conscience from dead works to serve the living God? (Heb. 9:14)

But to do good and to communicate forget not: for with such sacrifices God is well pleased. (Heb. 13:16)

19 Blessed is the man that endureth temptation: for when he is tried, he shall receive the crown of life, which the Lord hath promised to them that love him. (James 1:12)

20 Talk no more so exceeding proudly; let not arrogancy come out of your mouth: for the LORD is a God of knowledge, and by him actions are weighed. (1 Sam. 2:3)

Sacrifice and offering thou didst not desire; mine ears hast thou opened: burnt offering and sin offering hast thou not required. Then said I, Lo, I come: in the volume of the book it is written of me, I delight to do thy will, O my God: yea, thy law is within my heart. (Ps. 40:6–8)

For thou desirest not sacrifice; else would I give it: thou delightest not in burnt offering. The sacrifices of God are a broken spirit: a broken and a contrite heart, O God, thou wilt not despise. (Ps. 51:16–17)

Though the LORD be high, yet hath he respect unto the lowly: but the proud he knoweth afar off. (Ps. 138:6)

The wicked, through the pride of his countenance, will not seek after God: God is not in all his thoughts. (Ps. 10:4)

The fear of the LORD is to hate evil: pride, and arrogancy, and the evil way, and the froward mouth, do I hate. (Prov. 8:13)

A man's pride shall bring him low: but honour shall uphold the humble in spirit. (Prov. 29:23)

Hear ye, and give ear; be not proud: for the LORD hath spoken. (Jer. 13:15)

For from within, out of the heart of men, proceed evil thoughts, adulteries, fornications, murders, Thefts, covetousness, wickedness, deceit, lasciviousness, an evil eye, blasphemy, pride, foolishness: All these evil things come from within, and defile the man. (Mark 7:21–23)

Be of the same mind one toward another. Mind not high things, but condescend to men of low estate. Be not wise in your own conceits. (Rom. 12:16)

And these things, brethren, I have in a figure transferred to myself and to Apollos for your sakes; that ye might learn in us not to think of men above that which is written, that no one of you be puffed up for one against another. (1 Cor. 4:6)

But he giveth more grace. Wherefore he saith, God resisteth the proud, but giveth grace unto the humble. (James 4:6)

Likewise, ye younger, submit yourselves unto the elder. Yea, all of you be subject one to another, and be clothed with humility: for God resisteth the proud, and giveth grace to the humble. (1 Pet. 5:5)

For all that is in the world, the lust of the flesh, and the lust of the eyes, and the pride of life, is not of the Father, but is of the world. (1 John 2:16)

21 And there was also a strife among them, which of them should be accounted the greatest. (Luke 22:24)

22 Jesus knowing that the Father had given all things into his hands, and that he was come from God, and went to God; He riseth from supper, and laid aside his garments; and took a towel, and girded himself. After that he poureth water into a bason, and began to wash the disciples' feet, and to wipe them with the towel wherewith he was girded... So after he had washed their feet, and had taken his garments, and was set down again, he said unto them, Know ye what I have done to you? Ye call me Master and Lord: and ye say well; for so I am. If I then, your Lord and Master, have washed your feet; ye also ought to wash one another's feet. For I have given you an example, that ye should do as I have done to you. (John 13:3–5, 12–15)

23 If there be therefore any consolation in Christ, if any comfort of love, if any fellowship of the Spirit, if any bowels and mercies, Fulfil ye my joy, that ye be likeminded, having the same love, being of one accord, of one mind. Let nothing be done through strife or vainglory; but in lowliness of mind let each

esteem other better than themselves. Look not every man on his own things, but every man also on the things of others. Let this mind be in you, which was also in Christ Jesus: Who, being in the form of God, thought it not robbery to be equal with God: But made himself of no reputation, and took upon him the form of a servant, and was made in the likeness of men: And being found in fashion as a man, he humbled himself, and became obedient unto death, even the death of the cross. (Phil. 2:1–8)

Wherefore seeing we also are compassed about with so great a cloud of witnesses, let us lay aside every weight, and the sin which doth so easily beset us, and let us run with patience the race that is set before us, Looking unto Jesus the author and finisher of our faith; who for the joy that was set before him endured the cross, despising the shame, and is set down at the right hand of the throne of God. (Heb. 12:1–2)

24 But when the fulness of the time was come, God sent forth his Son, made of a woman, made under the law, To redeem them that were under the law, that we might receive the adoption of sons. (Gal. 4:4–5)

Let this mind be in you, which was also in Christ Jesus: Who, being in the form of God, thought it not robbery to be equal with God: But made himself of no reputation, and took upon him the form of a servant, and was made in the likeness of men: And being found in fashion as a man, he humbled himself, and became obedient unto death, even the death of the cross. (Phil. 2:5–8)

25 But they understood not this saying, and it was hid from them, that they perceived it not: and they feared to ask him of that saying. (Luke 9:45)

And they understood none of these things: and this saying was hid from them, neither knew they the things which were spoken. (Luke 18:34)

26 Then the Pharisees went out, and held a council against him, how they might destroy him. (Matt. 12:14)

And he taught daily in the temple. But the chief priests and the scribes and the chief of the people sought to destroy him. (Luke 19:47)

27 For whether is greater, he that sitteth at meat, or he that serveth? is not he that sitteth at meat? But I am among you as he that serveth. (Luke 22:27)

I can of mine own self do nothing: as I hear, I judge: and my judgment is just; because I seek not mine own will, but the will of the Father which hath sent me. (John 5:30)

28 For I came down from heaven, not to do mine own will, but the will of him that sent me. (John 6:38)

As thou hast sent me into the world, even so have I also sent them into the world. (John 17:18)

Then said Jesus to them again, Peace be unto you: as my Father hath sent me, even so send I you. (John 20:21)

29 Thou shalt not avenge, nor bear any grudge against the children of thy people, but thou shalt love thy neighbour as thyself: I am the LORD. (Lev. 19:18)

³⁰ Thou shalt not avenge, nor bear any grudge against the children of thy people, but thou shalt love thy neighbour as thyself: I am the LORD… But the stranger that dwelleth with you shall be unto you as one born among you, and thou shalt love him as thyself; for ye were strangers in the land of Egypt: I am the LORD your God. (Lev. 19:18, 34)

³¹ Bless them which persecute you: bless, and curse not. Rejoice with them that do rejoice, and weep with them that weep. Be of the same mind one toward another. Mind not high things, but condescend to men of low estate. Be not wise in your own conceits. Recompense to no man evil for evil. Provide things honest in the sight of all men. If it be possible, as much as lieth in you, live peaceably with all men. Dearly beloved, avenge not yourselves, but rather give place unto wrath: for it is written, Vengeance is mine; I will repay, saith the Lord. Therefore if thine enemy hunger, feed him; if he thirst, give him drink: for in so doing thou shalt heap coals of fire on his head. Be not overcome of evil, but overcome evil with good. (Rom. 12:14–21)

³² And, behold, a certain lawyer stood up, and tempted him, saying, Master, what shall I do to inherit eternal life? He said unto him, What is written in the law? how readest thou? And he answering said, Thou shalt love the Lord thy God with all thy heart, and with all thy soul, and with all thy strength, and with all thy mind; and thy neighbour as thyself. And he said unto him, Thou hast answered right: this do, and thou shalt live. But he, willing to justify himself, said unto Jesus, And who is my neighbour? And Jesus answering said, A certain man went down from Jerusalem to Jericho, and fell among thieves, which stripped him of his raiment, and wounded him, and departed, leaving him half dead. And by chance there came down a certain priest that way: and when he saw him, he passed by on the other side. And likewise a Levite, when he was at the place, came and looked on him, and passed by on the other side. But a certain Samaritan, as he journeyed, came where he was: and when he saw him, he had compassion on him, And went to him, and bound up his wounds, pouring in oil and wine, and set him on his own beast, and brought him to an inn, and took care of him. And on the morrow when he departed, he took out two pence, and gave them to the host, and said unto him, Take care of him; and whatsoever thou spendest more, when I come again, I will repay thee. Which now of these three, thinkest thou, was neighbour unto him that fell among the thieves? And he said, He that shewed mercy on him. Then said Jesus unto him, Go, and do thou likewise. (Luke 10:25–37)

³³ A new commandment I give unto you, That ye love one another; as I have loved you, that ye also love one another. By this shall all men know that ye are my disciples, if ye have love one to another. (John 13:34–35)

This is my commandment, That ye love one another, as I have loved you… These things I command you, that ye love one another. (John 15:12, 17)

Owe no man any thing, but to love one another: for he that loveth another hath fulfilled the law. For this, Thou shalt not commit adultery, Thou shalt not kill, Thou shalt not steal, Thou shalt not bear false witness, Thou shalt not covet; and if there be any other commandment, it is briefly comprehended in this saying, namely, Thou shalt love thy neighbour as thyself. Love worketh no ill to his neighbour: therefore love is the fulfilling of the law. (Rom. 13:8–10)

And walk in love, as Christ also hath loved us, and hath given himself for us an offering and a sacrifice to God for a sweet smelling savour. (Eph. 5:2)

And the Lord make you to increase and abound in love one toward another, and toward all men, even as we do toward you. (1 Thess. 3:12)

But as touching brotherly love ye need not that I write unto you: for ye yourselves are taught of God to love one another. (1 Thess. 4:9)

Let brotherly love continue. (Heb. 13:1)

Seeing ye have purified your souls in obeying the truth through the Spirit unto unfeigned love of the brethren, see that ye love one another with a pure heart fervently. (1 Pet. 1:22)

As every man hath received the gift, even so minister the same one to another, as good stewards of the manifold grace of God. (1 Pet. 4:10)

For this is the message that ye heard from the beginning, that we should love one another... And this is his commandment, That we should believe on the name of his Son Jesus Christ, and love one another, as he gave us commandment. (1 John 3:11, 23)

Beloved, let us love one another: for love is of God; and every one that loveth is born of God, and knoweth God... Beloved, if God so loved us, we ought also to love one another. No man hath seen God at any time. If we love one another, God dwelleth in us, and his love is perfected in us. (1 John 4:7, 11–12)

And now I beseech thee, lady, not as though I wrote a new commandment unto thee, but that which we had from the beginning, that we love one another. (2 John 1:5)

34 Salt is good: but if the salt have lost his saltness, wherewith will ye season it? Have salt in yourselves, and have peace one with another. (Mark 9:50)

Be of the same mind one toward another. Mind not high things, but condescend to men of low estate. Be not wise in your own conceits. (Rom. 12:16)

Let us therefore follow after the things which make for peace, and things wherewith one may edify another. (Rom. 14:19)

Now the God of patience and consolation grant you to be likeminded one toward another according to Christ Jesus. (Rom. 15:5)

Finally, be ye all of one mind, having compassion one of another, love as brethren, be pitiful, be courteous. (1 Pet. 3:8)

35 Be kindly affectioned one to another with brotherly love; in honour preferring one another. (Rom. 12:10)

Submitting yourselves one to another in the fear of God. (Eph. 5:21)

[36] Not forsaking the assembling of ourselves together, as the manner of some is; but exhorting one another: and so much the more, as ye see the day approaching. (Heb. 10:25)

But if we walk in the light, as he is in the light, we have fellowship one with another, and the blood of Jesus Christ his Son cleanseth us from all sin. (1 John 1:7)

[37] Behold, I send you forth as sheep in the midst of wolves: be ye therefore wise as serpents, and harmless as doves. (Matt. 10:16)

Giving no offence in any thing, that the ministry be not blamed. (2 Cor. 6:3)

To speak evil of no man, to be no brawlers, but gentle, shewing all meekness unto all men. (Titus 3:2)

[38] Let us therefore follow after the things which make for peace, and things wherewith one may edify another. (Rom. 14:19)

Wherefore comfort one another with these words. (1 Thess. 4:18)

Wherefore comfort yourselves together, and edify one another, even as also ye do. (1 Thess. 5:11)

But exhort one another daily, while it is called To day; lest any of you be hardened through the deceitfulness of sin. (Heb. 3:13)

And let us consider one another to provoke unto love and to good works. (Heb. 10:24)

[39] So we, being many, are one body in Christ, and every one members one of another. (Rom. 12:5)

Wherefore receive ye one another, as Christ also received us to the glory of God. (Rom. 15:7)

For I would that all men were even as I myself. But every man hath his proper gift of God, one after this manner, and another after that. (1 Cor. 7:7)

For to one is given by the Spirit the word of wisdom; to another the word of knowledge by the same Spirit. (1 Cor. 12:8)

That there should be no schism in the body; but that the members should have the same care one for another. (1 Cor. 12:25)

Wherefore putting away lying, speak every man truth with his neighbour: for we are members one of another. (Eph. 4:25)

Let the word of Christ dwell in you richly in all wisdom; teaching and admonishing one another in psalms and hymns and spiritual songs, singing with grace in your hearts to the Lord. (Col. 3:16)

[40] Let us not therefore judge one another any more: but judge this rather, that no man put a stumbling block or an occasion to fall in his brother's way. (Rom. 14:13)

For, brethren, ye have been called unto liberty; only use not liberty for an occasion to the flesh, but by love serve one another... But if ye bite and devour one another, take heed that ye be not consumed one of another... Let us not be desirous of vain glory, provoking one another, envying one another. (Gal. 5:13, 15, 26)

Wherefore putting away lying, speak every man truth with his neighbour: for we are members one of another. (Eph. 4:25)

Submitting yourselves one to another in the fear of God. (Eph. 5:21)

Lie not one to another, seeing that ye have put off the old man with his deeds. (Col. 3:9)

I charge thee before God, and the Lord Jesus Christ, and the elect angels, that thou observe these things without preferring one before another, doing nothing by partiality. (1 Tim. 5:21)

As every man hath received the gift, even so minister the same one to another, as good stewards of the manifold grace of God. (1 Pet. 4:10)

Likewise, ye younger, submit yourselves unto the elder. Yea, all of you be subject one to another, and be clothed with humility: for God resisteth the proud, and giveth grace to the humble. (1 Pet. 5:5)

Speak not evil one of another, brethren. He that speaketh evil of his brother, and judgeth his brother, speaketh evil of the law, and judgeth the law: but if thou judge the law, thou art not a doer of the law, but a judge. (James 4:11)

41 Hatred stirreth up strifes: but love covereth all sins. (Prov. 10:12)

But if ye bite and devour one another, take heed that ye be not consumed one of another. (Gal. 5:15)

Recompense to no man evil for evil. Provide things honest in the sight of all men... Be not overcome of evil, but overcome evil with good. (Rom. 12:17, 21)

Let all bitterness, and wrath, and anger, and clamour, and evil speaking, be put away from you, with all malice. (Eph. 4:31)

See that none render evil for evil unto any man; but ever follow that which is good, both among yourselves, and to all men. (1 Thess. 5:15)

From whence come wars and fightings among you? come they not hence, even of your lusts that war in your members?... Speak not evil one of another, brethren. He that speaketh evil of his brother, and judgeth his brother, speaketh evil of the law, and judgeth the law: but if thou judge the law, thou art not a doer of the law, but a judge. (James 4:1, 11)

Wherefore laying aside all malice, and all guile, and hypocrisies, and envies, and all evil speakings. (1 Pet. 2:1)

Not rendering evil for evil, or railing for railing: but contrariwise blessing; knowing that ye are thereunto called, that ye should inherit a blessing. For he that will love life, and see good days, let him refrain his tongue from evil, and his lips that they speak no guile: Let him eschew evil, and do good; let him seek peace, and ensue it. For the eyes of the Lord are over the righteous, and his ears are open unto their prayers: but the face of the Lord is against them that do evil. (1 Pet. 3:9–12)

42 Charity suffereth long, and is kind; charity envieth not; charity vaunteth not itself, is not puffed up, Doth not behave itself unseemly, seeketh not her own, is not easily provoked, thinketh no evil. (1 Cor. 13:4–5)

[43] With all lowliness and meekness, with longsuffering, forbearing one another in love. (Eph. 4:2)

Forbearing one another, and forgiving one another, if any man have a quarrel against any: even as Christ forgave you, so also do ye. (Col. 3:13)

Now therefore there is utterly a fault among you, because ye go to law one with another. Why do ye not rather take wrong? why do ye not rather suffer yourselves to be defrauded? (1 Cor. 6:7)

[44] And I myself also am persuaded of you, my brethren, that ye also are full of goodness, filled with all knowledge, able also to admonish one another. (Rom. 15:14)

And the servant of the Lord must not strive; but be gentle unto all men, apt to teach, patient, In meekness instructing those that oppose themselves; if God peradventure will give them repentance to the acknowledging of the truth; And that they may recover themselves out of the snare of the devil, who are taken captive by him at his will. (2 Tim. 2:24–26)

And others save with fear, pulling them out of the fire; hating even the garment spotted by the flesh. (Jude 1:23)

[45] For if ye forgive men their trespasses, your heavenly Father will also forgive you: But if ye forgive not men their trespasses, neither will your Father forgive your trespasses. (Matt. 6:14–15)

But I say unto you which hear, Love your enemies, do good to them which hate you, Bless them that curse you, and pray for them which despitefully use you. And unto him that smiteth thee on the one cheek offer also the other; and him that taketh away thy cloke forbid not to take thy coat also. Give to every man that asketh of thee; and of him that taketh away thy goods ask them not again. And as ye would that men should do to you, do ye also to them likewise... But love ye your enemies, and do good, and lend, hoping for nothing again; and your reward shall be great, and ye shall be the children of the Highest: for he is kind unto the unthankful and to the evil. Be ye therefore merciful, as your Father also is merciful. (Luke 6:27–31, 35–36)

Let us not therefore judge one another any more: but judge this rather, that no man put a stumbling block or an occasion to fall in his brother's way. (Rom. 14:13)

And be ye kind one to another, tenderhearted, forgiving one another, even as God for Christ's sake hath forgiven you. (Eph. 4:32)

Forbearing one another, and forgiving one another, if any man have a quarrel against any: even as Christ forgave you, so also do ye. (Col. 3:13)

There is one lawgiver, who is able to save and to destroy: who art thou that judgest another? (James 4:12)

Grudge not one against another, brethren, lest ye be condemned: behold, the judge standeth before the door. (James 5:9)

[46] But it shall not be so among you: but whosoever will be great among you, let him be your minister; And whosoever will be chief among you, let him be

your servant: Even as the Son of man came not to be ministered unto, but to minister, and to give his life a ransom for many. (Matt. 20:26–28)

But he that is greatest among you shall be your servant. (Matt. 23:11)

By love serve one another. (Gal. 5:13b)

And walk in love, as Christ also hath loved us, and hath given himself for us an offering and a sacrifice to God for a sweet smelling savour. (Eph. 5:2)

Yea, and if I be offered upon the sacrifice and service of your faith, I joy, and rejoice with you all. (Phil. 2:17)

47 Hereby perceive we the love of God, because he laid down his life for us: and we ought to lay down our lives for the brethren. But whoso hath this world's good, and seeth his brother have need, and shutteth up his bowels of compassion from him, how dwelleth the love of God in him? My little children, let us not love in word, neither in tongue; but in deed and in truth. (1 John 3:16–18)

48 That we henceforth be no more children, tossed to and fro, and carried about with every wind of doctrine, by the sleight of men, and cunning craftiness, whereby they lie in wait to deceive; But speaking the truth in love, may grow up into him in all things, which is the head, even Christ. (Eph. 4:14–15)

Preach the word; be instant in season, out of season; reprove, rebuke, exhort with all longsuffering and doctrine. (2 Tim. 4:2)

Holding fast the faithful word as he hath been taught, that he may be able by sound doctrine both to exhort and to convince the gainsayers. (Titus 1:9)

49 Take heed to yourselves: If thy brother trespass against thee, rebuke him; and if he repent, forgive him. (Luke 17:3)

Preach the word; be instant in season, out of season; reprove, rebuke, exhort with all longsuffering and doctrine. (2 Tim. 4:2)

50 But he answered and said, It is written, Man shall not live by bread alone, but by every word that proceedeth out of the mouth of God. (Matt. 4:4)

But he said unto them, Have ye not read what David did, when he was an hungred, and they that were with him;... Or have ye not read in the law, how that on the sabbath days the priests in the temple profane the sabbath, and are blameless? (Matt. 12:3, 5)

And he answered and said unto them, Have ye not read, that he which made them at the beginning made them male and female. (Matt. 19:4)

And said unto him, Hearest thou what these say? And Jesus saith unto them, Yea; have ye never read, Out of the mouth of babes and sucklings thou hast perfected praise?... Jesus saith unto them, Did ye never read in the scriptures, The stone which the builders rejected, the same is become the head of the corner: this is the Lord's doing, and it is marvellous in our eyes? (Matt. 21:16, 42)

He that rejecteth me, and receiveth not my words, hath one that judgeth him: the word that I have spoken, the same shall judge him in the last day. (John 12:48)

Believest thou not that I am in the Father, and the Father in me? the words that I speak unto you I speak not of myself: but the Father that dwelleth in me, he doeth the works. (John 14:10)

51 But speaking the truth in love, may grow up into him in all things, which is the head, even Christ. (Eph. 4:15)

52 Though I speak with the tongues of men and of angels, and have not charity, I am become as sounding brass, or a tinkling cymbal. And though I have the gift of prophecy, and understand all mysteries, and all knowledge; and though I have all faith, so that I could remove mountains, and have not charity, I am nothing. And though I bestow all my goods to feed the poor, and though I give my body to be burned, and have not charity, it profiteth me nothing. Charity suffereth long, and is kind; charity envieth not; charity vaunteth not itself, is not puffed up, Doth not behave itself unseemly, seeketh not her own, is not easily provoked, thinketh no evil; Rejoiceth not in iniquity, but rejoiceth in the truth; Beareth all things, believeth all things, hopeth all things, endureth all things. Charity never faileth: but whether there be prophecies, they shall fail; whether there be tongues, they shall cease; whether there be knowledge, it shall vanish away. For we know in part, and we prophesy in part. But when that which is perfect is come, then that which is in part shall be done away. When I was a child, I spake as a child, I understood as a child, I thought as a child: but when I became a man, I put away childish things. For now we see through a glass, darkly; but then face to face: now I know in part; but then shall I know even as also I am known. And now abideth faith, hope, charity, these three; but the greatest of these is charity. (1 Cor. 13:1–13)

53 And this is his commandment, That we should believe on the name of his Son Jesus Christ, and love one another, as he gave us commandment. And he that keepeth his commandments dwelleth in him, and he in him. And hereby we know that he abideth in us, by the Spirit which he hath given us. (1 John 3:23–24)

Beloved, let us love one another: for love is of God; and every one that loveth is born of God, and knoweth God. He that loveth not knoweth not God; for God is love. In this was manifested the love of God toward us, because that God sent his only begotten Son into the world, that we might live through him. Herein is love, not that we loved God, but that he loved us, and sent his Son to be the propitiation for our sins. Beloved, if God so loved us, we ought also to love one another. No man hath seen God at any time. If we love one another, God dwelleth in us, and his love is perfected in us... And we have known and believed the love that God hath to us. God is love; and he that dwelleth in love dwelleth in God, and God in him. Herein is our love made perfect, that we may have boldness in the day of judgment: because as he is, so are we in this world. There is no fear in love; but perfect love casteth out fear: because fear hath torment. He that feareth is not made perfect in love. We love him, because he first loved us... And this commandment have we from him, That he who loveth God love his brother also. (1 John 4:7–12, 16–19, 21)

I rejoiced greatly that I found of thy children walking in truth, as we have received a commandment from the Father. And now I beseech thee, lady, not as though I wrote a new commandment unto thee, but that which we had from the beginning, that we love one another. And this is love, that we walk after his commandments. This is the commandment, That, as ye have heard from the beginning, ye should walk in it. (2 John 1:4–6)

For I rejoiced greatly, when the brethren came and testified of the truth that is in thee, even as thou walkest in the truth. I have no greater joy than to hear that my children walk in truth. Beloved, thou doest faithfully whatsoever thou doest to the brethren, and to strangers; Which have borne witness of thy charity before the church: whom if thou bring forward on their journey after a godly sort, thou shalt do well. (3 John 1:3–6)

⁵⁴ He that saith he is in the light, and hateth his brother, is in darkness even until now. He that loveth his brother abideth in the light, and there is none occasion of stumbling in him. But he that hateth his brother is in darkness, and walketh in darkness, and knoweth not whither he goeth, because that darkness hath blinded his eyes. (1 John 2:9–11)

For this is the message that ye heard from the beginning, that we should love one another. Not as Cain, who was of that wicked one, and slew his brother. And wherefore slew he him? Because his own works were evil, and his brother's righteous. Marvel not, my brethren, if the world hate you. We know that we have passed from death unto life, because we love the brethren. He that loveth not his brother abideth in death. Whosoever hateth his brother is a murderer: and ye know that no murderer hath eternal life abiding in him. Hereby perceive we the love of God, because he laid down his life for us: and we ought to lay down our lives for the brethren. But whoso hath this world's good, and seeth his brother have need, and shutteth up his bowels of compassion from him, how dwelleth the love of God in him? My little children, let us not love in word, neither in tongue; but in deed and in truth. And hereby we know that we are of the truth, and shall assure our hearts before him. (1 John 3:11–19)

Beloved, if God so loved us, we ought also to love one another. No man hath seen God at any time. If we love one another, God dwelleth in us, and his love is perfected in us... If a man say, I love God, and hateth his brother, he is a liar: for he that loveth not his brother whom he hath seen, how can he love God whom he hath not seen? And this commandment have we from him, That he who loveth God love his brother also... Whosoever believeth that Jesus is the Christ is born of God: and every one that loveth him that begat loveth him also that is begotten of him. By this we know that we love the children of God, when we love God, and keep his commandments. For this is the love of God, that we keep his commandments: and his commandments are not grievous. (1 John 4:11–12, 20–5:3)

[55] And hereby we do know that we know him, if we keep his commandments. He that saith, I know him, and keepeth not his commandments, is a liar, and the truth is not in him. But whoso keepeth his word, in him verily is the love of God perfected: hereby know we that we are in him. He that saith he abideth in him ought himself also so to walk, even as he walked... And now, little children, abide in him; that, when he shall appear, we may have confidence, and not be ashamed before him at his coming. If ye know that he is righteous, ye know that every one that doeth righteousness is born of him. (1 John 2:3–6, 28–29)

Whosoever committeth sin transgresseth also the law: for sin is the transgression of the law. And ye know that he was manifested to take away our sins; and in him is no sin. Whosoever abideth in him sinneth not: whosoever sinneth hath not seen him, neither known him. Little children, let no man deceive you: he that doeth righteousness is righteous, even as he is righteous. He that committeth sin is of the devil; for the devil sinneth from the beginning. For this purpose the Son of God was manifested, that he might destroy the works of the devil. Whosoever is born of God doth not commit sin; for his seed remaineth in him: and he cannot sin, because he is born of God. In this the children of God are manifest, and the children of the devil: whosoever doeth not righteousness is not of God, neither he that loveth not his brother. (1 John 3:4–10)

[56] When the Son of man shall come in his glory, and all the holy angels with him, then shall he sit upon the throne of his glory:... Then shall the King say unto them on his right hand, Come, ye blessed of my Father, inherit the kingdom prepared for you from the foundation of the world: For I was an hungred, and ye gave me meat: I was thirsty, and ye gave me drink: I was a stranger, and ye took me in: Naked, and ye clothed me: I was sick, and ye visited me: I was in prison, and ye came unto me. Then shall the righteous answer him, saying, Lord, when saw we thee an hungred, and fed thee? or thirsty, and gave thee drink? When saw we thee a stranger, and took thee in? or naked, and clothed thee? Or when saw we thee sick, or in prison, and came unto thee? And the King shall answer and say unto them, Verily I say unto you, Inasmuch as ye have done it unto one of the least of these my brethren, ye have done it unto me. (Matt. 25:31, 34–40)

Remembering without ceasing your work of faith, and labourof love, and patience of hope in our Lord Jesus Christ, in the sight of God and our Father. (1 Thess. 1:3)

And the Lord make you to increase and abound in love one toward another, and toward all men, even as we do toward you: To the end he may stablish your hearts unblameable in holiness before God, even our Father, at the coming of our Lord Jesus Christ with all his saints. (1 Thess. 3:12–13)

We are bound to thank God always for you, brethren, as it is meet, because that your faith growth exceedingly, and the charity of everyone of you all toward each other aboundeth. (2 Thess. 1:3)

For God is not unrighteous to forget your work and labour of love, which ye have shewed toward his name, in that ye have ministered to the saints, and do minister. (Heb. 6:10)

Whosoever believeth that Jesus is the Christ is born of God: and every one that loveth him that begat loveth him also that is begotten of him. By this we know that we love the children of God, when we love God, and keep his commandments. For this is the love of God, that we keep his commandments: and his commandments are not grievous. (1 John 5:1–3)

57 Watch ye, stand fast in the faith, quit you like men, be strong. Let all your things be done with charity. (1 Cor. 16:13–14)

Can We Say It More Simply?

As a young boy, I borrowed a few coins from one of my companions. Concerned that I would remember to pay him back, he insisted that I write down what I had borrowed from him. Finding a scrap of paper and a pencil, I began to write a detailed explanation of the loan.

He interrupted me and said, "Just write that 'I owe you...' and the amount of money." Getting another scrap of paper, I began to write, "I owe you..."

He stopped me again and said, "Just write the letters *I-O-U*, the amount, and then sign it."

IOU

Those three simple vowel sounds are known all around the English-speaking world as denoting a debt to someone else. Later, as a new believer growing in the Lord, the letters *IOU* took on a different word meaning. Instead of *I Owe You*, they came to mean *Inward, Outward,* and *Upward.* Micah gives a perfect example of a simple summary:

> He hath shewed thee, O man, what is good;
> and what doth the LORD require of thee, but to
> do justly, and to love mercy, and to walk humbly
> with thy God? (Mic. 6:8)

The *Inward* focus is do justly. That is, walk honestly with integrity, guarding our heart. The *Outward* effort is to love mercy, walking with a spirit of forgiveness and service. The *Upward* aim is to walk humbly with God by faith—that is, with dependent trust and obedience.

Other Examples

Other wonderful summaries are these:

> Wherefore lift up the hands which hang down, and the feeble knees; And make straight paths for your feet, lest that which is lame be turned out of the way; but let it rather be healed. [Inward] Follow peace with all men, [Outward] and holiness, without which no man shall see the Lord: [Upward]. (Heb. 12:12–14)

Or

> Flee also youthful lusts: but follow righteousness [Inward], faith [Upward], charity, peace [Outward], with them that call on the Lord out of a pure heart. (2 Tim. 2:22)

Or this passage covered in previous chapters:

> And beside this, giving all diligence, add to your faith virtue; and to virtue knowledge; And to knowledge temperance; and to temperance patience; and to patience godliness; And to godliness brotherly kindness; and to brotherly kindness charity. For if these things be in you, and abound, they make you that ye shall neither be barren nor unfruitful in the knowledge of our Lord Jesus Christ. (2 Pet. 1:5–8)

If these things abound in us,
then our walk through the path of
this life will please our God.

About the Author

Jack began a personal relationship with Jesus at nine years old. Through his teen years and university schooling years, he was very active in leading youth groups, Bible clubs, and outreach ministries, eventually serving as deacon and then interim pastor of his local church. His future wife, Sandy, came to the Lord in one of the youth ministries. And they both felt called to medical missions in high school. Shortly after they were married, and just before starting his medical training, Jack served as president of International Christian Youth.

With Jack's training in surgery and Sandy's in nursing, they served as missionaries at a hospital in Bangladesh for part of a year. Later they led a missionary team to Brazil to start a hospital along the upper Amazon River. For sixteen years, Jack served in the hospital, directed and mentored others in church ministries, and guided traveling medical evangelism in the rural communities. For over twenty-five years, Jack has been heading medical teams to needy areas on five continents. While occasionally helping with emergency relief in disaster areas, he continues to lead medical teams, ministering with congregations in and through their local church.

CPSIA information can be obtained
at www.ICGtesting.com
Printed in the USA
BVHW061144030522
635995BV00026B/736